JAZZ AGE

Selected titles in ABC-CLIO's Perspectives in American Social History series

African Americans in the Nineteenth Century: People and Perspectives

American Revolution: People and Perspectives

Baby Boom: People and Perspectives

British Colonial America: People and Perspectives

Civil Rights Movement: People and Perspectives

Civil War: People and Perspectives

Cold War and McCarthy Era: People and Perspectives

Colonial America: People and Perspectives

Early Republic: People and Perspectives

Great Depression: People and Perspectives

Industrial Revolution: People and Perspectives

Jacksonian and Antebellum Age: People and Perspectives

Making of the American West: People and Perspectives

Reconstruction: People and Perspectives

Vietnam War Era: People and Perspectives

Westward Expansion: People and Perspectives

Women's Rights: People and Perspectives

PERSPECTIVES IN
AMERICAN SOCIAL HISTORY

Jazz Age

People and Perspectives

Mitchell Newton-Matza, Editor
Peter C. Mancall, Series Editor

A B C  C L I O

Santa Barbara, California • Denver, Colorado • Oxford, England

Library of Congress Cataloging-in-Publication Data
Jazz age : people and perspectives / Mitchell Newton-Matza, editor.
   p. cm. — (Perspectives in American social history)
  Includes bibliographical reference and index.
   ISBN 978-1-59884-033-9 (hard copy : alk. paper) — ISBN 978-1-59884-034-6 (ebook) 1. United States—History—1919–1933. 2. United States—Social conditions—1918–1932. 3. Popular culture—United States—History—20th century. I. Newton-Matza, Mitchell.
  E784.J38 2009
  973.91—dc22   2009019161

13 12 11 10 9   1 2 3 4 5

This book is also available on the World Wide Web as an eBook.
Visit www.abc-clio.com for details.

ABC-CLIO, LLC
130 Cremona Drive, P.O. Box 1911
Santa Barbara, California 93116-1911

This book is printed on acid-free paper (∞)

Manufactured in the United States of America

*This book is dedicated to the loving memories of
my sister Lisa and Aunt Joanie.
I'll never forget the craziness, laughter,
and love you always gave.*

Contents

Series Introduction, ix

Introduction, xiii

About the Editor and Contributors, xxvi

Chronology, xxxi

1 African Americans in the Jazz Age, 1
Jamie J. Wilson

2 Farmers, 17
Jeremy Bonner

3 Gangsters and Bootleggers, 37
Scott Allen Merriman

4 Jazz Age Evangelism, 53
John H. Barnhill

5 Consumers, 75
Susan Ferentinos

6 Musicians and Entertainment, 93
Kurt Gartner

7 Immigrants and Nativists, 109
Mitchell Newton-Matza

8 Reformers, Radicals, and Socialists, 129
Mitchell Newton-Matza

9 Writers, 149
Mitchell Newton-Matza

10 Businesspersons, 167
Sean O'Connor

Primary Documents, 187
Reference, 209
Bibliography, 223
Index, 237

Series Introduction

Social history is, simply put, the study of past societies. More specifically, social historians attempt to describe societies in their totality, and hence often eschew analysis of politics and ideas. Though many social historians argue that it is impossible to understand how societies functioned without some consideration of the ways politics works on a daily basis or what ideas could be found circulating at any given time, they tend to pay little attention to the formal arenas of electoral politics or intellectual currents. In the United States, social historians have been engaged in describing components of the population that had earlier often escaped formal analysis, notably women, members of ethnic or cultural minorities, or those who had fewer economic opportunities than the elite.

Social history became a vibrant discipline in the United States after it had already gained enormous influence in Western Europe. In France, social history in its modern form emerged with the rising prominence of a group of scholars associated with the journal *Annales Economie, Societé, Civilisation* (or *Annales ESC* as it is known). In its pages and in a series of books from historians affiliated with the École des Hautes Études en Sciences Sociale in Paris, brilliant historians such as Marc Bloch, Jacques Le Goff, and Emanuel LeRoy Ladurie described seemingly every aspect of French society. Among the masterpieces of this historical reconstruction was Fernand Braudel's monumental study, *The Mediterranean and the Mediterranean World in the Age of Philip II*, published first in Paris in 1946 and in a revised edition in English in 1972. In this work Braudel argued that the only way to understand a place in its totality was to describe its environment, its social and economic structures, and its political systems. In Britain the emphasis of social historians has been less on questions of environment, per se, than on a description of human communities in all their complexities. For example, social historians there have taken advantage of that nation's remarkable local archives to reconstruct the history of the family and details of its rural past. Works such as Peter Laslett's *The World We Have Lost*, first printed in 1966, and the multiauthored *Agrarian History of England and Wales*, which began to appear in print in 1967, revealed that painstaking work could reveal the lives and habits of individuals who had never previously attracted the interest of biographers, demographers, or most historians.

Social history in the United States gained a large following in the second half of the 20th century, especially during the 1960s and 1970s. Its development sprang from political, technical, and intellectual impulses deeply embedded in the culture of the modern university. The politics of civil rights and social reform fueled the passions of historians who strove to tell the stories of the underclass. They benefited from the adoption by historians of statistical analysis, which allowed scholars to trace where individuals lived, how often they moved, what kinds of jobs they took, and whether their economic status declined, stagnated, or improved over time. As history departments expanded, many who emerged from graduate schools focused their attention on groups previously ignored or marginalized. Women's history became a central concern among American historians, as did the history of African Americans, Native Americans, Latinos, and others. These historians pushed historical study in the United States farther away from the study of formal politics and intellectual trends. Though few Americanists could achieve the technical brilliance of some social historians in Europe, collectively they have been engaged in a vast act of description, with the goal of describing seemingly every facet of life from 1492 to the present.

The 16 volumes in this series together represent the continuing efforts of historians to describe American society. Most of the volumes focus on chronological areas, from the broad sweep of the colonial era to the more narrowly defined collections of essays on the eras of the Cold War, the baby boom, and America in the age of the Vietnam War. The series also includes entire volumes on the epochs that defined the nation, the American Revolution and the Civil War, as well as volumes dedicated to the process of westward expansion, women's rights, and African American history.

This social history series derives its strength from the talented editors of individual volumes. Each editor is an expert in his or her own field who has selected and organized the contents of his or her volume. Editors solicited other experienced historians to write individual essays. Every volume contains first-rate analysis complemented by lively anecdotes designed to reveal the complex contours of specific historical moments. The many illustrations to be found in these volumes testify too to the recognition that any society can be understood not only by the texts its participants produce but also by the images they craft. Primary source documents in each volume will allow interested readers to pursue some specific topics in greater depth, and each volume contains a chronology to provide guidance to the flow of events over time. These tools—anecdotes, images, texts, and timelines—allow readers to gauge the inner workings of America in particular periods and yet also to glimpse connections between eras.

The articles in these volumes testify to the abundant strengths of historical scholarship in the United States in the early years of the 21st century. Despite the occasional academic contest that flares into public notice, or the self-serving cant of politicians who want to manipulate the nation's past for partisan ends—for example, in debates over the Second Amendment to the U.S. Constitution and what it means about potential limits to the rights of gun ownership—the articles here all reveal the vast increase in knowledge of the American past that has taken place over the previous half century. Social historians do not dominate history faculties in American colleges and universities, but no one could deny them a seat at the intellectual table. Without their efforts, intellectual, cultural, and political historians would be hard pressed to understand why certain ideas circulated when they did, why some religious movements prospered or foundered, how developments in fields such as medicine and engineering reflected larger concerns, and what shaped the world we inhabit.

Fernand Braudel and his colleagues envisioned entire laboratories of historians in which scholars working together would be able to produce *histoire totale*: total history. Historians today seek more humble goals for our collective enterprise. But as the richly textured essays in these volumes reveal, scholarly collaboration has in fact brought us much closer to that dream. These volumes do not and cannot include every aspect of American history. However, every page reveals something interesting or valuable about how American society functioned. Together, these books suggest the crucial necessity of stepping back to view the grand complexities of the past rather than pursuing narrower prospects and lesser goals.

Peter C. Mancall

Series Editor

Introduction

Defining any time period can be difficult. When the term *Jazz Age* is brought to mind, so are countless images, mostly of the 1920s: the music, fashion, Prohibition, movies, radio, and the rise of automobiles. More importantly, the words *Jazz Age* conjure up an atmosphere never previously before seen. For purposes of this book, the period of the Jazz Age will encompass the years 1918–1930. This range has been chosen for several reasons. First, obviously, this is the period in which jazz music gained a wide audience. Second, it is also a period in which so many changes in the country's culture accompanied the rise of jazz music, whether or not the music had a direct influence. Third, in terms of American social history, it is a distinct period in which so much was not only happening but was also interconnected in some way.

What is meant exactly by the term *Jazz Age*? Is it defined solely by the musical form that gained strong popularity during the 1920s? First, we can address some conceptions and misconceptions. Typical conceptions of the Jazz Age relate to the music, fashion, social behavior, and great developments in art, literature, economics, and political battles. As far as misconceptions go, many would suggest that the Jazz Age was a time when social norms were thwarted and so-called proper behavior was suddenly thrown out the window, all because of this new form of music that many believed was corrupting long-cherished values.

The era of World War I is often considered to be an era of lost innocence, the end of the Victorian era. The common perception of Victorian society was this was a time when the Western world supposedly behaved according to a strict moral code. With the end of World War I the world entered a new age, one in which the beliefs of the past no longer seemed valid. Some people wished to hold on to the norms of the past, and some desired to move forward and embrace the sweeping changes the new era presented. The Jazz Age is the period of time in which society was emerging from a devastating period and allowing a new generation to define its own social code.

In reality, this period was one of incredible contradictions. On one hand, the country was opening up in a more liberal fashion in terms of social and cultural behavior and the ways in which such behavior was expressed; on the other hand, it was a time in which conservatism was on the rise. The resurgence of the Ku Klux Klan (KKK), a very conservative Supreme Court, the supposed decline of the labor movement, censorship of movies, immigration restriction, the drive for U.S. isolationism on the world stage, and the end of the Progressive Era are all ways in which the perceived liberal agenda had strong opposition. This was a very complex time in which a nation, tired of playing international politics, turned inward and concentrated more on domestic ideas.

However, this was not necessarily a liberal versus conservative battle, nor was it a "good guy/bad guy" situation. These statements are not meant to be taken that one side was absolutely right and the other embarrassingly wrong. Each side had its arguments, however valid or invalid. Furthermore, being liberal on one agenda did not mean being liberal on all. Human emotions are very flexible. Support for such issues as Prohibition or immigration restriction could come from both liberal and conservative sides. For the purposes of this discussion, the terms "liberal" and "conservative" are to be taken in a very general sense.

For those who considered themselves conservative, a variety of factors were at work during this period: the strength of the religious community, isolationism, increased xenophobia, fear of radicalism, and the need to control the morality of the country. After all, was the need to control morality a response to the growing trends in entertainment and fashion, or was this a collection of deep-rooted fears simply reacting to growing trends that appeared to be dangerous to society?

From the conservative view, the Jazz Age contained many elements that needed to be controlled, starting with the music, which many viewed as vile, primitive, and destructive to the morals of society because it appealed to society's most base instincts. Much of this response was rooted in racism. As a music form, jazz began in the African American community, and during this time a goodly number of the musicians were black. This in itself was alarming to many because the music's appeal crossed racial lines. It was considered appalling to see whites, especially white women in short skirts, dancing to what was considered "jungle music." Many whites saw jazz music as an attempt by the black community to undermine the morality and superior lifestyle of whites.

Along those same lines, the changes in fashion also challenged more conservative views. The hemlines in women's skirts and dresses became considerably shorter. In much earlier times, the display of female legs was mostly considered improper. With the Jazz Age, women were expressing themselves in a way that was considered to be shocking to modern society. Women's bodies were not meant to be exposed.

Another concern during the Jazz Age was immigration. If the racial concerns of the period were not bad enough, the growing influx of immigrants from what were considered the less sophisticated parts of Central and Eastern Europe, Latin America, and Asia merely added to the problem.

Immigrants from these areas were seen as particularly undesirable, especially as so many were Catholic or Jewish (especially those from Central and Eastern Europe). Furthermore, ever since the 19th century, European immigrants were viewed as the cause of American society's woes. Many of that century's problems were blamed on the radical notions European immigrants injected into American society. Socialism, anarchism, and communism were not true American ideals, so the introduction of these beliefs must have come from abroad. Therefore, to protect the "correct" religious and philosophical fabric of American society, the immigration door must be shut.

This does not even take into account the immigration restrictions toward those from other areas of the world. Mexican immigrants especially streamed into the United States during the Jazz Age. Asian immigrants had been regarded as the dregs of the earth since the 19th century, even though the need for their labor in building the nation's railway system was imperative. To restrict immigration from any such areas was therefore seen as essential to the protection of American society.

One group especially personified these feelings of racial and ethnic hatred. The resurgence of the KKK during the Jazz Age presented conservative white America with a form of expression against those who were considered to be unacceptable to proper American society. Begun as a southern organization dedicated to the suppression of African Americans, the KKK sought to protect what it believed to be the norms of proper—meaning "white"—society. During the Jazz Age, this focus expanded across the nation. Not restricted to the South, the KKK managed to reach into northern states, especially those areas in which the new influx of immigrants would be more liable to settle. The northern state with the highest KKK population was Indiana. Not only were blacks the target of the KKK's wrath, but so were Catholics, Jews, and any nonwhite population, not to mention anyone of mixed race. The expressions of music and fashion of the Jazz Age only fueled the doctrine espoused by the KKK. Such a decline in morality was thought to be the work of the blacks, who were clearly (in the eyes of the KKK) being funded by the Jews. American society was to be protected.

Probably nothing better personified the period's battle between liberalism and conservatism than the infamous Scopes "Monkey" Trial of 1925. John Scopes was arrested and tried in Dayton, Tennessee, for violating that state's law against teaching evolution in the public schools. Although the entire trial was itself a setup by the American Civil Liberties Union, it marked a confrontation between those who wanted to move forward and those who wished to protect what they held to be long-cherished beliefs. Speaking for the prosecution was the three-time presidential candidate William Jennings Bryan (who had also served as secretary of state under Woodrow Wilson), and the defense had a fire-breathing attorney from Chicago, Clarence Darrow. Although the two had enjoyed a friendship in the past, these figureheads of conservatism versus liberalism helped make the trial a true media circus and showed the divisions within society. The clash between progress and tradition was never more pronounced.

The Jazz Age also saw an increase in the battle over how education was to be handled in the United States. For years there had been controversy over compulsory education, and during the Progressive Era (ca. 1890–1920) the debate over how to go about educating the public took on two points of view. In an argument that stretched back to America's earlier Age of Reform (ca. 1820–1860), and espoused by reformer Horace Mann, an educated public was an informed electorate. People with an education would make better, informed decisions. It was also argued that providing the public with a workable educational system would make society more equitable; it was believed that with an education, everyone would have an equal chance to succeed. As immigration increased throughout the 19th century, and into the 20th, educational reformers held that providing Americanization classes would help ease the new groups into American society. They would be able to speak the language, understand the legal system, and know how to integrate themselves into society.

But the counterargument was just as vehement. Compulsory education for children was opposed by many middle- and lower-class parents who needed the additional income provided by their working children. Sending their children to school would cut into the family budget. Also, many wondered who would really benefit from such an educational system. Many believed people—whether children or immigrants—would not be educated so much as they would be indoctrinated. It was argued that the "three Rs" might be taught, but so also would intolerance. Many believed people would be taught to be docile citizens who did not question the system. As evidenced by the controversy over American Education Week during the early years of the 1920s (see the chapter on *Reformers, Radicals, and Socialists*), control over the educational system was a battle between those who believed only "true" American ideals belonged in the nation's classroom and those who advocated free thought and expression.

The era of the Jazz Age is also remembered for the meteoric rise of radio and film. Although film had been around for a considerable time, with the Jazz Age many now became concerned with censoring the content of movies. Hollywood was considered (and not all that wrongfully so!) a haven of decadence and filth, something many feared would be shown to audiences on the big screen, and, thus, influence improper behavior. Relationships between men and women on screen were carefully monitored.

Hollywood was certainly not without its sex symbols or sexually suggestive themes. Names such as the infamous Rudolph Valentino and Clara Bow were household words and certainly inflamed many passions and fantasies. Historical period pieces often depicted men and women in various states of dress and undress. Hollywood certainly engaged in its share of titillation, but there were certainly enough watchdog groups to monitor Hollywood's output and make trouble in case they thought any lines were crossed.

Again, these are not necessarily conservative issues per se; supporting these issues did not make one a conservative. These points tend to be placed into the "conservative" category, however, because they were seen as trying to preserve the established order. The liberal side of society had its own agenda. Like the conservatives, liberals thought they had much to promote. Both thought they were protecting society. For the liberal side, the changes in society were for the best. Progress was good; society could never remain in a stagnant state. But this assumption was often unfair; conservatives were not opposed to progress in itself. The point was how such progress affected society.

As the name implies, the Jazz Age first conjures up the musical form itself. Jazz was very much an American invention, one whose appeal was embraced overseas, especially in Europe. Whereas the more conservative portions of society considered the music to be vulgar, others found its free-form style and improvisational potentials to be exhilarating. This same sort of attitude would reemerge during the 1950s with the advent of rock and roll music. Although nightclubs might have been segregated, white audiences flocked to clubs to hear predominantly black artists perform. Two particular aspects of this shocked "proper" society; fashion and dancing. The changes in fashion, particularly that of women, were considered improper as hemlines grew considerably shorter. Also, the dancing was considered to be as vulgar as the music, and that men and women were touching each other in a manner considered to be too sexual in nature.

The liberation many felt was beyond compare. Men and women were congregating in a manner never before seen. Gone were the days when chaperones were a necessity and requirement. Both sexes were more freely associating in these clubs, smoking, drinking, and traveling to and from these places in automobiles—and alone. This in itself was considered shocking. Many feared what men and women were doing together when riding unescorted in a car or, worse yet, what might happen should they park somewhere isolated.

The changes in fashion were exciting and wonderful, and women enjoyed the sense of liberation that came with a new form of self-expression in clothing. Whether it can be attributed to the rebelliousness of a new generation, or the overall thrill of change, the excitement in new fashions has always been a cause for celebration in any society.

The Jazz Age also brought a sexual revolution. Although each generation seems to believe it invents and defines sexuality, all that really changed throughout these years were the ways such feelings and practices were expressed. Probably the most shocking change in sexuality was the increased emphasis on birth control. For women to control their bodies through such a method was seen as improper because it would also mean sexual freedom.

For women, there was more going on than simply new forms of fashion or sexual expression. Women were starting to have a greater share in American society. In 1920, women were allowed to vote in their first presidential election. In that election they tended to vote along the same lines as the men, that is, conservatively. Warren G. Harding won the White House easily in a landslide. Women were also expressing themselves culturally. Many more women were making a name for themselves in art, literature, fashion design, and political action. The brazen and outspoken Russian anarchist Emma Goldman was one such woman. Although they were still hardly on the top rung of society, women were finding new avenues opening to them.

For African Americans, the Jazz Age was also home to the movement known as the Harlem Renaissance. This flourishing of African American culture crossed several genres—music, literature, and art (in all its various forms). It was a celebration of black culture, and the expression came from within the community. This was important to blacks as their image in much of popular American culture was anything but positive. The images of African Americans, especially in film, portrayed them as simpleminded, often drunkards, incapable of any sort of skilled labor or respectable professions, and, especially in the case of black men, preying on white women. An example of this was D.W. Griffith's classic (or notorious, depending on one's point of view) 1915 film *The Birth of a Nation*. Based on the book *The Klansman*, the film presented a sympathetic portrayal of the KKK and a negative portrayal of African Americans. The film remains controversial and is often banned.

The Harlem Renaissance gave a voice to the black community. Publications such as *The New Negro* and *The Crisis* provided a forum for black writers such as Langston Hughes, Zora Neale Hurston, and Claude McKay. It was a way for the community to provide an image of black America from an African American perspective.

The expression of black pride was especially seen in the Back to Africa movement as advocated and promoted by the Jamaican-born Marcus Garvey and his Universal Negro Improvement Association (UNIA). Through the Black Star Line Steamship Company, Garvey planned to conduct trade with the West Indies and bring black Americans to Africa because white society would not protect African Americans. Garvey wanted to create a strong black Africa. On the flimsiest of evidence, Garvey was convicted of mail fraud in 1925, only to be paroled by President Calvin Coolidge two years later. Garvey was eventually deported back to Jamaica.

One form of recklessness that certainly permeated the Jazz Age had nothing to do with the music but could absolutely be compared with how many viewed jazz: playing the stock market. Whereas jazz music was thought to be uncontrolled and wild, so were the ways in which Americans participated in an unregulated marketplace. Whereas jazz musicians relied on improvisation to give life to the music, so did stock market speculators—whether professional or amateur—go with the moment. But for jazz musicians, the results of improvisation and free-form expression were far more pleasant.

As Calvin Coolidge said, "the business of America is business," and to a great deal of American society, participating in the market meant being a part of the nation's economic machinery. However, it must be noted that although playing the market was considered to be a popular form of speculation and amusement, in reality, only a small percentage of the American population owned any sort of stock. A large number of investors bought stock on margin, which meant the buyer needed to put down only a percentage of the stock's value.

Stories of stock market successes were popular. One particular theme was that of the lowly person who, having purchased stock, sold at a much higher price and made a profit large enough to live a comfortable life. But at this time the stock market was not regulated by the federal government, and professional investors, and those who knew the market quite intimately, were able to artificially inflate stock prices, enabling them to unload their own supply for a tidy profit at the expense of those who had no idea phony manipulation was at work. The losers were those outside this inner circle, usually the amateurs. Whereas it was possible to earn a nice profit one day, it was also possible to lose considerable sums the next.

Along with a growing interest in playing the stock market was the growing interest in land speculation. For those looking to make a quick buck in real estate, Florida was the place to go. People bought unimproved lots and saw their value rise sometimes in as little as one day. Quickly selling these lots brought a nice, fast profit. It was said that more than 2 million people participated in the Florida land boom. However, the bottom fell out of the market, helped by Mother Nature. As with stocks, many bought property on installment, and many banks found it difficult to keep up with the financial demands. As for Mother Nature, a severe hurricane in September 1926 wiped out not only developments but also the desire to invest in an area that was at the mercy of such potentially violent weather.

The Jazz Age was also marked by considerable growth in the consumer market and the increased influence of big business. Men such as Henry Ford were on the cutting edge of factory technology, employee compensation, and making products more accessible to the masses. Although he was not the inventor of the assembly line, Ford certainly perfected the process. Furthermore, Ford offered his workers the previously unheard of sum of $5 a day salary. This, however, came with a caveat. To be eligible for such a high rate of pay, workers had to pass a series of investigations to prove their moral character was in keeping with what Ford believed to be correct.

Scientific management was also popular among many employers. The way workers went about their daily tasks was studied to see how productivity could be increased by having employees do double duty. Instead of a worker performing one particular aspect of a job at a time, productivity experts studied how a worker could perhaps perform more than one task simultaneously. However, the constant pressure to produce goods at such a breakneck speed took a mental toll on many workers. Although it is satire, Charlie Chaplin's classic 1936 film *Modern Times* shows how such work could affect a person. Chaplin's Little Tramp character works on an assembly line and uses wrenches to tighten screws all day. He eventually goes crazy and on a comedic rampage, twisting anything, and everyone, in sight. The film also presents an interesting image of workers as being merely parts of factory machinery as the Little Tramp becomes caught up in the machine gears.

In keeping with 19th-century folklore of "the little person who could," becoming the owner of one's own business was still very much a part of the American system. To rise up from humble beginnings to control an industrial empire was still seen as the measure of a man's success. In theory, anyone could perform such a feat. As with playing the stock market, such opportunities were supposedly open to all.

For consumers, access to goods had never appeared to be better. However, although the Jazz Age appeared to provide workers with greater access, during this time the wages of workers actually did not rise and did not keep pace with growth in other areas. Producers encouraged consumers to purchase more goods in an increasingly aggressive fashion. For instance, Ford devised a system that made it easy to purchase an automobile by offering low prices and access to credit. Other businesses also offered credit to the public on a greater scale than before. And, as was noted earlier, even the purchase of stock did not require the full amount. People bought on margin, which required only a small percentage of the stock's value.

The Jazz Age was also marked by some changes in the labor movement. It is generally acknowledged that this period was unfriendly to labor. Irving Bernstein's book *The Lean Years* describes the many woes faced by the labor movement during this time. Union membership was down, and the U.S. Supreme Court, headed by former president William Howard Taft, handed down numerous conservative decisions that tended to favor big business. Many companies experimented with what was termed "welfare capitalism." In this program, which varied from company to company, employers were starting to offer many of the benefits promoted by unions and other reformers—wage scales, vacation time, stock options, and other benefits now considered standard. Many employers were sincere about offering such perks to their workers. Others were not, for some believed the best way to counter the actions of any reformers was to take such actions oneself. Offering benefits such as vacation time would undercut the lure of union membership, but this often came at a price. To be eligible for benefits a person must be employed for a specific period of time. Quite often, just as one was about to become eligible, layoffs would suddenly occur. If these employees were brought back to work after so much as one week, they would start over again from day one.

The fear of radicalism was very prominent during the Jazz Age. Besides the belief that newer immigrants were a lesser class of people, the drive for immigration restriction was especially based on two ideas: religion and radicalism. Many did not like the influx of Roman Catholics and Jews into the country because they believed such groups would undermine American society. In addition, many believed radical agitation was the work of immigrant fanatics who wished to disrupt American morals. Such fears stretched back into the 19th century. For instance, the infamous Haymarket Riot in Chicago in 1886 was blamed on the foreign born. In 1912, the socialist presidential candidate Eugene V. Debs garnered close to 1 million votes, or approximately 6 percent of the popular vote. Then, when the Bolshevik Revolution occurred in Russia in late 1917, there was fear that such an outbreak was possible in the United States.

In 1919, several events gave credence to this fear. First of all, there was a massive wave of strikes. In Seattle, workers actually seized control of the city for a brief period. Then, in that same year, came the formation of the Communist Party and the Communist Labor Party. Born out of a schism within the Socialist Party, these two groups immediately went underground and sought the approval and recognition of the new Soviet

Union. During the early 1920s was the first Red Scare, whereby radicals—whether real or perceived—were persecuted. This was especially prominent during the infamous Palmer raids. Led by U.S. attorney general A. Mitchell Palmer, and with blanket approval from the government, the homes and offices of radicals were raided. Many were deported. A clear signal was sent to the radical sector of society: Don't rock the boat.

No incident describes the issues involving radicalism and immigration restriction greater than the Sacco and Vanzetti case. Nicola Sacco and Bartolomeo Vanzetti, two Italian anarchists, were convicted and executed for a robbery/murder in Massachusetts. With their guilt in doubt, they were convicted more on who and what they were rather than on any actual evidence, which was in itself quite flimsy. To those who favored immigration restriction and the persecution of radicals, Sacco and Vanzetti were the perfect excuse for the government's need to clamp down on such elements. In recent years, however, the case has been reexamined by several historians who concluded that Sacco might very well have been guilty. However, Sacco's guilt has not been adequately proven.

No discussion of the Jazz Age would be complete without mentioning Prohibition. With the passage of the Eighteenth Amendment on January 16, 1920, alcoholic beverages were supposed to be banned in the United States. *Were supposed to be banned* is the operative phrase here, for as is well known, people hardly went thirsty.

The question that crosses many minds is that if there was so much opposition to Prohibition, how did it pass? To understand this one must go back to the 19th century. During the Age of Reform, the temperance movement began to pick up steam. It was argued that a sober population was a productive population. Sober parents worked to support their families, and sober people did not abuse their loved ones. Furthermore, sober people were spiritual people. There was a debate as to what types of liquor, if any, were to be allowed. Some believed that wine and beer were acceptable beverages as they contained lower alcohol contents (as if that made a difference to someone on a drinking binge). They held that it was the spirits—hard liquor—that was to be avoided.

This attitude carried throughout the 19th century and into the 20th. So what does this mean for the passage of the Eighteenth Amendment? The answer is simple: the anti-liquor forces were simply better organized. Those who upheld the right for people to enjoy an alcoholic beverage did not have their own organization to fight for their rights. Many simply argued that people had the right to drink if they wished. The Roman Catholic Church also became involved in this fight. Consecrated wine was essential to their masses as they believed the wine was transformed into the blood of Jesus Christ.

Regardless of the controversy, Prohibition passed, and was a total failure. Thwarting the law became big business. President Warren G. Harding himself kept a supply of liquor on hand. The infamous speakeasies, where one could drink to one's heart's (or stomach's!) content, thrived. All one needed to enter such places was to know somebody who could direct one to such an establishment. Organized crime also flourished with Prohibition. Besides running speakeasies and other establishments where liquor was readily available, the mob also made money through bootlegging, or providing liquor to "employees" who would sell to individual buyers on the streets.

Although the presence of the mob was hardly new, providing illegal goods, such as alcohol, became a cash cow. The most famous mobster of the Jazz Age was Chicago's own Al Capone. A vicious criminal, Capone knew how to control the flow of alcohol, especially by eliminating his competition. During the Great Depression many actually saw Capone as a hero. His soup kitchens helped feed a great many people, all of whom were grateful for the free meal. In an ironic twist, Capone was never knocked off his lofty perch by another mobster. The government was able to convict Capone on income tax evasion. He later died an ignominious death for a major crime boss: syphilis. One of the country's most ruthless mobsters died in bed (literally and figuratively).

People also responded to Prohibition by learning how to produce their own alcoholic stash. In many places easy instructions on how to produce certain types of liquor were provided. Quite often bootleggers, unaffiliated with the mob, would make their own version of alcoholic beverages—often termed "bathtub gin"—and provide their product to whomever had the money. However, a lot of this self-produced alcohol was dangerous. Many people suffered severe physical reactions, including blindness, to badly made booze, and many died from drinking what would best be deemed poison.

For law officials, enforcing Prohibition was certainly an uphill battle. There were simply too few agents to enforce the law. Furthermore, with the widespread opposition to Prohibition, many people simply had no intention of going along with the law. In theory, the availability of liquor was supposed to stop, but it was anything but impossible to obtain a drink. As the well-known phrase went, "Prohibition is better than no Prohibition."

Fashion, music, racial and gender interaction, sexual expression, and illegal alcoholic use all came together to influence the cultural aspects of the Jazz Age. It was an exciting time for those who wished to break free of tradition and establish their own lifestyle, to participate in something fresh and new, something of their own making. It was a time for celebration.

The census of 1920 provided one very interesting spin on the Jazz Age. For the first time in American history more people lived in urban as opposed to rural settings. The Jeffersonian ideal of the United States being a nation of small farmers would never be realized. Although farmers still played a pivotal role in the nation's economy, they were now in a minority position. Cities, the centers of industry, were now on top.

For many in rural settings, the lure of the city was beyond exciting. This was seen as both positive and negative. On the positive side, men and women from farm communities saw the big city as a chance to make their own way in the world. Young women especially took jobs in industrial centers as a way to supplement the family income. This goes back to antebellum times when young ladies flocked to places like the textile mills of Lowell, Massachusetts, as a way to earn a living until marriage. For many young men, especially those who would not inherit the family farm, the industrial centers offered a chance to establish themselves. Although they might certainly send a portion of their earnings back home, the lure of the city gave them a chance to be on their own.

The negative side of big city lure was argued by those who saw such centers as cesspools of sin and vice, which was also in keeping with the old Jeffersonian ideals of urban centers being detrimental to the health of a nation. The stories of young men and women corrupted by the city's temptations were many, and not just related by those in rural areas. In the cities young people, from otherwise more proper backgrounds, were exposed to indecent forms of dress, drinking and smoking, improper forms of entertainment, and social interaction on a level that was unsupervised and unrestrained.

This was especially seen in Theodore Dreiser's 1900 book *Sister Carrie*. Although this novel was written well before the Jazz Age, it showed many what could happen to an innocent young farm girl in the big city. This was the story of Carrie, an attractive young girl who travels to Chicago in hopes of finding a better life. She struggles with menial labor and the low pay offered in such positions. Her beauty certainly has an effect on men, and in one of the novel's more shocking elements (for its time), she loses her virginity. She later becomes involved with an older man who steals money from his company to provide a life of luxury for Carrie. They flee the country briefly. Winding up in New York, Carrie makes a name for herself as a stage actress, and her relationship with this man falls apart as she moves on with her new life, leaving him far behind, broke and forgotten. To many, this book was a moral tale of what could happen in the big city if one was not too careful and did not adhere to appropriate moral standards.

For farmers, this period began with worry. During the war years, the demand for agricultural products, both at home and abroad, brought nice profits. But, as is typical after a war ends, the marketplace changed and prices dropped. Part of the farmers' economic woes was the result of the financial focus shifting from an agricultural to an industrial base. Several historians also argued that farmers felt a loss of prestige during this time. The Jeffersonian ideal of the farmer as the mainstay of American society was no longer true. Now the urban centers held the allure.

For religious leaders, the Jazz Age provided innumerable topics for discussion. The Prohibition issue alone allowed many to preach about the hazards and moral implications of the use of alcohol. Furthermore, changes in fashion, music, and social interaction provided more than enough material for the pulpit, not to mention the fear of radicalism and issues such as evolution, which was perceived (in some cases rightfully so) as the antithesis to Christianity. Yet this is not to imply that all evangelists had a conservative agenda. Many religious leaders were reformers in their own right. It was argued that moving forward did not have to mean abandoning religious beliefs. Furthermore, to enforce conformity was to take away a person's moral choice. While it was hoped that people would make the right moral choice, forcing people to conform to a single set of beliefs was to take away individuality. Jesus did not preach intolerance. Listening to jazz music or having a beer did not make one sinful; excesses did.

So what exactly was the Jazz Age? Perhaps this period leaps out so much because it is sandwiched between the end of the Progressive Era and World War I and the start of the Great Depression. In contrast to the eras preceding and following the Jazz Age, it certainly stands out with a character all its own. To be sure, many of the elements of the Jazz Age hardly ended with the start of the Depression, just as many elements were not necessarily invented by the age. Society is fluid and forever changing, and although the use of the word "inevitable" is often dangerous, was this period bound to happen? Traditional society cannot always maintain its mainstream status and will eventually be replaced by newer styles. What is traditional today may seem laughable tomorrow. For the Jazz Age, it was a chance for a generation to make its own traditions. Whether these traditions endured is not the issue; what is the issue is that the opportunity was there, and people seized it.

The Jazz Age is one of the most fascinating periods in American history. Whether easily defined or enigmatic, the era definitely saw a society going through a time of growth. With the onset of the Great Depression the nation's priorities changed, but the memories left by the Jazz Age continue to hold this country's interest into modern times. Hollywood films often revisit the era. Historical museums often have exhibits depicting specific aspects of the times. The Jazz Age may sometimes come across as reckless and wild, but there was much in this period to capture the imagination of contemporary spectators.

Acknowledgments

The changes that have taken place in my life since I first signed the contract with ABC-CLIO to produce this book have been truly amazing. In some ways it is difficult for me to let this book go. But now that it is finished, and I can take a very short break until my next project, I wish to take this opportunity to thank those who helped me along the way.

I cannot say enough about those who contributed excellent chapters to this work. John Barnhill, Jeremy Bonner, Susan Ferentinos, Kurt Gartner, Scott Merriman, Sean O'Connor, and Jamie Wilson all provided exceptional, and original, pieces that I thoroughly enjoyed reading. Thank you for your hard work!

I would be most remiss not to mention the extremely helpful and very patient staff at ABC-CLIO who not only provided guidance through this project but were understanding when I underwent not one, but two computer breakdowns. Their willingness to answer questions and provide much valuable feedback helped me more than I can say. Kim Kennedy White, James Sherman, and Steve Danver were terrific, and I hope we work together again soon. Kim's remarkable skills as an editor still amaze me. Her keen eye helped spot numerous errors, and her good humor helped make any revisions easy.

There are others who have been invaluable to my life over the past several years. Those who gave me encouragement and support, and were there for me during difficult times, include Carlos Cortes, Robert Moore, Kristin Vanderbilt, Freddy Atkins, Jillian Campbell, Janelle Gilbert, John Nestler, Bob Brown, Dennis McGuire, Sarah Pickett, Jason Travis, Kathleen Krupica, Rick Kay, James Hogg, Marvin McClure, Art Armstrong, and Katie Glover, who just gave me an assignment I hope I will live up to. Of course, my parents and family deserve a nod of credit for putting up with me as I got back on my feet. If I neglected to mention your name, I am sorry!

There are five very precious people—my very dearest friends—who especially deserve credit. Karen Brad, Carlita Bruton, Kelly Carevic, Lilienne Li, and Josie Brissette have all been a major part of my life. You have no idea how much I appreciate and love you for what you have done for me. You had faith in me during the times I had none in myself. I wish I could give you each an acknowledgment chapter as you deserve.

But most of all I must acknowledge my 11-year-old daughter, Safira. She read my chapters and had the most interesting comments to make, helping me to correct unclear and convoluted statements. Saffy also serves as my personal adviser. I can talk to her about anything, and she provides insights and advice that go well beyond her young age. She is the light of my life and is probably better known at the Museum of Science and Industry than I am, and I work there.

About the Editor and Contributors

Mitchell Newton-Matza is a Chicago native. He received his B.A. in history from Eastern Illinois University and an M.A. from DePaul University. He earned his Ph.D. from the Catholic University of America, in Washington, D.C., where he concentrated on the history of law and labor, with minor fields in Habsburg Austria and U.S. radical literature. He also has a love for world history, especially that of Asia and Latin America. He currently resides in Chicago, Illinois, where he completed his dissertation *Intelligent and Honest Radicals: The Chicago Federation of Labor and the Illinois Legal System, 1919–1932*, which is a study of the relationship between the Chicago labor movement and Illinois law. It is scheduled for publication in 2009 by the University Press of America. He also contributed two chapters for the *Railroads* volume in the nine-volume series *The Industrial Revolution in America—Lives of the Workforce and Labor Organizations and Reform Movements*. He has been previously published in journals such as *The Journal of Juvenile Law, Proceedings of the Association for Living Historical Farms and Agricultural Museums,* and *The Journal of the Illinois State Historical Society*, and he has written more than 30 encyclopedia and reference articles. He has been teaching history for several years at various universities and colleges throughout the Chicago area and is currently on staff at Westwood College, O'Hare campus, where he teaches history, critical thinking, research methods, and college writing. Mitchell has also presented, or commented on, numerous papers at conferences such as the Illinois History Symposium, Popular Culture Conference, and the Working Class Studies Conference. He also works at the world-famous Museum of Science and Industry as a facilitator, providing educational and interactive experiences for museum guests. His favorite exhibits to work are the coal mine, the U-505 submarine, and Pocket Science.

John H. Barnhill is an independent scholar. He received his Ph.D. from Oklahoma State University, Stillwater, in 1981. His professional experience includes teaching at the university level as well as working in a museum, the Oklahoma state archives, an Air Force field history office, and, strangely, a

Department of Defense computing facility. He has published a book and hundreds of journal and encyclopedia articles and reviews. He currently resides in Houston, Texas.

Jeremy Bonner is an independent scholar in Pittsburgh.

Susan Ferentinos is the public history manager for the Organization of American Historians. She holds a master's of library science and a Ph.D. in history from Indiana University and has been the recipient of numerous grants and awards for her research in the history of family, gender, and sexuality. She is currently working on a book with a working title of *An Unpredictable Age: Sex, Consumption, and the Emergence of the American Teenager, 1900-1950.*

Kurt Gartner has served as an associate professor of music at Kansas State University since 1999. Gartner's 2007–2008 responsibilities included an assignment as special assistant to the provost and a spring 2008 sabbatical leave. As a 2006–2007 Big 12 Faculty Fellow, he collaborated with the percussion studio and jazz program at the University of Missouri. Since 2004, he has served the Percussive Arts Society as music technology editor for the journal *Percussive Notes*. Before his appointment at KSU, Dr. Gartner served as an associate professor of bands at Purdue University in West Lafayette, Indiana. In 2001, he completed his doctor of arts degree at the University of Northern Colorado (Greeley), where he studied percussion and jazz performance and pedagogy, directed a jazz band and a percussion ensemble, taught jazz history, and was the assistant director of the UNC/Greeley Jazz Festival. Gartner received the Graduate Dean's Citation for Outstanding Dissertation for his research on the late percussion legend Tito Puente. In association with this research, Dr. Gartner has also studied percussion and arranging at the prestigious Escuela Nacionál de Música in Havana, Cuba.

Scott Allen Merriman is a lecturer in history at Troy University, Montgomery, Alabama. Among his published works are *Religion and the Law in America* and *The History Highway 4.0.* In addition, he has written numerous articles and encyclopedia entries. He received his Ph.D. in history from the University of Kentucky. He previously taught at a number of universities, including the University of Cincinnati, Thomas More College, and the University of Maryland University College. His current research projects include a study of the Espionage and Sedition Acts in the Midwest.

Sean O'Connor was born in Oak Park, Illinois, and has been a lifelong resident of the Chicago area. He studied history and political science at Northern Illinois University (NIU), earning a B.A. with honors in 2002 and an M.A. in 2005. While an undergraduate, he was president of NIU's History Club (2000–2002) and the Eta-Eta Chapter of Phi Alpha Theta (2001–2002). He was twice named Outstanding Student of the Year by the History Department (2001, 2002) and won the History Department's Undergraduate (491) Essay Prize in 2002. His theses have been on resistance to standard time and daylight saving time in the United States and the United Kingdom. In March 2008, he was appointed interim archivist of Chicago's Museum of Science and Industry (MSI) after working there as an assistant to the archivist

(2005–2009) and a program interpreter (2001–2008). He has spoken at the 9th and 10th conferences on Illinois history on, respectively, time regime resistance in Illinois and the architecture of MSI. Mr. O'Connor is a member of the American History Association, the American Association of Museums, the Society of American Archivists, the Midwest Archives Conference, the Association of Midwest Museums, Chicago Area Archivists, and Chicago Area Medical Archivists. In his spare time, he writes movie reviews for his friends. His first conference paper was titled "Chicago Time," and he is creating an extensive PowerPoint presentation called *A Temple for the Muses: The Museum of Science and Industry*, a summary of his paper *A Temple for the Muses: The Architecture, Construction, Dilapidation, Reconstruction, and Expansion of the Museum of Science & Industry's House, the Palace of Fine Arts in Chicago's Jackson Park.*

Jamie J. Wilson received his Ph.D. from New York University and is an assistant professor of United States and African American history at Salem State College in Salem, Massachusetts. His research on the African American experience has appeared in academic and popular journals. Currently, he is working on a manuscript about black urbanization in Harlem, New York, during the interwar period.

Chronology

1918

General Developments Spanish influenza sweeps through the United States, Europe, and Asia. An estimated 20–30 million people die in an epidemic that lasts through 1919.

The U.S. Marines engage in their first World War I battles at Cantigny and Château-Thierry.

Russian Bolshevik leader Vladimir Lenin signs a pact with Germany, effectively pulling Russia out of World War I, an act that puts additional burdens on the Allies.

January U.S. president Woodrow Wilson introduces his Fourteen Points to Congress, outlining his plans for post–World War I peace. This document is a plan for restructuring the postwar world. Part of this restructuring includes national self-determination. Many areas that were previously part of the Habsburg Empire, also known as Austria-Hungary, were consolidated into new nations, such as the former Czechoslovakia. The plan also called for a League of Nations, a precursor to the modern United Nations.

October President Wilson suffers a stroke. Not only are vital presidential duties thrown into a turmoil, but so are the negotiations of the postwar world. Wilson recovers enough to take over his duties, but in a weakened state.

October 25 President Wilson appeals to American voters to provide the Democrats with majority control of both houses of Congress.

November 11 Signing of the Armistice bringing the end of World War I hostilities.

December 29 In what would eventually develop into the national Farmer-Labor Party, the Chicago Federation of Labor creates the Labor Party of Cook County.

1919

General Developments The Treaty of Versailles is signed, the peace treaty formally ending World War I.

Mass strikes by thousands upon thousands of workers break out across the country in various commercial and industrial centers. People fear a radical overthrow on the level of the two revolutions that occurred in Russia during 1917, leading to numerous activities by U.S. government agencies to curb radicalism.

John Lloyd Wright (son of the famous architect Frank Lloyd Wright) invents Lincoln Logs, which he markets with the Red Square Toy Company.

George B. Hansburg patents the pogo stick, which becomes immensely popular during the Jazz Age.

February 6–11 More than 65,000 workers in Seattle call a general strike. Although the strikers run the city for a time, Seattle is shut down. Pressure from the government and national labor leaders helps end the strike.

May 3 The U.S. Supreme Court decides the case *Schenck v. United States*, which was a challenge to the constitutionality of the World War I Espionage and Sedition Acts. These acts were considered to be an infringement on the right of free speech and political dissent against the war. This case upholds the acts by establishing the famous "clear and present danger" doctrine.

July 17 A young African American child swimming in Lake Michigan accidentally crosses into the white section and is pelted with rocks. One of the rocks hits the child in the head and he drowns, touching off race riots in Chicago, which are marked by several days of violence, at the end of which 38 people are dead.

September In a debate over support for the Soviet Union, in Chicago the left wing of the Socialist Party is expelled leading to two subsequent events: On September 1, the Communist Labor Party is formed by such people as famed author John Reed; and on September 2, the Communist Party is formed, led by such people as Louis Fraina. Both parties identify with the Bolsheviks of the Soviet Union and seek recognition. The Russians refused to acknowledge either faction and order the two to combine, which they eventually do.

October 28 Over President Wilson's veto, Congress passes the National Prohibition Enforcement Act (also known as the Volstead Act), providing enforcement of the 18th Amendment, which takes effect the following year, banning alcoholic beverages.

November 10–12 The first national convention of the newly formed American Legion takes place in Minneapolis, Minnesota. The American Legion contains members of the World War I American Expeditionary Forces.

December 24 President Wilson announces that the railroads would be returned to private control on March 1, 1920.

1920

General Developments The national census reveals that for the first time in U.S. history more people lived in urban rather than rural settings.

The population of the United States is 106.4 million people.

Harry Burt invents the Good Humor bar, an ice cream bar on a stick covered with chocolate.

The League of Nations has its first meeting in Geneva, Switzerland.

The U.S. Senate rejects the United States becoming a member of the League of Nations, despite the fact that the League was created at the prompting of President Wilson.

F. Scott Fitzgerald publishes *This Side of Paradise*.

Edna St. Vincent Millay publishes *A Few Figs from Thistles*.

Sinclair Lewis publishes *Main Street*.

Trojan condoms make their debut. The idea of birth control becomes a major moral controversy during the Jazz Age.

January 2 U.S. attorney general A. Mitchell Palmer instructs federal agents to arrest thousands of suspected radicals, mostly communists, in what are known as the Palmer raids. Many are deported, although the majority of those rounded up were innocent. Approximately 6,000 people in 36 cities are rounded up.

January 3 The Boston Red Sox trade baseball great Babe Ruth to the New York Yankees for the previously unheard of sum of $125,000.

January 10 The newly created League of Nations, the forerunner to the United Nations, ratifies the Treaty of Versailles.

January 16 The Eighteenth Amendment goes into effect and Prohibition becomes national law. The manufacture, sale, or possession of alcoholic beverages is prohibited.

February 13 Secretary of State Robert Lansing resigns from office at the request of President Wilson, who accuses Lansing of holding unauthorized cabinet meetings when Wilson had a physical collapse in 1919.

February 14 The League of Women's Voters is created in Chicago.

February 28 The Transportation Act, also known as the Esch-Cummins Act, is passed. The law provides for the return of railroads to private control. The act also expands the powers of the Interstate Commerce Commission to include such activities as setting minimum and maximum rates and regulating service and traffic.

March 28 Hollywood continues to be big national news with the marriage of movie stars Douglas Fairbanks and Mary Pickford.

April 17 The American Professional Football League is created.

April 20 Deadly tornadoes sweep through Mississippi and Alabama, killing 219 people.

May 2 The Negro National League plays its first baseball game in Indianapolis, Indiana.

May 5 Italian immigrants and Anarchists Nicola Sacco and Bartolomeo Vanzetti are arrested for a robbery and murder in Braintree, Massachusetts. This touches off a worldwide controversy over the subsequent trial and conviction. They are executed in 1927.

May 8 The Socialist Party convention meets in New York and again nominates Eugene V. Debs as its presidential candidate, although he is still in prison.

June 5 The Merchant Marine Act, also known as the Jones Act, is passed. The law repeals the emergency war regulations concerning shipping. The act also creates a Shipping Board, which is authorized to propose shipping routes, and allows the sale of ships built by the government to private parties. $25 million of the money raised would be used for loans to those constructing new vessels.

June 8 The Republican convention meets in Chicago and nominates Warren G. Harding for president and Calvin Coolidge for vice president.

June 10 The Water Power Act is passed, which creates a Federal Power Commission. This law addresses water power reserves on public lands, excluding Native American reservations. The commission is authorized to provide 50-year licenses to construct power-producing facilities, after which the government will assume control.

June 28 The Democratic convention meets in San Francisco and nominates James Cox for president and future president Franklin D. Roosevelt as vice president.

July 11–13 The Farmer-Labor Party, a development of the Labor Party created by the Chicago Federation of Labor, is formed in Chicago and nominates Parley Parker Christensen for president.

August 26 Women are given the right to vote with the ratification of the Nineteenth Amendment.

September 8 Airmail service begins between New York and San Francisco.

September 28 Eight players on the Chicago White Sox baseball team are indicted for intentionally losing the 1919 World Series in the infamous Black Sox Scandal. Federal judge Kenesaw Mountain Landis would go on to become the first commissioner of baseball.

October 19 John Reed, the famed Socialist writer and cofounder of the Communist Labor Party, dies of typhus in the Soviet Union.

November 2 Warren G. Harding is elected president in a landslide. The Farmer-Labor Party candidate, Parley Parker Christensen, fails to garner even 1 percent of the vote, and Socialist Party candidate Eugene V. Debs, running from an Atlanta penitentiary, gains 3.4 percent.
Pittsburgh radio station KDKA goes on the air in the first broadcast for the industry.

1921

General Developments Johnson & Johnson launches the Band-Aid bandages
product.

Popular candy bar Peter Paul Mounds bar makes its debut.

Cecile B. de Mille begins a string of films using sex and sensation, sparking a considerable amount of controversy and calls for more stringent censorship of Hollywood films.

The Pan African Congress meets in London and Brussels in the late summer and fall.
W. E. B. Du Bois, Walter White, and Jessie Redmon Fausett attend as representatives of the National Association for the Advancement of Colored People (NAACP).

Ezra Pound publishes *Poems 1918–1921.*

John Dos Passos publishes *Three Soldiers.*

Edith Wharton wins the Pulitzer Prize for *Age of Innocence.*

January 2 The Pittsburgh radio station KDKA makes the first religious radio
broadcast.

March 4 Harding is inaugurated as president.

March 18 Members of the Universal Negro Improvement Association (UNIA), the
group founded by Marcus Garvey, travel to Monrovia, Liberia, as part of Garvey's Back to Africa movement in order to discuss a program with the
government.

May 19 The Emergency Quota Act is passed. In the first of two major legislative acts
during the 1920s, immigration is cut by more than 95 percent by setting
quotas according to a group's population number as listed in the 1910
census.

May 31 At least 39 die in the Tulsa race riots. The riots are touched off by an elevator
incident involving Dick Rowland, a black man, and Sarah Page, a white
woman, who was said to have screamed. Some people accused Rowland of
an attempted sexual assault, but other accounts noted that he accidentally
stepped on her feet. While a white mob went to lynch Rowland, who was in
a jail cell, a black mob was prepared to protect him. A discharged gun set off
a flurry of violence.

June 10 The Budget and Accounting Act is passed to reform the national budget.
The act requires the president to submit a budget of estimates for both
expenditures and receipts and to submit a statement of the government's financial status.

July 14 After a highly questionable trial, Sacco and Vanzetti are found guilty.

July 21 Aviator Billy Mitchell demonstrates air power by using an aircraft to demonstrate how a battleship could be destroyed from the air.

August 9 The Veterans Bureau is created as an independent unit responsible for
administering veterans' relief.

August 15 The Packers and Stockyards Act is passed. The law bans unfair practices, such as price manipulations, and requires stockyards to register with the U.S. Department of Agriculture.

August 24 The Grain Trading Futures Act regulates contract markets selling grain for future delivery with the intention of preventing unfair market manipulations.

September 7–8 The inaugural Miss America beauty pageant is held in Atlantic City, New Jersey.

October 5 The first baseball game to be broadcast over the radio is game one of the World Series. WJZ, from Newark, New Jersey, provides the broadcast.

October 18 Charles P. Strite patents the first bread toaster.

November 11 Speaking at Arlington National Cemetery, Washington, D.C., to commemorate Veterans Day, President Harding's speech is broadcast in two cities.

November 23 Congress passes the Sheppard-Towner Act authorizing $1 million in federal aid to the states to promote the welfare and health of maternity and infancy.

1922

General Developments Herbert T. Kalmus develops the Technicolor process.
Albert H. Taylor and Leo C. Young develop radar for the Navy, using past studies and experiments.
The Society for the Preservation of Negro Spirituals goes on tour. Members perform for segregated audiences on the East Coast.
The self-winding wristwatch is invented.
Reader's Digest is founded.
The first all-African American Broadway show, *Shuffle Along*, debuts.
F. Scott Fitzgerald publishes *Tales of the Jazz Age*.
Sinclair Lewis publishes *Babbitt*. Despite its indictment of modern life, cities across the country claim to be the model for the book's fictional town of Zenith.
James Weldon Johnson publishes *Book of American Negro Poetry*.
Claude McKay publishes *Harlem Shadows*.

February 18 The Cooperative Marketing Act, also known as the Capper-Volstead Act, exempts agricultural producers and cooperatives from antitrust laws.

May 30 The Lincoln Memorial is dedicated in Washington, D.C.

June 24 In Tulsa, Oklahoma, the KKK initiates more than 1,000 new members.

August 28 Radio station WEAF in New York City airs the first commercially sponsored program.

September 4 James H. Doolittle flies across the United States in under 24 hours, setting a new record.

September 22 The Cable Act is passed, providing married women U.S. citizenship independent of their husbands.

December 1 In what would become a world phenomenon, Howard Carter discovers the tomb of Egyptian pharaoh King Tutankhamen. The curse of King Tut's tomb becomes part of world folklore.

1923

General Developments John D. Hertz purchases a rental car company and renames it the Hertz Drive-Ur-Self System.

The Committee of One Hundred is established in Mississippi by African American leaders to discuss and express black people's political and economic concerns.

Back to Africa and UNIA leader Marcus Garvey is convicted of mail fraud, despite the flimsy and questionable evidence against him.

The first legal birth control clinic opens in New York City.

March 3 Henry R. Luce and Briton Hadden publish the first issue of *Time* magazine.

August 2 President Harding suddenly dies of a heart attack in San Francisco. Rumors about the true cause of his death run rampant as corruption within his administration becomes more publicized. Arguments persist that Harding's death is too mysterious and that he was murdered to cover up the alleged corruption. Vice President Calvin Coolidge is sworn in as the new president the following day.

September 15 The governor of Oklahoma declares martial law as the KKK becomes out of control.

October 16 Walt and Roy Disney create the Walt Disney Company.

December 6 Coolidge gives the first official presidential address over the radio.

December 10 The first version of the Equal Rights Amendment is introduced and defeated in Congress.

1924

General Developments The McCormick-Patterson chain begins the first publication of the *New York Daily News*, a tabloid. The paper features sensational news, crime, and sex stories.

The first Macy's Thanksgiving Day parade is held.

Kleenex Kerchiefs, innovations in facial tissues, are introduced by the Kimberly-Clark Corporation.

J. Edgar Hoover is appointed director of the Bureau of Investigation, which would be renamed the Federal Bureau of Investigation in 1935.

The KKK reaches its height of influence across the United States.

February 3 Former president Woodrow Wilson dies.

February 12 The very first performance of *Rhapsody in Blue*, by George Gershwin, takes place in New York City at the Aeolian Hall.

April 9 The Dawes Plan is reported. In a response to Germany's difficulties paying reparations for World War I, the plan called for a way to stabilize the German economy and set up a schedule of payments.

May 18 The Chicago Federation of Labor officially severs all ties with the Farmer-Labor Party, which had since been taken over by the communists, and returns to the American Federation of Labor's political stance of nonpartisanship.

May 19 The World War Adjusted Compensation Act, also known as the Soldiers' Bonus Act, provides for compensation for veterans below the rank of captain. The adjusted rates are $1.25 a day for overseas duty and $1 for U.S. service.

May 21 In what would become a nationally known sensational case, Nathan Leopold and Richard Loeb, two students at the University of Chicago, murder 14-year-old Bobby Franks. They will later be spared from the death penalty by famed attorney Clarence Darrow.

May 26 The National Origins Act, also known as the Johnson-Reed Act, passes placing new restrictions on immigration. In superseding the 1921 Emergency Quota Act, immigration is restricted to 2 percent of a group's population number as listed in the 1890 census. This is especially directed at preventing large numbers of Eastern European immigrants.

June 15 The Ford Motor Company produces its 10 millionth car.

June 30 Secretary of Interior Albert Fall is implicated in the Teapot Dome scandal. He is the first cabinet member to go to prison.

August 24 The Agricultural Marketing Act is passed. In an effort to prevent the dumping of agricultural goods on the market, which could lead to farm foreclosures, loans are provided to cooperatives and dealers to hold products from the marketplace.

October The comic strip *Little Orphan Annie* makes its debut in New York City's *Daily News*.

November Coolidge is elected president in his own right.

December 11 James B. Duke presents a $40 million grant to Trinity College, changing its name to Duke University.

December 13 Samuel L. Gompers, the longtime leader of the American Federation of Labor, dies.

1925

General Developments *The New Negro,* edited by Alain Locke, makes its debut. As part of what would be known as the Harlem Renaissance, this book is a collection of writings by African American authors examining their role in American culture and society.

A. Philip Randolph organizes the Brotherhood of Sleeping Car Porters.

The Louisville *Courier-Journal* begins the first children's National Spelling Bee.

Mein Kampf, written by future Nazi dictator Adolf Hitler, is published. The book, which outlines Hitler's hatred toward the Jews and his plans for domination, receives little notice in the United States.

Marcus Garvey begins serving his five-year prison sentence for mail fraud.

New York's Madison Square Garden opens.

John Dos Passos publishes *Manhattan Transfer.*

George Bernard Shaw wins the Nobel Prize for Literature.

Sinclair Lewis publishes *Arrowsmith.*

The Book of American Negro Spirituals is published.

Gertrude Stein publishes *The Making of Americans.*

Hollywood's first big war movie, *The Big Parade,* is released. It is a story of World War I that follows its characters from patriotic fervor to the realities of war. Also presented are the relationships many U.S. soldiers had with French women while overseas.

January 3 In Italy, Benito Mussolini announces he is seizing power.

January 5 Nellie Tayloe Ross becomes the first woman governor in history, taking over in Wyoming upon the death of her husband.

February 16 Floyd Collins dies in Sand Cave, Kentucky, after being trapped for 18 days. The event becomes a virtual media circus, and many reporters provide frequent updates.

March The American Negro Congress is formed.

April 10 F. Scott Fitzgerald publishes *The Great Gatsby.*

June 2 Lou Gehrig, a player for the New York Yankees baseball team, begins his streak of 2,120 consecutive games, a record that lasts for decades.

June 6 Walter Percy Chrysler forms the Chrysler Corporation.

June 29 A devastating earthquake destroys Santa Barbara, California.

July 10–21 The Scopes "Monkey" Trial in Dayton, Tennessee, becomes nationwide news and a media circus. John Scopes is indicted, tried, and convicted for violating the state's law against teaching evolution. Acting for the prosecution is former presidential candidate and secretary of state William Jennings Bryan. For the defense is the famous Chicago lawyer Clarence Darrow, who recently convinced jurors to spare the lives of Leopold and Loeb.

August 8 With approximately 40,000 members, the KKK stages a march down Pennsylvania Avenue in Washington, D.C., its largest parade ever.

August 16 The *Gold Rush*, by and starring Charlie Chaplin, debuts.

September 13 The first university for African Americans, Xavier University, opens its doors.

October 28 Col. William "Billy" Mitchell is court-martialed for insubordination and resigns from the army. Mitchell, an advocate of the use and importance of air power in military conflicts, earns a five-year suspension from service for his open criticism of the high brass.

1926

General Developments Soviet film director Sergei Eisenstein's classic work, *The Battleship Potemkin*, is screened in the United States. This groundbreaking work uses the idea of montage in filmmaking.
Langston Hughes publishes *The Weary Blues*.
Kodak introduces the 16mm film.
The Book-of-the-Month Club debuts. This club becomes enormously popular as it not only encourages more people to read but also to discuss literature.
Ernest Hemingway publishes *The Sun Also Rises*.
Carl Van Vechten publishes *Nigger Heaven*.
Evangelist preacher Aimee Semple MacPherson claims to have been abducted, despite no evidence to prove it happened. Her reputation takes further hits as rumors of improper behavior, including illicit relationships, are circulated.
The National Broadcasting Company (NBC) creates the first radio network across the country.

January The U.S. Senate approves the entry of the United States into the World Court.

February The Revenue Act is passed reducing personal income and inheritance taxes.

March 7 The first transatlantic telephone conversation takes place between New York and London.

March 16 Robert H. Goddard launches his first rocket.

May 9 Richard E. Byrd and Floyd Bennett make the first flight over the North Pole.

August 6 Gertrude Ederle is the first woman to swim the English Channel.

August 23 Silent film star Rudolph Valentino dies.

September 18 A severe hurricane hits Florida, resulting in the deaths of more than 300 people. The storm also puts an end to the land boom previously engulfing the area.

1927

General Developments Noted writer Sinclair Lewis publishes *Elmer Gantry*, which is an indictment of the use of organized religion for personal monetary gain.

President Coolidge commutes the prison sentence of Marcus Garvey, who is then deported back to Jamaica.

Langston Hughes publishes *Fine Clothes to the Jew*.

The Harlem Globetrotters, a basketball team that becomes noted for its sporting skills and humorous shows, makes its debut.

The first tunnel for vehicles opens between New York and New Jersey.

James Weldon Johnson rereleases his 1912 work *Autobiography of an Ex-Colored Man*, but this time his name is placed on the book.

The McNary-Haugen Farm Relief bill is vetoed by President Coolidge, arguing that it is an unwarranted intrusion of the federal government in the national economy.

The U.S. Supreme Court allows for the sterilization of "feeble-minded" people in *Buck v. Bell*.

Cecile B. De Mille's biblical film *King of Kings*, about the life of Jesus, makes its debut.

Duke Ellington and his band do a live broadcast from New York's famed Cotton Club.

February 23 To regulate the radio industry, Congress creates the Federal Communications Commission (FCC).

March 3 The Treasury Department creates the Prohibition Bureau to fight bootlegging.

May 16 The first Academy Awards are held. *Wings* is the first film to win the Best Picture award.

May 20–21 Charles Lindbergh makes his historic solo transatlantic flight from New York to Paris in a $33^{1}/_{2}$ hour trip.

September 27 New York Yankees slugger and baseball icon Babe Ruth hits his 60th home run for the season. The record is not broken until the end of the century.

October 6 The first sound film, *The Jazz Singer*, opens in New York and is a huge success. Although a good portion of the film is silent, the famous phrase at the end of the film, "You ain't heard nothing yet," becomes a legend in film history.

December Giving in to pressure for new models, Henry Ford ceases production of his famous Model T, instead marketing his new Model A.

1928

General Developments Oscar DePriest becomes the first African American from the North to be elected to Congress. DePriest, who is from Chicago's First Congressional District, serves three terms.

Colonel Jacob Schick receives a patent for an electric razor.

D. H. Lawrence publishes his highly controversial *Lady Chatterley's Lover*.

Margaret Mead publishes *Coming of Age in Somoa*.

W. E. B. DuBois publishes *Dark Princess*.
Claude McKay publishes *Home to Harlem*.

January Ruth Snyder, a known adulteress and convicted murderer, is the first woman to be executed in the electric chair in New York's Sing Sing prison.

February 25 The FCC grants the first television license to Charles Jenkins Laboratories.

April 13 The Socialist Party convention meets in New York and nominates Norman Thomas for president.

May 11 General Electric starts regular broadcasts out of WGY in Schenectady, New York. Programming is for two hours, three days a week.

May 15 The Flood Control Act provides $325 million for levee work in the Mississippi Valley.

May 22 The Merchant Marine Act, also known as the Jones-White Act, increased the amount of government loan money available to private shipbuilders. The amount is increased from $125 million to $250 million and allows government ships to be sold at low prices.

May 27 The Workers' (Communist) Party convention meets in New York and nominates William Z. Foster for president.

June 12 The Republican Party convention meets in Kansas City, Missouri, and nominates Herbert Hoover for president.

June 17 Amelia Earhart begins her successful attempt to be the first woman to fly across the Atlantic Ocean.

June 26 The Democratic Party convention meets in Houston and nominates Alfred E. Smith for president.

June 30 Kodak produces the first color motion picture film.

August 27 The Kellogg-Briand Pact is signed in Paris, outlawing war.

October 15 Germany's Graf Zeppelin dirigible arrives at Lakehurst, New Jersey. Though dirigibles are considered to be the most elegant means of travel, they fail to gain huge successes.

November 6 Herbert Hoover wins the presidential election.

November 16 More than 6.6 million shares are traded on the New York Stock Exchange, a new record.

November 18 Walt Disney releases the first sound cartoon, *Steamboat Willie*. The character of Steamboat Willie eventually becomes the famous cartoon character Mickey Mouse.

December Congress approves the Boulder Dam Act, making the way for the construction of the famous dam in Nevada.

1929

General Developments Ernest Hemingway writes *A Farewell to Arms*.

Robert and Helen Lynd publish *Middletown*, an examination of life in a small Midwest town.

The Museum of Modern Art in New York opens its doors immediately after the stock market crash. Despite the economic downturn, the museum manages to survive.

Construction begins on the Empire State Building in New York. The building takes 14 months to complete.

Scotch tape is invented.

William Faulkner publishes *The Sound and the Fury*.

Thomas Wolfe publishes *Look Homeward Angel*.

February 14 Seven members of the George "Bugs" Moran gang are murdered in a garage in what is termed as the St. Valentine's Day Massacre. Although it is never proven in court, the gang hit is ordered by rival Chicago mobster Al "Scarface" Capone.

April 15 The Export Debenture Plan addresses the issue of farm relief by providing export bounties of specified commodities. However, controversy over the measure led to its defeat.

June 15 The Agricultural Marketing Act creates a Federal Farm Board, which includes the secretary of agriculture. Low-interest loans are provided to help stabilize the marketplace and allow for fluctuations in the prices.

October 24 On Black Thursday stock prices take a steep fall.

October 29 On Black Tuesday, the stock market crashes. More than $13 billion is lost, and the country soon enters the Great Depression.

1930

General Developments In spite of the growing Depression, President Hoover maintains his opposition to direct relief for the unemployed. He instead believes in decentralized work policies whereby the federal government leads a voluntary program working with agencies on state and local levels.

March 30 Created to establish guidelines for what is appropriate for movies, the Motion Pictures Production Code begins operation.

July 3 Veterans Administration Act creates the Veterans Administration as a way to place all federal activities concerning former servicemen under one organization.

November 4 In national elections the Republicans lose their Senate majority and see their majority in the House greatly reduced.

December 2 Hoover requests $100 to $150 million in appropriations for public works construction.

African Americans in the Jazz Age | 1

Jamie J. Wilson

Perceptions of African Americans

A popular misrepresentation persists regarding African Americans in the 1920s that stems at least partially from the term *Jazz Age*. The term conjures ideas of carefree living, sipping gin in black neighborhood speakeasies, American prosperity, and the expansion of creative artistic spaces for black Americans. These characterizations are only partially true, of course, and depending on them to discuss the position of black people in the United States during the 1920s obfuscates rather than illuminates the complicated political geography within which African Americans found themselves. Most black folks during the 1920s were not living it up at rent parties or discussing poetry in literary salons. Although many did, in the decade after World War I, most were continuing on the path that generations before them had tread. They were trying to fashion a life in a country that did not want them, a country that promised democracy to the world while denying citizenship to the children of those who built this country as slaves.

The Great Migration

African Americans were geographically, politically, and culturally in transition during the Jazz Age. During World War I, more than 400,000 African Americans left the South for opportunities in northern industries, and during the 1920s, more than 800,000 continued what historians have called the Great Migration, a seven-decade-long movement out of the South that would not end until the 1970s. The Great Migration was an extension of the long road to freedom, respect, and full citizenship African Americans had begun and traversed centuries before during slavery, Reconstruction,

The movement of African Americans en masse to northern and western cities of the United States in the early 20th century is referred to as the Great Migration. The movement was the result of increased industrialization and opportunities in the North, and the limitations and Jim Crow laws of the rural South. However, the racism of the North was often as harsh as that of the South. (*North Wind Picture Archives*)

and redemption. The reasons for migrating were as varied as the thousands of individuals who left. Some left for economic and political opportunities, and others fled for fear of legal and extralegal lynching, racial violence, and domestic abuse. Together, the underlying causes of the Great Migration, as sociologist Carol Marks observes, were economic stagnation and state policies that subjugated African Americans (Marks 1989, 5).

In the opening decades of the 20th century, the American South was continuing the slow process of industrialization that began shortly after the Civil War, but most of the southern population, about 57 percent, was still engaged in farming cotton as sharecroppers. Sharecropping was an economic system wherein plantation owners divided their land into smaller lots that were rented to poor whites and blacks who, in theory, received seeds, farming equipment, and provisions from the plantation owner, grew cotton, and received their share of the profits after the harvest. In actuality, sharecropping was an unequal system wherein cheating and chicanery kept sharecropping families in perpetual poverty and tied to the land. This arrangement would change, however, with the infestation of boll weevil.

The boll weevil arrived in the United States from Mexico in the early 1890s, and by 1912 the insect had spread throughout much of the Deep South, destroyed cotton crops, and forced plantation owners to decrease cotton cultivation in favor of other crops and release their poor black and white laborers. Consequently, thousands of rural laborers flocked to southern cities and towns looking for work in the floundering industrial sector. Before the arrival of rural agricultural laborers, industrialization exacerbated the competition between white and black industrial workers as black workers were displaced by white workers. The arrival of rural laborers led to increased competition for jobs, unemployment, and underemployment for black industrial workers. For those blacks who were employed, working conditions were hazardous and wages were 30 to 40 percent less than wages paid in other parts of the country. For many with sparse means and little hope of improving them, migration seemed to be the only choice.

Disenfranchisment and violence propelled others to leave the home of their ancestors. Using poll taxes, voter examinations, property qualifications, and other means, southern state legislatures effectively disenfranchised blacks at the turn of the 20th century and continued to legally deny them the right to vote until the 1960s. During the 1920s in Alabama, for example, potential black voters were required to own at least 40 acres of land on which taxes were paid. Similarly, throughout the South, the understanding clause was used to disqualify potential black voters. To vote, so the notion went, one had to a have a basic understanding of one's specific state and federal constitutions. In practice, however, spurious questions like "how many bubbles does a bar of soap make?" or "how many raindrops fall in an hour?" were asked (British Broadcasting Corporation 1995).

Without the right to vote, blacks were at the mercy of the Jim Crow system: second-class citizens, legally separated from whites, and unable to encourage politicians to consider issues of black civil rights, especially with regards to lynching. During the 1920s, there were 315 reported lynchings, of which 218 victims were black. Although they may have been statistically rare events according to historical sociologists, they had an enormous influence on African Americans and their reasons to leave the South (Figures in Stovel 2001, 843–880; Stephens 1999, 655–671). White southerners often lynched black men for allegedly raping white women; but more often, whites lynched blacks when white economic power and white privilege were threatened. One migrant offered a poignant response to violence in a letter to the *Chicago Defender*, the Chicago-based black newspaper and staunch advocate of migration, stating that "After twenty years of seeing my people lynched for any offense from spitting on the sidewalk to stealing a mule, I made up my mind that I would turn the prow of my ship toward the part of the country where the people at least made a pretense of being civilized" (Henri 1975, 130).

Northern Promises and Realities

Encouraged by the information they received from industry labor recruiters, black northern newspapers, black social welfare organizations, and family and friends who had already moved North, African Americans left the South for northern and western cities. Some fled alone, families migrated as a group, and, at times entire churches moved in cars and by foot, train, and steamship such that by 1920 almost 40 percent of African Americans in the North lived in Detroit, Cleveland, Cincinnati, Columbus, New York City, Philadelphia, Pittsburgh, and Chicago (Trotter 1991, 128).

In Chicago during the 1920s, African Americans faced discriminatory hiring practices, irregular employment, rising unemployment, and segregated housing. During the 1910s, especially during World War I, African Americans had gained a foothold in most of the major industries in Chicago. Blacks working in meatpacking, for example, increased by 363 percent during that decade, and the proportion of blacks in manufacturing and mechanical industries increased from 18.5 percent to 36.1 percent during the war. The continued migration and the return of white soldiers from abroad, however, led employers to replace thousands of black workers with white ones. Though some black women obtained clerical jobs, they were denied employment in most industries. Consequently, many African American women in Chicago were employed as domestic servants. Employment discrimination, combined with the recession of late 1920, led to marked deterioration in black Chicago's opportunities and life chances. As the decade progressed, charitable groups discussed high unemployment rates and opened shelters to house the black poor. In 1926, an employee of the U.S. Employment Service observed, "Many Negroes come to this city seeking employment which in many cases there [sic] are unable to secure. The result is they become destitute." Historian Gareth Canaan, has noted:

> . . . in 1927, the Chicago Urban League's Annual Report stated that the 1926–1927 fiscal year had the highest unemployment of any year since 1921. There were 2,414 placements that year compared to 3,515 in 1925–1926 and an average of 238 applicants for each 100 job openings during the year (Canaan 2001, 153).

Growing unemployment, decreased wages, and segregated housing policies and customs led African Americans to live in segregated housing options in the South Side of Chicago. Like blacks in other major cities, during the period, the Southside was an emerging ghetto wherein families paid exorbitant amounts for rent and lacked access to health care options, adequate schools, and recreation facilities, all of which led to compromised health. Although it is true that the black community in Chicago was better off than their southern relatives and that they had created homes in Chicago, one should be cautious in creating images of carefree, Jazz Age black communities filled with gaiety.

The urban industrial North was not the only destination of African American migrants. Many went to rural industrial areas and urban industrial centers in the upper South. In southern West Virginia the black population increased nearly 50 percent by 1920 to a total of approximately 60,000. Throughout the decade, migration would continue to expand the population to about 80,000 by 1930. Drawn by the coal mining industry, fewer incidents of racial violence, and better political opportunities, the 1920s saw the creation of stable black communities in the central Appalachian region. Similarly, African Americans left lower southern areas, traveled the Mississippi River corridor, and settled in Norfolk, Virginia, to find employment opportunities in the tobacco, shipping, and oil industries. Between 1910 and 1930, Norfolk's black population increased by 20,000.

Political Actions and Aspirations

Wherever they went, migrants were the fulcrum for political leverage in African Americans communities. Nonmigrant blacks throughout the South used the migration to speak out against discrimination and the causes of the migration, while black communities in destination areas used the increase in their population to form political organizations. One of the most pertinent examples of the ways in which nonmigrant blacks used the Great Migration as political leverage is the Committee of One Hundred in Mississippi. Founded by African American leaders, the organization was established in 1923 to discuss and express black people's political and economic concerns and negotiate with white local and countywide business and civic leaders. Capitalizing on white fears of losing more of their black laboring class, the committee successfully negotiated for the restoration of Alcorn Agricultural and Mechanical College Latin curriculum and encouraged the Mississippi state legislature to increase appropriations to statewide black vocational training. The group and other blacks appealed to white planters' and industrialists' self-interest to win temporary improvements in the working conditions in sawmills, as well as in the diets and living accommodations of sharecroppers.

Garvey and the UNIA

Migrants and nonmigrants also joined the Universal Negro Improvement Association (UNIA). Throughout the United States between 1918 and 1927, Africans Americans were galvanized by Marcus Garvey and the UNIA. Born in 1887 in Jamaica, Garvey organized the UNIA in Jamaica in 1914. After touring the United States to obtain support for vocational education in Jamaica, Garvey became convinced that Harlem, New York, would offer fertile ground in which to plant the seeds for his new organization. There the UNIA was incorporated in 1918 with the aims to

> . . . establish a Universal Confraternity among the race; to promote the spirit
> of pride and love; to reclaim the fallen; to administer to and assist the
> needy; to assist in civilizing the backward tribes of Africa; to assist in the
> development of Independent Negro nations and communities; to establish a
> central nation for the race, where they will be given the opportunity to
> develop themselves; to establish Commissaries and Agencies in the principal
> countries and cities of the world for the representation of all Negroes; to
> promote a conscientious Spiritual worship among the native tribes of Africa; to
> establish Universities, Colleges and Academies and Schools for racial education

Portrait of Marcus Garvey, publisher and founder of the Universal Negro Improvement Association and African Communities League.
(*Library of Congress*)

and culture of the people; to improve the general conditions of Negroes everywhere (Stein 1986, 31–32).

During that same year, Garvey, with the assistance of Madame C. J. Walker, purchased Liberty Hall, the headquarters for his organization, and began publishing the *Negro World,* the UNIA's periodical. Sold for 5¢ per copy in New York City and 10¢ outside the city, *Negro World* presented Garvey's views on black nationalism, featured essays on African and African American history, and provided reports on the projects of UNIA branches throughout the African Diaspora. At its height in 1921, the paper had a distribution of 75,000.

Marcus Garvey appealed to black working and middle classes by providing a "quasi-religious theory of race pride and advancement," a black capitalist economic plan, and fraternal bonds and relationships. In the postwar world of competing nations and empires, the UNIA created images of a black empire wherein African Americans and West Indians would not be under the heel of white racists and exploiters. The UNIA's Black Star Line and the

Black Cross Navigation and Trading Company, shipping ventures created in 1919 and 1924, respectively, aimed to unify the African Diaspora and be the cornerstone for black economic independence, encouraged African Americans, and provided a symbol for racial advancement to a people who had been left out of the American Dream. Blacks had already seen and heard of Garvey's dreams of black independence in the *Negro World*. More importantly, the paper practiced what its writers preached by employing large numbers of blacks. The UNIA annual August conventions, which first convened in 1920, included parades on Lenox Avenue in Harlem and made the UNIA a community organization. In August 1924, the biblical Jesus was canonized as the "Black Man of Sorrows" and his mother, Mary, as a black woman. Followers were given a political and economic plan to follow on earth and the promise of meeting their loving, black God after death.

Spreading the Word

Under the UNIA banner, hat factories and laundries were established in Chicago, restaurants in New York, and a publishing company in Pittsburgh. Branches were found in the Deep South, in Mississippi and Alabama; the Midwest, in Chicago and Cleveland; and as far west as Bakersfield, California. The UNIA continued to exist until Garvey's death in 1940 and was involved in citywide elections throughout the country in the mid-1920s, but by 1921 the proverbial die was cast and the organization began to wane. During that year the Black Star Line was dissolved, Garvey was under investigation for mail fraud, and black leaders like W. E. B. DuBois, A. Philip Randolph, Chandler Owen, and Robert Abbott began calling for his ouster. In 1922, Garvey was convicted of mail fraud. Despite appeals, he was imprisoned in 1925 and deported to Jamaica in 1927.

Garvey's UNIA was especially significant in the postwar world as it embodied a new political sensibility among black Americans; it represented what historians and contemporaries called the "New Negro." As political scientist Dean Robinson notes, with Garvey "support for black nationalism arguably reached an all-time high in the United States, until the expansion of the Nation of Islam in the late 1950s" (Robinson 2001, 24). Conservative estimates of his constituents indicate that the UNIA at its zenith had 2 million dues-paying members and 6 million supporters nationwide. Although the actual number of Garvey's adherents will never be known for sure, the UNIA provided a training ground for future black activists, offered a political awareness that would be appropriated by later black nationalists like Malcolm X, and electrified a decade with hope and political struggle.

African Blood Brotherhood

The UNIA was not the only black political organization operating in the 1920s. During the postwar period, Harlem was home to black socialists like

African Americans and the Communist Party

Many studies of the role of African Americans during the Jazz Age generally concentrate on two areas: the Harlem Renaissance and racial discrimination, especially as the KKK rose to national prominence. But, as with any other group of people, there was far more to note and celebrate. What is not always discussed are influences on African American thinking and behavior.

To the Communist Party, blacks were prime territory. Communism, in its pure form, promotes equality among all, regardless of race or gender. Communist organizers were active in the southern states, especially among sharecroppers and farm workers.

As some studies of communist activities in the south have pointed out, all too often organizers did not take into account that blacks were not quite as ignorant as commonly believed. Organizers did not always understand what it meant to be a black American, especially in the southern states. Although many blacks did not have the benefit of an education, that was not to imply

A. Philip Randolph and Chandler Owen, the editors of the *Messenger*, who advocated trade unionism, socialism, and political equality. It was also the home to the African Blood Brotherhood (ABB), a secret Afro-Marxist organization founded in Harlem during World War I and made up of African American and West Indian radicals, including Ben E. and Theodore Burrell, Grace Campbell, W. A. Domingo, Ottow Huiswood, and William Jones, all of whom were members of the Supreme Council of the Brotherhood. Wedding socialist ideas with tenets of black nationalism and Pan-Africanism, the ABB espoused independence and self-determination for Africans and all people of African descent. Initially, these ideas led the group to attempt a political relationship with the UNIA, but Garvey castigated the group for being too radical. As Garvey was a black capitalist, the ABB's socialist ideas were too much for him to consider, and the budding relationship withered in 1921, the same year the ABB received national attention when the Oklahoma chapter provided armed self-defense for blacks during the race riots in Tulsa, Oklahoma.

Throughout the early 1920s, the ABB grew in size and attracted thousands of black working- and middle-class members. Organizing discussion and lectures, writing newspaper articles, and speaking on street corners, the ABB radicalized parts of African American communities nationwide. Simultaneously, the Communist Party was developing its approach to the race question in the United States and its relationship to African Americans. In 1925, the ABB dissolved as members joined the American Negro Labor Congress (ANLC) of the Communist Party, which though short-lived and opposed by segments of African America, placed African Americans on the communist agenda and made the Communist Party an important political group among blacks.

they were unintelligent. Some could not sufficiently argue political and economic theory, but blacks were well aware of what needed to be done to improve their lot. Communism was just one possible way. Communist organizers needed to realize that black Americans were not so easily led, for they had their own ideas.

Many blacks did in fact join the Communist Party, which was in itself a very risky move. Communism was anathema to American society, and for a racial group who already faced enormous discrimination to join an organization forced to operate underground would do little to improve their status. The KKK despised communism as being anti-American. The Klan operated in every state in the United States, and for blacks, who already suffered at their hands, being a communist merely meant courting even more trouble. But for those African Americans who embraced communism, the benefits seemed worth the risk.

Pan-African Congresses

The politics of the UNIA and the ABB demonstrates that African Americans' creative capacities and political sensibilities during the Jazz Age went beyond the geographical constraints of the United States as many continued a dialogue and political discourse regarding African Americans' relationship with Africa and diasporic communities. Between 1919 and 1927, W. E. B. DuBois organized several Pan-African congresses attended by leading black intellectuals and activists from the United States, Europe, the Caribbean, and Africa. The first meeting convened in Paris, France, in February 1919 and was attended by 57 delegates, four of whom represented the governments of France, Belgium, Portugal, and the United States—nations responsible for the colonial administration of Africa. Resolutions were passed to encourage the League of Nations to formulate ways to monitor and regulate colonial rule in Africa in the areas of government and labor, native African enfranchisement by colonial governments, universal education of native Africans, and the exploitation of African natural resources by European powers. The 1921 Pan-African Congress, which met in London and Brussels in the late summer and fall, was more radical in its approach and better attended than the previous congress of 1919; of the 110 delegates, three—DuBois, Walter White, and Jessie Redmon Fausett—attended as representatives of the National Association for the Advancement of Colored People (NAACP). The growing anticolonial sentiment throughout the African Diaspora was expressed in the Congress's resolutions that criticized African colonial powers and white supremacy. Together, these two conferences, along with the 1925 London Pan-African Congress and the 1927 conference in New York City, indicate that African Americans saw themselves as possessing similar social, political, and economic concerns and aspiration with other people of African descent throughout the world.

The Continued Presence of the NAACP

For the NAACP, these concerns included civil rights for African Americans. Founded in 1909 by progressive whites and blacks who had been affiliated with the Niagara Movement, the moderately nationalist NAACP, now the oldest black political organization, was entering its second decade of operation in the 1920s. Black nationalists of the era often characterized the NAACP as a bourgeois organization, out of touch with the black working class. This perception, however, is misleading. The NAACP's leadership was an interracial coalition of middle-class individuals who may have had bourgeois tastes and perspectives, but many of its members were workers and rural farmers. Reading the *Crisis*, the monthly periodical of the NAACP, which was edited by W. E. B. Du Bois during the period, one more fully understands the organization's appeal. Unlike Garvey's UNIA, which called for repatriation to Africa or political separation, the NAACP stood for full and complete equality for African Americans in all sectors of American life. Throughout the 1920s, the NAACP used mass action, lobbying, and litigation to achieve that goal. As historian Mark Schneider recalls, "In the vast America beyond [New York City], three hundred to four hundred African-American branches of the NAACP fought for voting rights and education, against segregation and lynching, in a thousand battles both spectacular and quotidian" (Schneider 2002, 4).

Throughout the 1920s, the NAACP fought residential segregation through litigation. In Washington, D.C., in 1922, the group fought the use of restrictive covenants, pacts between white property owners to refuse to sell property to African Americans, when Helen Curtis was denied the purchase of a home in a white neighborhood. NAACP lawyers argued that restrictive covenants violated the Fourteenth and Fifteenth Amendments, and after a series of appeals and setbacks, the case *Corrigan v. Buckley* was heard before the Supreme Court in 1926. The Court upheld restrictive covenants, and the NAACP lost its case, but in doing so they laid the foundation for the 1948 *Shelley v. Kramer* case, which overturned restrictive covenants. Similarly, in 1927, the NAACP shook the foundation of residential segregation with *Harmon v. Tyler*, when the United States Supreme Court ruled for the elimination of residential ordinances in New Orleans. That same year, the organization successfully defended Dr. Ossian Sweet of Detroit who was charged with murder and attempted murder after he and his family defended their home against a white mob.

The Harlem Renaissance

The NAACP was also instrumental in creating a literary space for African American writers in the *Crisis*, the organization's periodical, and by doing so helped usher in the Harlem Renaissance, a political, cultural, and

As jazz musicians ventured to Northern cities during the 1920s, new regions of the country got the opportunity to experience live jazz performance in dance clubs and night clubs. (*Michael Ochs Archives/Getty Images*)

literary movement centered in Harlem, New York, from 1919 to 1929. The political foundation of the Harlem Renaissance was best stated by James Weldon Johnson, one of the foundational supports of the movement:

> The final measure of the greatness of all peoples is the amount and standard of the literature and art they have produced. The world does not know that a people is great until that people produces great literature and art. No people that has produced great literature and art has ever been looked upon by the world as distinctly inferior . . . and nothing will do more to change the mental attitude and raise his status than a demonstration of intellectual parity by the Negro through the production of literature and art.

With blacks being effectively shut out of unions, jobs, and politics, the arts appeared to be a place where they would be recognized. This recognition, in turn, would provide political rights, according to Charles Johnson, a sociologist and the primary energy behind the Renaissance (Lewis 1997, 125–130). Others saw the Renaissance as a multifaceted endeavor to depict the lives, voice the concerns, and intimate the desires of African Americans. (For more information, also see the chapter entitled Writers.)

Many writers and visual artists participated in the Harlem Renaissance, and many volumes have been written about them. Some lived and worked in Harlem; others did not but made Harlem the subject of their work. All shared an aesthetic and common purpose of representing African Americans. Two of the most important Harlem Renaissance writers were Claude McKay and Langston Hughes.

McKay and Hughes

Claude McKay was born into a peasant farming family in Jamaica, and in 1912, at the age of 23, he was awarded a literary prize for two collections of poetry, *Songs of Jamaica* and *Constab Ballads*. During that same year, McKay immigrated to the United States, attended college, worked menial jobs, and published his writing in progressive literary magazines in New York City. At the end of World War I, McKay's radical politics led him to the Soviet Union, where he stayed until 1934 and published two more books of poetry and four works of fiction. His best-known poem, "If We Must Die," is a battle cry for African Americans to fight against lynching politically through the courts, but also physically, if necessary. As a portion of McKay's poems relates:

> O kinsmen! we must meet the common foe!
> Though far outnumbered let us show us brave,
> And for their thousand blows deal one deathblow!
> What though before us lies the open grave?
> Like men we'll face the murderous, cowardly pack,
> Pressed to the wall, dying, but fighting back!
> (Quoted in Young 1996, 378)

Langston Hughes was arguably the most prolific of Harlem Renaissance writers, as his writing career spanned four decades. His talent was demonstrated early as a teenager when he wrote "The Negro Speaks of Rivers"—perhaps the most read and memorized poem in the African American literary canon. After his poetry was published in Alain Locke's 1925 *The New Negro*, Hughes's writing abilities continued to be demonstrated with publication of two volumes of poetry, *The Weary Blues* in 1926 and *Fine Clothes to the Jew* in 1927. By the end of his career, Hughes had written ten volumes of poetry, nine works of fiction, nine plays, and two autobiographies. His lyrical style, combined with the local color of Harlem, made Hughes the ideal person to write about the everyday events and people who traversed the streets of Harlem. The most successful of this genre was the Jesse B. Semple series. According to Al Young, "Hughes captur[ed] in verses the way that average folks spoke and sang about the dark ironies and quiet glories of everyday living" (Young 1996, 388). In "Mother to Son," Hughes provides the reader with age-old wisdom from the African American experience. In this excerpt, Hughes writes

> Well son, I'll tell you:
> Life for me ain't been no crystal stair.
> It's had tacks in it,
> And splinters,
> And boards torn up,
> And places with no carpet on the floor—
> Bare.
> But all the time
> I'se been a-climbin' on
> And reaching landin's,

And turnin' corners,
And sometimes goin in the dark
Where there ain't been no light.
(Young 1991, 391)

The Importance of Jazz Music

If McKay, Hughes, and others provided the literary dimension, jazz and blues provided the musical score for the Harlem Renaissance. Linking musical forms that had developed in the American South at the turn of the 20th century with new styles, arrangements, and ideas, jazz musicians made the art form the dominant musical idiom of the decade. Similarly, blacks from the South brought with them a blues tradition that originated in slavery and found new expression in what has come to be known as the urban blues. Many African American musicians recorded with race records, recording companies that catered to African American audiences. Mamie Smith, for example, recorded "Crazy Blues" with the Okeh Record Company and sold 7,500 recordings per week. Through the distribution of their records, musicians popularized jazz for mainstream audiences and created new avenues and possibilities for black musicians and singers who traversed the country playing for black and white audiences at rent parties, cabarets, and jazz clubs. Big bands emerged under the leadership of Fletcher Henderson and Jelly Roll Morton in Chicago, Clarence Love in Kansas City, and Duke Ellington in New York City. Black women blazed new paths in blues singing. One of the most important was Bessie Smith, whose style laid the foundation for later jazz, blues, and gospel singers. Although her music was not popular with many middle-class blacks, who thought the subjects of drinking and female sexuality found in her music did not portray African Americans in a positive light, she continued to perform songs that spoke to the everyday realities of African American life. During the era Smith performed with leading jazz musicians, including Louis Armstrong and Fletcher Henderson. One of her most popular songs is "Gimme a Pigfoot," excerpted here:

> Up in Harlem every Saturday night When the highbrows get together its just so right. They all congregate at an all night hop And what they do is Oo Bop Bee Dap Oh Hannah Brown from way cross town Gets full of corn and starts breaking 'em down And at the break of day, you can hear ol' Hannah say 'Gimme a pigfoot and a bottle of beer.' Send me again. I don't care. I feel just like I wanna clown. Give the piano player a drink because he's bringing me down! He's gotta rhythm, yeah! When he stomps his feet. He sends me right off to sleep. Check all your razors and your guns. We gonna be arrested when the wagon comes (Quoted in Davis 1998, 281–282).

Beyond Harlem

Undoubtedly, the writers and musicians of the Harlem Renaissance were not the first black artists, and although Harlem may have been the center of black creativity, it was certainly not the only place. Between 1896 and 1906, Paul Laurence Dunbar published numerous books of poetry and fiction, and during the same period, Charles Chestnut published three novels. During the Jazz Age blacks in Boston held poetry circles; black theater groups formed in other black urban centers in Chicago, Detroit, and Philadelphia; and black writers throughout the country published literary and scholarly articles. Black musicians existed for generations. However, what is essential for students of history to remember is that the Harlem Renaissance was the first time in history in which there was a large output of work by African American artists; concentrated in one location, African American arts and letters were taken seriously by white publishers and the dominant white culture. The Harlem Renaissance ended with the 1929 stock market crash and subsequent Great Depression as white patrons' coffers could no longer support black artists and intellectuals, and the African American ceased to be a novel topic for mainstream publishers. Nevertheless, by the end of the Harlem Renaissance black artists had created "twenty-six novels, ten volumes of poetry, five Broadway plays, innumerable essays and short stories, two or three ballets and concerti, and [a] large output of canvas and sculpture" (Wintz 1998, 63; Lewis 1997, 121).

Conclusion

African Americans entered the 1920s with a heightened race consciousness and political unrest as a result of World War I and the Great Migration. Having had their sons and fathers serve in World War I and hearing the promises of democracy, many expected to become full citizens. Surely, they had no illusions that racism would be eradicated, their experience and their ancestors' time in this country had proven that such a dream would be generations in coming, but they did expect citizenship rights. For many, they sought this in lands far from where they and generations before had toiled. In the North they found economic opportunity, the right to vote, and spaces where they could feel free. It was not the Promised Land, but it would do. In the North and South, by creating new political organizations, forging diasporic identities, and engaging and challenging what it meant to be black in the United States, African Americans laid the foundation for the civil rights movement of the 1950s and 1960s. The imaginative and innovative styles of black artists, intellectuals, and musicians of the 1920s continue to inspire peoples around the globe as we re-envision and re-imagine their medium. Most importantly, African Americans' achievements and survival speak to the tenacious spirit of a people who, despite structural inequality, racism, and capitalism, continue to make their mark in the United States against almost insurmountable odds.

References and Further Reading

Boyle, Kevin. *Arc of Justice: A Saga of Race, Civil Rights and Murder in the Jazz Age.* New York: Henry Holt and Company, 2004.

British Broadcasting Corporation and Discovery Communications. *The Promised Land: Take Me to Chicago,* 1995.

Canaan, Gareth. "Part of the Loaf: Economic Conditions of Chicago's African American Working Class During the 1920s." *Journal of Social History* 35, no. 1 (Fall 2001): 149, 150.

Davis, Angela. *Blues Legacies and Black Feminism.* New York: Vintage Books, 1998.

Esedebe, P. Olisanwuche. *Pan Africanism: The Idea and Movement, 1776–1991.* Washington, D.C.: Howard University Press, 1994.

Harrison, Alferdteen, ed. *Black Exodus: The Great Migration from the American South.* Jackson: University of Mississippi Press, 1991.

Henri, Florette. *Black Migration: Movement North, 1900–1920.* Garden City, NJ: Anchor Press/Doubleday, 1975.

Jacques-Garvey, Amy, ed. *Philosophy and Opinions of Marcus Garvey.* New York: Atheneum, 1992.

Kuykendall, Ronald A. "African Blood Brotherhood, Independent Marxist During the Harlem Renaissance." *The Western Journal of Black Studies* 26, no. 1 (2002): 16–21.

Lewis, David Levering. *When Harlem Was In Vogue.* New York: Penguin Books, 1997.

Marks, Carole. *Farewell—We're Good and Gone: The Great Black Migration.* Bloomington: Indiana University Press, 1989.

Martin, Tony. *Race First: The Ideological and Organizational Struggles of Marcus Garvey and the Universal Negro Improvement Association.* Westport, CT: Greenwood Press, 1976.

Naison, Mark. *Communists in Harlem during the Depression.* Urbana: University of Illinois Press, 1983.

Ottley, Roi, and William Weatherby, eds. *The Negro in New York: An Informal Social History, 1626–1940.* New York: Praeger Publishers, 1969.

Robinson, Dean. *Black Nationalism in American Politics and Thought.* New York: Cambridge University Press, 2001.

Schneider, Mark Robert. *We Return Fighting: The Civil Rights Movement in the Jazz Age.* Boston: Northeastern University Press, 2002.

Shawki, Ahmed. 2006. *Black Liberation and Socialism.* Chicago: Haymarket Books.

Stein, Judith. *The World and Marcus Garvey: Race and Class in Modern Society.* Baton Rouge: Louisiana State University Press, 1986.

Stephens, Judith. 1999. "Racial Violence and Representation: Performance Strategies in Lynching Dramas of the 1920s." *African American Review* 33, no. 4 (Winter): 655–671.

Stovel, Katherine. 2001. "Local Sequential Patterns: The Structure of Lynching in the Deep South, 1882–1930." *Social Forces* 79, no. 3 (March): 843–880.

Trotter, Joe William, ed. *The Great Migration in Historical Perspective*. Bloomington: Indiana University Press, 1991.

Weldon Johnson, James. *The Book of American Negro Poetry*. New York: Harcourt Brace, 1959.

Wintz. Cary D. *Black Culture and the Harlem Renaissance*. Houston: Rice University Press, 1998.

Young, Al. *African American Literature: A Brief Anthology*. New York: HarperCollins, 1996.

Farmers | 2

Jeremy Bonner

Facing Changes

If the status of farmers in 1920s America was ambiguous, this was no more than a reflection of the farmers' inner uncertainty about their future in an industrialized world. The golden age of American agriculture, when foreign demand for American crops and livestock seemed limitless, lasted from 1900 to 1918, but came to a grinding halt when European nations began to look to Asia and South America for less expensive foodstuffs. Overproduction, geared to serving war-torn Europe, produced a glut of such staple crops as wheat and cotton, which drove down domestic prices, even as the cost of the manufactured goods farmers wanted to purchase continued to rise. Encouraged by city-based agrarian reformers to accommodate themselves to the culture of consumption prevalent in urban America for over a decade and increasingly dependent on the prosperity of the industrial sector for their livelihood, Jazz Age farmers confronted an ever-widening gap between income and expenses that only heightened their resentment of the city.

Although the 1920s enjoyed a justifiable reputation for political conservatism, American farmers, especially on the Great Plains, proved an exception to the rule. The reaction to the status quo politics of Warren Harding and Calvin Coolidge, however, represented less the revolt of a downtrodden rural proletariat than the protest of aspiring middle-class farmers against their failure to emulate the gains of urban white-collar workers. In the South, where tenancy and sharecropping combined to create an agrarian underclass, politics remained in the hands of the social elite, but in the Midwest and West, commercial farmers mobilized behind insurgent Republicans dedicated to restoring the purchasing power of their rural constituency. While embracing more culturally conservative attitudes than those of city dwellers, farmers increasingly accommodated themselves to the interest-group politics of the 1920s. The shift that took place during the 1920s set the seal on a transformation that had been under way since the failure of the Populist movement during the 1890s.

The Country Life Movement and World War I, 1907–1919

At the beginning of the 20th century, the world of the typical American farmer was characterized by physically demanding labor and comparative social isolation. Standing apart from industrial society and cultivated using agricultural methods not vastly different from those of the mid-19th century, the typical American farm was a largely self-sufficient social organism, promoting an ethic of hard work that extended to all family members (including children) and disdained the preoccupation with leisure of the wider society. Although rural health, diet, and sanitation did not decline, social reformers helped bring about dramatic advances in the quality of urban life that further widened the economic gap between the two worlds. Farmers' preoccupation with self-reliance led them to disdain forms of organization that went beyond the county level. They were strong defenders of the country school, which was less well equipped than its urban counterpart, boasted a much shorter school year, and yet provided the rudimentary form of education that corresponded closely with what most farmers desired for their children. Their preference for local oversight applied equally to rural government, where the prevailing concern was not with the impact of federal or state legislation, but with justice, education, and roads, all of which were handled at the township or community level. "The idea that government should carry out broad functions of amelioration was repugnant to farm people," writes David Danbom. "Illness, hardship, education, or failure were all matters to be handled by the family, or if it failed, informally by the neighborhood" (Danbom 1979, 18).

In the early 1900s, agrarian idealists, social scientists, and agricultural economists came together to form the country-life movement, dedicated to breathing new life and vigor (as they saw it) into the rural backwater. Although their interest in the countryside ranged from an idealistic belief in the farmer as the moral bedrock of the nation to the practical issue of increasing the food supply to America's cities, they agreed on the program of reforms proposed by President Theodore Roosevelt's Country Life Commission in 1909. This commission—on which few farmers served—recommended an entirely reconstructed local education system that would encourage both adults and children to better understand the need for more organization of the countryside. Such a change would necessitate a great degree of school consolidation and the provision of practical courses in scientific agriculture, industrial arts, and domestic science. The commission also embraced the idea of cooperative farming, which it hoped would contribute to social regeneration and give farmers greater access to electricity and telephones.

These proposals were not received with universal approbation by many farmers, however, because they were seen as overly invasive. School consolidation was openly resisted and had stalled by the early 1920s; one-room schoolhouses endured in much of the rural North and Midwest. Even a 1925 campaign by Governor Al Smith of New York, which offered considerable financial inducements for rural school districts to consolidate, did not achieve much success, and the state retained many country school districts well into the 1930s. By the same token, many rural teachers proved unsuited to the task of creating a new generation of scientific farmers and lacked the skills to inculcate such expertise.

The entry of the United States into World War I in 1917 obliged Congress to address the question of agricultural mobilization. The Food Production Act led to a vast increase in the numbers of farm demonstration agents; by 1918, more than three-quarters of the nation's counties had such an agent. In many rural areas, where other government activity was minimal, these agents not only sought to meet the federal government's objective of increased production, to which most farmers responded enthusiastically, but also to conform the rural population (who in some parts of the country were not entirely convinced of the wisdom of participating in the conflict) to national priorities. County agents increasingly oversaw many aspects of government that elsewhere were the responsibility of state and city governments, including Liberty Loan drives, the activities of local draft boards, and the allocation of scarce resources like seed and fertilizer. It was also at the instigation of U.S. Department of Agriculture (USDA) agents that the first farm bureaus, the forerunners of the agricultural organizations of the 1920s and 1930s, were organized.

The Rural Economy

European demand for American staple crops led to a boom in agricultural land prices between 1921 and 1922, most notably in the Midwest, especially in Corn Belt states such as Iowa, Illinois, and Indiana. This, together with more intensive cultivation of existing land during the early 1920s, led to an unacceptably high level of wheat production. Having overextended themselves financially only a few years previously, farmers were taken unawares by the abrupt decline in commodity and land prices that began in 1920. While food prices declined, the cost of all commodities (including machinery and manufactured goods) steadily increased, leaving most farmers unable to increase income (because further increases in production would only reduce food prices further) or reduce costs (because fixed charges and taxes still had to be paid).

The crisis proved most acute in the Midwest and West, where the greatest expansion had taken place and mortgages were high. Bankruptcy and repossession by the banks that issued those mortgages was inevitable. A knock-on effect was felt by agricultural villages that serviced these farming communities, resulting in bank failures, decreased lines of credit, and the closing of businesses dependent on a prosperous agricultural economy. Although the situation improved somewhat after 1923, most farmers found themselves more than ever dependent on the nonfarm U.S. economy and increasingly vulnerable to economic shocks, given their inability to break into foreign markets as the United States moved from the status of debtor to creditor to the nations of Europe.

The Farmers' Struggle to Survive

The role of the farmer in American history is indispensible. The United States was an agricultural society beginning in the earliest colonial times, but the importance of the farmer would diminish over time.

For the economic status of farmers, the market was not kind. Agriculture, along with industry, took full advantage of the prices available during the World War I years. The price index for agricultural goods continued up to 1920, two years into the Jazz Age. But with the onset of the 1920s, farmers saw their income drop, whereas urban workers saw their disposable income rise about 1 percent per year. During World War I, a bushel of wheat could go as high as $2; after the war the price dropped as low as 32 cents.

What did rise was the amount of debt farmers faced. In 1920, farm mortgage was approximately $7.8 million. In 1923, the number reached $10.7 million at one point. In terms of foreclosures and bankruptcies, between 1924 and 1933, the number

Farmers' Associations

Two possible solutions to this dilemma presented themselves. One was the creation of marketing institutions for farmers that would reduce the need for government intervention. The greatest success was achieved by groups like the California Fruit Growers' Association and Land O'Lakes Creamery in the Midwest, which used standardized grading and inspections, established storage and processing systems, and coordinated sales. In the state of Washington, the Lewis-Pacific Dairymen's Association was formed in 1919 to achieve precisely that degree of control of market share. Aiming at taking on the whole of the local market, the association limited membership to local farmers engaged in dairy farming who purchased a $10 share for each cow owned. Unlike the Grange cooperatives that already existed, the association saw its role as purely economic—not community building—and on these terms it successfully defied the economic downturn of 1921 and even weathered the Great Depression.

By way of contrast, the American Farm Bureau Federation (AFBF) advocated centralized marketing strategies, but, in doing so, lost the support of many farmers' elevators and many thousands of members. The AFBF's inclusion of nonfarmers involved in agricultural marketing, even the bankers and merchants whom the Farmers' Union had excluded, was a red flag to those who thought the organization favored big farmers and businesspeople. Despite successful recruitment campaigns by the AFBF in the early 1920s, it made little effort to establish itself at a community level. The failure of U.S. Grain Growers Inc., launched in 1921 to provide a general marketing organization for all grain growers in the country, demonstrated that most farmers were resistant to notions of the compulsory practically quadrupled. The midwestern states were especially hit hard.

The federal government was not entirely blind to the situation. In 1924, Congress passed the Agricultural Credits Act. In an effort to prevent the dumping of agricultural goods on the market, which could lead to low prices for crops, lost income, and eventually farm foreclosures, loans were provided to cooperatives and dealers in order to hold products from the marketplace. By 1932, approximately $304 million in loans were given.

In 1929, the government passed the Agricultural Marketing Act. The law created a Federal Farm Board, which included the secretary of agriculture. Low-interest loans were provided to help stabilize the marketplace and provide for fluctuations in the prices. Future federal attempts at price-support programs did not succeed as farmers were not willing to alter their harvesting patterns. With the onset of the Great Depression, overproduction and price controls would again become issues.

pooling of wheat and to corporate control of the fruits of their labor. By 1923, the organization was moribund.

An alternative solution, which ultimately became one of the great political issues of the 1920s, was direct government intervention. Although Republican administrations gave the USDA regulatory power over grain exchanges and stockyards and raised tariffs on agricultural products, these measures failed to dramatically lift prices. Into the vacuum stepped George N. Peek, an Illinois farm equipment manufacturer who proposed establishing a government corporation to purchase enough of the surplus of certain agricultural commodities to raise domestic prices. The surplus would then be sold on the world market at whatever price could be achieved, and the loss would be paid for by means of an equalization fee levied on all farmers. By its compulsory nature—which foreshadowed New Deal agricultural policy—the measure extended the principle of tariff protection to farmers. Although the McNary-Haugen bill eventually passed both houses of Congress, it was the subject of persistent presidential vetoes and was never enacted into law.

The changes in agricultural production set in motion during World War I only accelerated in the postwar period, as bankers and technical experts sought to impress upon farmers the necessity of such practices. In this, they were assisted by the wave of foreclosures that accompanied the agricultural depression of the early 1920s. Where banks sought to find the most profitable way to manage their newly acquired properties, recent graduates of agricultural colleges looked on repossessed farms as laboratories for comparing the various forms of scientific management of agriculture. Deborah Fitzgerald (2001) has described how both groups exerted pressure on farmers to track income and expenses through questionnaires or in account books supplied by rural banks (the incentive being that farm loans would only be extended to those who could produce detailed records).

A woman sells a Parkway Motor Co. Fordson tractor, ca. 1921; tractor sales skyrocketed in the United States during the 1920s. (*Library of Congress*)

Work Initiatives

Farmers were also encouraged to standardize work routines and make use of farm machinery, particularly tractors. The unreliability of many tractors actually inspired Nebraska's agricultural engineers to press for passage of a law in 1919 requiring all tractor manufacturers to submit their machines to efficiency tests at the state university, and the Nebraska Tractor Test subsequently became the model for many other agricultural states. Perhaps the most striking illustration of how the agricultural world had changed came with the growing number of corporate farms, launched by investors who sought to operate their properties on the factory model. They took the form of either "chain farms," where responsibility for different phases of production was allocated to adjoining farms controlled by one owner, or something resembling the industrial company town, such as the Taft Ranch in Texas, which covered 100,000 acres and employed 4,500 workers in four small towns.

One of the great initiatives of the 1920s was the Montana Farming Corporation launched in 1918 by Thomas Campbell. With land leased from Native Americans in southeastern Montana, Campbell created a 95,000-acre tract divided into a number of semiautonomous farms with bunkhouses, kitchens, and dining rooms to serve his workforce. An enthusiast for mechanization, Campbell purchased large numbers of tractors, trucks, and combines and was an advocate of managerial oversight of his work-force to a degree not commonly found in the ranching culture of the Great Plains. Campbell saw the future in terms of industrial farming, a practice also adopted in other wheat regions of the country, including Kansas, Oklahoma, North Dakota, Washington, and California.

The trend toward the agribusiness of the late 20th century was also foreshadowed in the transformation of California's irrigation district system during the 1920s. Concern about recurrent drought prompted calls from Californian farmers for greater irrigation, a trend that raised the cost of such projects from around $10 per acre in 1900 to at least $50 per acre by the 1920s. Increasingly, large landowners pushed through measures that allowed the formation of water storage districts, where voting was weighted to reflect land ownership, rather than the irrigation district principle of one person, one vote. When such a district was formed at the instigation of the Kern County Land Company in the San Joaquin Valley, the measure only passed because the company cast half the votes by virtue of its land ownership. Increasingly too, small California farmers would find themselves subject to the behests of the state water bureaucracy charged with implementing the Central Valley Project, which was finally adopted in 1929. Not even lip service was now paid to the standard arguments for irrigation advanced throughout the 19th century, namely restoring the autonomy of the yeoman farmer, housing the urban jobless, or bolstering the rural lifestyle. Irrigation was now to serve first the cities—in terms of the electricity generated by hydroelectric dams—and second the growing numbers of corporate farms that dotted the California landscape. A new form of agriculture was emerging in the Pacific West.

Resistance to mechanization was evident only in the South, where planters kept intact the system of fragmented plantations that had emerged from the Civil War. Lulled into a false sense of security by the high prices of cotton and tobacco from 1915 to 1919, Southern farmers were unprepared for the rising price of nonagricultural consumer goods. Southern farms continued to lag behind those of the North and West. Half were still smaller than 50 acres in 1920, and few were self-sufficient in basic foodstuffs. Only 18 percent of farms had telephones (compared with 38.7 percent of farms nationwide) and only 12 percent of farmers owned an automobile (figures in Fite 1984, 101).

As prices began to fall in 1920, some farmers endorsed production limits. In 1921, J. S. Wannamaker of the American Cotton Association called for legally binding contracts on farmers to reduce cotton production by 50 percent. Most resisted the McNary-Haugen legislation until 1927, however, because 50 percent of cotton was exported, compared with only 15 percent of wheat. Southern farmers generally failed to mechanize—except in western Texas and Oklahoma—as cheap abundant labor, coupled with the widespread use of mules, proved a more effective means of cultivation. Most efforts at cooperative marketing of cotton and tobacco were as unsuccessful as those aimed at wheat. Although some Southern farmers benefited from advice to switch from cotton to higher-value crops like peaches and pecans, they were very much in the minority.

Society and Culture

For American farmers, the 1920s were a time when technological advances produced a dramatic expansion of the network of family and community-centered relationships that had hitherto characterized their daily lives. In his study of the impact of the automobile on rural society, Michael Berger (1979) makes the point that while increasing the opportunities for recreation—and thus lessening the monotony of farm life—the automobile also increased opportunities for farm families, especially the young, to pursue activities apart from the family. It also sapped the familial relationship that had existed between farmers and hired workers: the farmers no longer needed to house and feed workers away from the local town, and farm workers could more easily move away from an unsatisfactory assignment. However, the automobile also permitted communities to redefine their enclave community over a wider area, as inter-town associations were able to meet more frequently, and county fairs were revitalized by the ability of farmers to drive to them.

If farmers and their spouses experienced a profound culture shock, it was nothing compared with that of their children. Of course, there were constraints, not least that, unlike urban workers, rural youths employed on family farms did not receive cash wages and were dependent on the largesse of their parents for entertainment expenses. Most farm families spent less than 10 percent of their household budget on recreation, although this varied depending on the region of the country and whether or not the farmer was a tenant. Many adults objected to the new commercial forms of recreation that brought young people together away from community supervision, and girls tended to have less access to family automobiles than their male siblings.

Rural Participation in New Cultural Pursuits

Even so, most farm youths expressed the same aspirations to be "modern" as their urban counterparts. In their access to new forms of entertainment, rural youths encountered different degrees of resistance from the older generation. The increasing ownership of family radios was seen as least threatening, because it could form part of family entertainment (during a communal meal, for example), but even here there could be conflicts with existing ethnic or religious traditions, and radio advertising frequently challenged established rural values and practices.

Moviegoing required travel to locations at some distance from the family homestead and was only a family activity among the more progressive farmers who belonged to 4-H clubs and farmers' organizations. In many marketing centers, Saturday night became known as "farmers' night," when farm families would come into town en masse to shop, play a game of pool, or see a movie. Here was an opportunity for people from neighboring farms to meet and reinforce their sense of community. "Farmers then," writes Hal Barron, "used their cars primarily to go to marketing centers rather than the big cities and metropolitan centers. There they found an environment that catered to them and in which they felt comfortable, and where they could pick and choose among activities that were both new and old in ways that resonated with and reinforced their values instead of threatening them" (Barron 1997, 73–75).

Many rural adolescents, by contrast, were inspired in their clothing and hairstyles by those worn in Hollywood, and it was they who pioneered newer forms of courtship and social interaction across the old ethnic divides. Even more communally divisive were the commercial dances, which many farm families deplored because they featured liquor and suggestive dancing styles. It was in this setting that rural adolescents were most able to indulge in countercultural rebellion.

Even as recreation subtly undermined some of the bonds of family life, traditional social structures also underwent transformation. For farmers, the farm bureau or the farmers' union was the centerpiece of local activities, be they economic, educational, or social. "Politics is an annual event," declared one North Dakota farmer. "[T]he Farmers' Union is something that you work with every day . . . it's a way of life" (Bonner 2001, 97–98). Not only did farmers' organizations shape the social life of men, but they also helped advance the work of women's organizations and children's clubs. Women became increasingly involved in work outside the home, especially in the Midwest and West, where the traditional gender divide was less pronounced than in the South. There was also a renewed interest in continuing education, evidenced by an increasing number of county library systems (especially in California), greater interest in university extension courses, and a wide range of rural newspapers, many of which were operated by the local farmers' organizations.

Women operate tractors on a farm, ca. 1918. The presence and importance of farm women in U.S. history had often been greatly understated in the past. (*National Archives and Records Administration*)

One notable exception was the *Producers' News*, published in Sheridan County in western Montana by Charles Taylor, a Socialist state senator for much of the 1920s. Owned by local farmers, the paper stressed its credentials as a "paper of the people, by the people and for the people," but it was also the publicity organ of the Farmer-Labor Party organized by Taylor and others in 1923, many of whose members were rural communists. The Farmer-Labor Party grew out of the efforts by the Chicago Federation of Labor (CFL) to create a viable national labor party, but was a dismal failure, with the exception of winning some local elections. By keeping in close touch with his rural constituency and cultivating a folksy manner, Taylor was able to counteract charges of sedition and even take control of the county government. It was significant that when operation of the paper shifted from Taylor to a communist official sent from New York and the newspaper abandoned its local columns in favor of propaganda on behalf of the class struggle, its fortunes—and those of the Farmer-Labor Party—dramatically declined, even though the region was entering a period of acute agricultural depression. The CFL, among others, abandoned the Farmer-Labor Party when the communists took control.

Although farmers' organizations adjusted to the new economic and political realities, other rural institutions fared less well. The rural church lost prestige as farmers exploited their new mobility to attend more prestigious town churches or even neglected Sabbath day attendance in favor of listening to a sermon broadcast on the radio. Rural regions were over-churched even before the 1920s, and most congregations had small memberships. Outside the South, the country church consistently lost members to the village, with two-fifths of rural church members attending village churches. Only a third of country churches had weekly services (compared with three-quarters of village churches), most proved more successful in attracting women than men, and, except in the South, few boasted the range of church organizations that could be found in their urban counterparts.

Cultural Interactions

Rural church consolidation transformed many Protestant congregations into community social centers, especially as the principle of the union church (one that united congregations from several different denominations) took hold. In such an environment, Protestant revivalism (particularly the Pentecostal sects), which made use of the radio and mass marketing to spread its message, could be particularly alluring. Such religious fervor helped fill the gap left by an increasingly professionalized form of politics, lacking in any sort of enthusiasm, and it proved particularly effective in the Far West. It appealed mainly to disgruntled members of existing churches, especially the young, who were fascinated by the role played by faith healing and ecstatic utterance in religious belief and practice.

Relations between farmers and nearby towns and cities remained lukewarm, at best, during the 1920s. The farmer's historic resentment at the

economic power of the city was only reinforced by antipathy to the perceived way of life of urban dwellers, especially the new immigrants who
had transformed the urban centers during the 1910s. Farmers considered
the immigrant enclaves to be un-American and to pose a threat to American democracy. At times, even a note of anti-Semitism characterized the
rural press and the pronouncements of such agrarian spokespersons as
Milo Reno.

Another phenomenon promoted by increased use of the automobile
was the rise of what Michael Berger (1979) has termed "rural suburbs."
Located at some distance from any city, these suburbs were settled by people who lived, worked, and played in a rural environment and had little
dependence on the city. Nevertheless, they had been schooled in the new
agrarian orthodoxy (many were college educated), and it was rural subur-
banites who pressed for further rural improvements.

Town and country relations were generally at their worst in the Midwest, where the agricultural depression was most severely felt. Sometimes
farmers believed their needs were overlooked as when, in one instance, a
township telephone company charged rural users a fee to call other rural
users but charged no fee to call those in the village (where most of the
stockholders lived) and no fee to a village resident who called a rural number (Bruner, Hughes, and Patten 1927, 99). Village incorporation also pro-
voked conflict, because farmers no longer shared in the government of a
village as they did under a township structure, and similar conflict arose as
the drive for school consolidation accelerated. Some farmers not only
resisted pressure to consolidate at the ballot box but also challenged local
government decisions in court and even secured passage of bills in the
state legislature to protect country schools.

Consumerism and Mass Consumption

The expansion of the new consumer economy to rural districts was one of
the most striking features of the 1920s. Despite participation in mail-order
buying, most farmers had rejected the gospel of mass consumption during
the 1900s and 1910s. As the number of farmer-owned automobiles
increased, however, a shift away from localism became evident. The
number of Model T Fords on American farms exceeded 2 million by 1920,
and farmers no longer viewed it as the "devil wagon," though they
still stressed its practical rather than its recreational possibilities. The automobile permitted greater discrimination in the stores that could be patronized, exposing many farm families to a much wider range of choice—
particularly in clothing styles—and speeding the demise of the general
store merchant. Many farm families also patronized chain stores, ignoring
the plaintive cries of merchants to buy locally and citing the lower prices,
fresher produce, and more frequent sales offered by these establishments.

As farmers expanded the range of stores they patronized, the social
function of the country store was increasingly undermined by the use of
delivery trucks and, later, the ability of customers to place telephone orders.

In many areas, indeed, the gasoline station took the place of the country store, providing a place where young people could meet and socialize. It also served as a way station for the new tourism that steadily reshaped the countryside in the 1920s, as urban residents discovered the joys of long-distance vacations. By 1925, there were more than 5,000 motor camps throughout the nation, providing farmers with opportunities to interact with Americans coming out of very different cultures from their own.

It is striking how much the USDA helped contribute to the remaking of the rural environment in the 1920s to conform to the new economic realities, not only on the farm but also in the home. Federal officials sought to transform farm women from fellow toilers with their husbands on the family farm to full-time homemakers and domestic managers. Through the Extension Service, farm women were exposed to a battery of propaganda designed to convince them of the importance of the urban domestic ideal. Rather than challenging the patriarchal family structure by seeking to improve female access to communications technology such as automobiles and telephones (which many farm families owned but to which few women had ready access), USDA officials chose to focus on household modernization. Such an approach favored white, commercially advanced farm families and penalized more marginal agrarian communities that relied on nonscientific agricultural techniques (such as the Mennonites). A parallel drive for modernization was inspired by the Department of Commerce, which, in 1922, launched the Better Homes in America movement, with a special focus on the provision of water, heating, sewage, and lighting systems to individual farm homes.

The object of the Extension Service was reinforced by an increasing effort on the part of American manufacturing industries to develop a market for their products in the rural hinterland. Their marketing strategies sought to persuade rural consumers of their need to become part of the "modern" way of life. To this end, the Extension Service helped promote the sale of washing machines by arguing that farm women washed more clothing than their urban counterparts and could not rely on commercial laundries as did the latter. Sometimes, however, commercial advertising even broke through the traditional gender division favored by the Extension Service, emphasizing the ability of rural women to drive a car or manage a business on her own account. Equally conducive to fostering a sense of community that went beyond the immediate locale was the radio, on which the USDA sponsored *National Farm and Home Hour*, which began broadcasting on NBC affiliates in 1928. Radio ownership was extensive and exceeded all other forms of farm technology except automobiles and telephones by 1930. For most farm women, however, the modernization goals of the Extension Service proved unachievable in the economic context of the agricultural depression of the 1920s.

The new consumer culture exerted a powerful allure, but farm families' choices of what items to acquire suggested a pragmatic approach rather than a substantive cultural shift. In the absence of rural electrification, farm electric power plants were an expensive addition, and the cultural imperative to acquire labor-saving household devices could create

Farmer listens to radio, ca. 1923. The radio was an indispensable tool in how different segments of society came to learn how the "other half" lived. (*Library of Congress*)

gendered tensions between farmers and their wives, not least because of the concurrent pressure for equipment modernization on the farm. Most farm families resisted the urban impulse toward installment purchases, and few acquired a complete range of devices. Radio also helped sell national brand-name products, as did magazine advertising, but country people's choices continued to be driven as much by personal preference as anything else. Many farm families bought a greater range of manufactured goods as farm production grew more specialized and commercialized, but they still continued to favor products like Red Circle coffee, which were not advertised in national journals. Families also appeared to make their choice of toiletries like Palmolive soap and Colgate toothpaste based on utility and price, rather than on the appeals to health and beauty often employed by national advertisers.

Radio purchases proved an exception to this rule because, like the automobile, the radio had practical as well as recreational application, and it could easily be adapted to the rhythm of the rural lifestyle. Families often listened to broadcasts while eating dinner, and women listened while performing household chores. Radio broke down barriers of distance, and some rural residents would listen late into the night trying to pick up faraway stations. From national sporting events to the 1928 presidential election and evangelists of the airwaves, residents of the rural North acquired new insights into the changes taking place in the United States. Not all broadcasting was urban centered. Station WLS in Chicago was acquired by an Illinois farm periodical in 1928 and became affiliated with NBC in 1933. Its most popular program was the *National Barn Dance*, which pioneered the broad-casting of country music from the South and West. WLS helped foster a new national sense of rural community, particularly through *RFD Dinnerbell*, in which the host read mail from farmers and reported on acts of neighborli-ness in farm communities across the Midwest.

The Politics of Protest

In 1919, legislators endorsed by the Nonpartisan League (NPL) held more than two-thirds of the seats in both chambers of the North Dakota legisla-ture. Among various measures proposed were bills to create an industrial commission to manage state enterprises, establish a state bank, and de-velop a state system of flour mills and terminal elevators. The proposed Bank of North Dakota was seen as key to the whole process of reform, because it would provide low-cost rural credits for farmers. It was to be the repository for all state and local government funds, and it was empow-ered to redeposit funds in any bank or make loans to political subdivisions and state or national banks to stabilize credit conditions.

Passage of the NPL program was swiftly followed by Governor Lynn Fraz-ier's decision to call a statewide referendum on the measures adopted. At the same time, however, the three "nonfarmer" Leaguers, including Attorney General William Langer, turned against the movement. Despite these defec-tions, all the measures passed with clear popular majorities. The Bank of North Dakota immediately went into operation, offering 30-year mortgages to farmers at a 7.0 percent interest rate (the average interest rate in North Dakota was around 8.7 percent). By the end of 1919, $1 million in farm loans had been made, and farmers were saving almost 3 percent interest.

Such successes were buttressed by a number of unwise appointments to state commissions and an increasing intolerance by NPL members to any dissent from their program in the smallest detail, something their adversaries in the Independent Voters' Association (IVA) were quick to exploit. The IVA was also assisted by the adoption, late in the legislative session, of a number of measures that could be portrayed as repressive of legitimate criticism by those in positions of authority. The repercussions of the North Dakota scene carried through to the 1920 Republican primary in Minnesota where Henrik Shipstead was anointed the NPL nominee for governor. After a hotly contested campaign, Shipstead lost by only 8,000 votes compared to the party's 50,000 vote deficit in 1918. He carried 54 counties (30 more than in 1918). In Colorado and Montana, the NPL also won victories in the Democratic primaries. In North Dakota, by contrast, the campaign of 1920 drew smaller crowds, as many farmers concluded that the NPL program was now enacted and there was a recognition that the NPL had not shown itself to be beyond reproach in office. The results in the primaries were consequently closer, although most NPL candidates still emerged victorious. In the general election, however, despite victories at the top of the ticket, control of the state house passed to the opposition, while the NPL clung to control of the state senate by a single vote.

One of the initiated measures passed during the election was the removal of the obligation on local governments to deposit their funds with the Bank of North Dakota. As the agricultural depression had hit home in western North Dakota in 1920, the bank had redeposited more than $1 million in banks in the western part of the state, and the fear arose that if large amounts were withdrawn by hostile officials those redeposits would have to be called in, resulting in bank failures and ruin for many farmers. In the face of this threat, the bank launched a campaign to secure individual deposits and sold small-denomination bonds to individual investors throughout the country, supported by the Public Ownership League and the American Federation of Labor. Despite relative success, many other NPL enterprises were seriously affected by the Depression, some going into bankruptcy.

In September 1921, the IVA filed petitions calling for recall of the NPL administration as well as constitutional amendments to establish a state debt limit, set limits for bond issues, and place restrictions on much of the state industrial enterprises. By this stage farmers had little money available for political campaigns, and their opponents were well organized. Governor Frazier was ousted from office, but in a curious twist the measures on the ballot that would have gutted the NPL agenda were all repudiated, leaving Frazier's successor with the task of administering a program that his faction wished to restrict. The charges of mismanagement had borne fruit, even though farmers continued to believe in the program for which the NPL had fought for five years.

The aftermath of the recall election saw the eclipse of the NPL as a national force but the emergence of new political entities that owed their success to NPL organizing. In 1922, Lynn Frazier, fresh from his recall, was elected to the U.S. Senate, where he was joined by Henrik Shipstead, the candidate of the entirely independent Farmer-Labor Party of Minnesota. Both men joined the now growing farm bloc, a cluster of progressive senators, almost all Republicans, who would spend the 1920s pressing the administrations of Warren Harding and Calvin Coolidge for greater government intervention in agriculture. Although the NPL failed to regain control of the North Dakota state legislature, it remained an influential force into the 1930s, and the essential features of its program were never dislodged, even though they may not have been developed to the fullest extent for which its founders had hoped.

Although North Dakota represented the most extreme example of 1920s agrarian insurgency, it was not the sole one. In Idaho, where the NPL made considerable inroads, the third-party approach pursued with some success in Minnesota was seen as a viable alternative after the failure of the NPL ticket in 1918 and the subsequent repeal of the direct primary by conservatives. Repudiating Arthur Townley's strategy, NPL leader Ray McKaig proposed a third party that would attract progressive Republicans and support the state's progressive U.S. senator, William Borah. Idaho farm groups formed the Idaho Farmers' Political Association in 1921, which subsequently became the Progressive Party, although some dissidents noted Senator Borah's lack of commitment to the new third party.

The Progressive platform was less specifically agrarian than that of the North Dakota NPL, but it did contain a commitment to government ownership of railroads and a one-year moratorium on farm mortgage foreclosures. Although they failed in statewide contests, the Progressives took control of three county governments that had formerly been NPL strongholds. In 1924, the Progressives ran a strong second in many races and made advances even in traditionally hostile Mormon country in the east. After 1924, however, their influence receded, and pressure for change would ultimately come from a resurgent Democratic Party, with which McKaig had persistently refused to consider alliance arrangements during the 1920s.

If the NPL failed to display great staying power, farmers' organizations nevertheless soon filled the policy-making void in Washington, D.C. At the suggestion of Farm Bureau Federation lobbyist Gray Silver, a farm bloc led by two Iowans, Senator William S. Kenyon and Representative Lester J. Dickinson, came into being in the summer of 1921. This bloc exerted pressure to get a number of pending agricultural bills passed in defiance of the Republican Party leadership. Although no other confrontation took place that session, farmers elected four new senators with agrarian credentials, including Smith Brookhart of Iowa, in 1922. In practice, members of the bloc remained divided over the appropriate solution to the problems of agriculture, and farm organizations were also divided over George Peek's proposal for an equalization fee. Only when the Peek plan was endorsed by USDA Secretary Henry Wallace Sr. did the farm bloc begin to come around to the idea.

Not until 1926 were supporters of the legislation able to bring it to the floor for consideration, largely due to the development of connections between midwestern legislators and farm groups. The much vaunted independence of congressmen in the early 1920s had been replaced by a commitment to interest-group negotiation. In 1925, moreover, the Farm Bureau replaced the conservative Oscar Bradfute with Sam Thompson, head of the Illinois Agricultural Association, who had condemned President Coolidge for his refusal to sign any price-fixing bill. In this election, it was the votes of farmers from the Midwest and South that carried the day, and many legislators took note, particularly as the independent presidential candidacy of Robert LaFollette in 1924 had failed to win the votes of many farmers. Increasingly, previously hostile congressmen converted to McNary-Haugenism, and farm organizations took to announcing their views on a congressman's performance, thereby encouraging or discouraging challengers. Beginning in 1927, the coalition extended to embrace southern congressmen, who until then had stood aloof from a largely Republican conflict. Although Republican presidents continued to veto such legislation, the "marriage of corn and cotton" was set to reap dividends once a Democratic administration was back in power.

The failure of midwestern insurgents to inflict any lasting transformation of the economic scene—outside a few local settings like North Dakota—promoted a defensive mentality among many voting farmers. At the local level, persistent antipathy to the rule of so-called experts meant low-level political conflict continued at the state level between rural and urban legislators over many practical issues. For example, the Federal

Highway Act of 1921 represented a compromise between interest groups like the American Automobile Association, which endorsed a federally financed system of transcontinental highways, and farmers, who favored a focus on farm-to-market routes.

Postwar reaction to government activism in the rural North was frequently hostile. In upstate New York, fear of the metropolis translated into a reaction against the more powerful state government erected during the 1910s, and frequent were rural demands to abolish boards and commissions and reduce the high taxes and regulatory framework established during World War I. At the same time, farmers appreciated the need to understand the new political system. Local newspapers reported political debates not only at the state but also at the county and township level, with a degree of detail unknown half a century before. Increasingly, too, political candidates were assessed less on their partisanship than on their qualifications and experience, and they were expected to provide specific evidence of the legislation they would introduce or support. In such a climate, much of the enthusiasm that had characterized earlier decades declined. "Discussions of precise issues and policies that reduced politics to a relatively narrow and technical matter," writes Paula Baker, "diminished the capacity of formal politics to address broad questions that still greatly engaged voters: for example, the social and economic direction of the nation and the place of moral teaching in public life" (Baker 1991, 163).

Concern about community morality sometimes saw rural communities exploit the otherwise despised state power to address their concerns. Campaigns in support of Prohibition enforcement and against cigarettes and immoral movies were undertaken in upstate New York. At the same time, antipathy to socialism and communism was a staple of politics in the rural North, in stark contrast to the situation prevailing in much of the Midwest, with the Allegheny and Clinton County Granges endorsing the deportation of people who supported socialism, anarchism, or bolshevism.

In the Midwest, rural legislators tried to compel urban dwellers to submit to rural standards of morality. Prohibition was ratified by the Illinois state legislature with the support of 80 percent of rural delegates and the opposition of three-quarters of those from Chicago. As it became clear that the law was being seriously flouted, rural delegates introduced bills that provided for monies confiscated from bootleggers to go to the state attorney general if the bootlegger was prosecuted by that office, or divided evenly between county enforcement and county schools if secured by another agency. Thus, not only was an incentive provided for enforcement, but an additional source of revenue was secured for the public schools (in contrast to their general antipathy to state commissions, rural legislators even proposed to set up a state Prohibition commission, at a cost of up to $20,000). Similar efforts were undertaken to regulate urban amusements like prizefighting and horse racing.

For many farmers, there was a strong incentive during the 1920s to make use of their disproportionate influence in state elections to block further gains by the metropolitan portions of the state. Farmers in Illinois and Iowa sought to use all means at their disposal to block bureaucratic expansion and shape state tax policy to favor their interests. Proposals for even minor increases in the pay of state officials were firmly opposed for fear of the precedent this might set, while attempts to introduce new commissions to regulate professional standards and working conditions (in such areas as housing, town planning, and electrical installation) were seen as penalizing rural areas, where many practical jobs were handled by gifted amateurs. (Farmers had no difficulty with regulatory commissions that dealt with such subjects as animal vaccines, which were of interest to them.) Rural delegates also made strenuous efforts to change the method of taxation during the 1920s, to lift the burden of property taxation. Farmers in Iowa and Illinois rallied behind income tax bills, but such efforts suffered defeats thanks to the opposition of delegates from the urban areas that extended across party lines.

As the decade wore on, farmers found it impossible to block urban pressure to increase county borrowing limits, for the new government machinery required injections of capital that could not be avoided. Indeed, the debate over road expenditures testified to a struggle both over where the new roads would be built and whether they would be financed by property taxes or (the farmers' preference) a gasoline tax. Iowa farmers sought to abolish the state highway commission in 1921 because it favored centralized planning and primary highways over farm-to-market roads. In Illinois, a 1923 road bill required a compromise in which a gasoline tax paid for road construction, of which two-thirds of the revenue was reserved for secondary roads, a clear triumph for the agrarian bloc. Alliances moved back and forth in the course of the decade, however, as farmers sought to find compromises that would draw delegates from the smaller towns into alignment with their cause.

Preparing for a New Deal, 1929–1932

The election of 1928 was widely interpreted—rightly or wrongly—as the defeat of the "city" candidate, Governor Al Smith of New York, by the farm boy turned president, Herbert Hoover. Neither candidate offered much in the way of consolation to the farmer, however. President Hoover had expressed great interest in helping farmers develop mechanisms that would enable them to participate in interest group bargaining while Secretary of Commerce. In 1924, he had endorsed creation of the Federal Cooperative Marketing Board, which would have provided marketing services, an inspection and certification system, and a market news service, but the legislation was rejected by Congress. Opposed to the McNary-Haugen proposals because of their coercive nature and interference with international trade, Hoover threw his authority behind the Agricultural Marketing Act of 1929, which established the Federal Farm Board to educate farmers and the public in the principles of cooperative marketing and to encourage the formation of agricultural cooperatives. The board was authorized to make low interest loans from a $500 million fund to cooperatives and to create clearing houses and stabilization corporations.

In practice, the marketing associations sustained by the Federal Farm Board were built from the top down and demonstrated little interest in the welfare of ordinary farmers, often competing with each other for active members. They proved ill-suited to handle staple commodities—such as wheat and cotton—that were sold in a variety of markets, and by 1931 many cooperatives were kept alive only with federal funding. A similar crisis affected the Federal Farm Loan System, which, from its establishment in 1916, had suffered from excessive centralization and bureaucratic red tape. The federal land banks, which had been intended to supplement rural credit, proved excessively cautious in their dealings, preferring to refinance existing loans rather than provide new long-term loans, and gave little encouragement to the establishment of farmer credit corporations that might have filled the gap.

While farmers were less immediately affected by the Great Crash of 1929 than other sectors of the economy, the knock-on effects were not slow to materialize. Far more serious was the nationwide drought of 1930, which caused a dramatic decline in income for the more prosperous farmers of the Midwest and West. In the wake of the drought, dust storms ravaged the Great Plains states, wiping out the livelihoods of many. It was in the Corn Belt that the greatest resistance was recorded as local farmers joined vigilante groups and directly intervened to prevent sales by foreclosure. Demonstrations and protests convinced many that the farmer—previously the bedrock of social stability—was now capable of violent revolution. Many farmers now looked to federal intervention on a massive scale, something of which Democratic presidential nominee Franklin Roosevelt took careful note.

The new prescription for agriculture, however, though it would depart from the 1920s stress on voluntarism, would continue to stress the necessity of agrarian organization. Under Henry Wallace Jr., the USDA would oversee a program of direct control of farm production and price-support loans, an approach that would tend to favor the large farmer, especially in the South, at the expense of the family farm. While small farmers would benefit from such programs as rural electrification, the march toward agribusiness would only accelerate in the 1930s and 1940s.

References and Further Reading

Baker, Paula. *The Moral Frameworks of Public Life: Gender, Politics and the State in Rural New York, 1870–1930.* New York: Oxford University Press, 1991.

Barron, Hal. *Mixed Harvest: The Second Great Transformation of the Rural North, 1870–1930.* Chapel Hill: University of North Carolina Press, 1997.

Berger, Michael L. *The Devil Wagon in God's Country: The Automobile and Social Change in Rural America, 1893–1929.* Hamden, CT: Archon, 1979.

Bonner, Jeremy. "Faith of Our Fathers: Religion, Politics and Social Change in the Trans-Mississippi West, 1924–1940." PhD diss., The Catholic University of America, Washington D.C., 2001.

Bruner, Edmund deS., Gwendolyn Hughes, and Margorie Patten. *American Agricultural Villages*. New York: George H. Doran Company, 1927.

Danbom, David. *The Resisted Revolution: Urban America and the Industrialization of Agriculture, 1900–1930*. Ames: Iowa State University Press, 1979.

Fite, Gilbert C. *Cotton Fields No More: Southern Agriculture, 1865–1980*. Lexington: University Press of Kentucky, 1984.

Fitzgerald, Deborah. "Accounting for Change: Farmers and the Modernizing State." In *The Countryside in the Age of the Modern State: Political Histories of Rural America*, edited by Catherine M. Stock and Robert D. Johnston, 189–212. Ithaca, NY: Cornell University Press, 2001.

Hamilton, David E. *From New Day to New Deal: American Farm Policy from Hoover to Roosevelt, 1928–1933*. Chapel Hill: University of North Carolina Press, 1991.

Hansen, John M. "Choosing Sides: The Creation of an Agricultural Policy Network in Congress, 1919–1932." *Studies in American Political Development* 2 (1987): 183–229.

Jellison, Katherine. *Entitled to Power: Farm Women and Technology, 1913–1963*. Chapel Hill: University of North Carolina Press, 1993.

Kirby, Jack T. *Rural Worlds Lost: The American South, 1920–1960*. Baton Rouge: Louisiana State University Press, 1987.

Kirschner, Don S. *City and Country: Rural Responses to Urbanization in the 1920s*. Westport, CT: Greenwood, 1970.

Lichtman, Allan J. *Prejudice and the Old Politics: The Presidential Election of 1928*. Chapel Hill: University of North Carolina Press, 1979.

Lovin, Hugh. "The Nonpartisan League and Progressive Renascence in Idaho, 1919–1924." *Idaho Yesterdays* 32, no. 3 (Fall 1988): 2–15.

McDonald, Verlane S. "'A Paper Of, By, and For the People:' the Producers News and the Farmers' Movement in Northeastern Montana, 1918–1937." *Montana: The Magazine of Western History* 48, no. 4 (Winter 1998): 18–33.

Morlan, Robert L. *Political Prairie Fire: The Nonpartisan League, 1915–1922*. 1955. Reprint, St. Paul: Minnesota Historical Society Press, 1983.

Neth, Mary. "Leisure and Generational Change: Farm Youths in the Midwest, 1910–1940." *Agricultural History* 67 (Spring 1993): 163–184.

Pisani, Donald J. *From the Family Farm to Agribusiness: The Irrigation Crusade in California and the West, 1850–1931*. Berkeley: University of California Press, 1984.

Watkins, Marilyn P. *Rural Democracy: Family Farmers and Politics in Western Washington, 1890–1925*. Ithaca, New York: Cornell University Press, 1995.

Gangsters and Bootleggers · 3

Scott Allen Merriman

Night life was a major element of the Jazz Age—both fueled largely by a desire for alcohol. This was illegal alcohol, for this was the era of Prohibition. Speakeasies provided customers with illicit drink and a place to dance, but the enjoyable atmosphere came at a high cost, as police raids spelled disaster, and owners had to deal with organized criminals to acquire their booze. Indeed, the trade in illicit alcohol helped to fuel a rise in organized crime, and high-profile gangsters come instantly to mind when the 1920s are discussed. For instance, even those who are not students of history have generally heard of the notorious bootlegger and organized crime boss Al "Scarface" Capone (1899–1947). Though some considered the gangster lifestyle to be exciting, many, particularly rural dwellers and farmers, whose crops became increasingly unproductive throughout the era, viewed the liquor and loose morals associated with bootlegging in an increasingly negative light.

Just as famous as the gangsters and bootleggers were the underfunded and undermanned federal agents pursuing them. Although the government employed fewer than 2,000 federal agents to prevent bootlegging, this group became well known for its brutal tactics and ruthless pursuit of gangsters. Headed up by Eliot Ness (1903–1957), the most famous of these groups was based in Chicago. Nicknamed the "Untouchables," this group targeted Capone and his operations.

Besides the crime associated with illicit alcohol, there was also a general rise in crime during the period, which, along with the wild and free lifestyles, contributed to the image of the time period as "roaring." Throughout the country, but particularly in the Western and Midwestern states, gangs of bank robbers unrelated to bootleggers went on crime sprees. The gangs of the 1920s served as springboards for some criminals who would become more famous during the early 1930s, when Midwestern bank robberies were often associated with poverty and desperation.

For example, George "Baby Face" Nelson (b. Lester Gillis, 1908–1934) began his career in the 1920s. John Dillinger (1903–1934), who was one of the most famous bank robbers of the 1930s, first robbed a local grocer in his hometown of Brightwood, Indiana, in 1924.

Temperance

The United States has a long history of conflict between government efforts to regulate alcohol and public rebukes to the government's efforts. Between 1791 and 1794, the Whiskey Rebellion erupted when Appalachian settlers opposed the federal government's new whiskey tax. Secretary of the Treasury Alexander Hamilton's rationale behind the tax was that increased taxes on whiskey would lower the consumption of alcohol. The tax was eventually reduced, but the struggle to impose government control on alcohol consumption was far from over. Indeed, the Whiskey Rebellion shows that from an early period in American history there was a concern over how much people drank, and an effort by the government to limit consumption.

The focus turned more toward the individual in the early 19th century, as many argued that Americans were drinking too much, and temperance societies sprang up. A great deal of this activity came during a time known as the Age of Reform (ca. 1820–1850). These temperance societies urged people, particularly men, to take pledges to either limit or wholly abstain from drinking. Some even took it to the next step, urging states to pass their own bans on alcohol. The state of Maine did listen, passing such a measure in 1851. Several other states followed, but federal law still allowed liquor to flow. Many statewide efforts were aimed at reforming individuals and imposing a societal code of morality on others. This effort ebbed and flowed throughout the 1800s, gaining real steam around the end of the 19th century.

There was a debate within the temperance movement as to whether drinking alcohol itself was morally wrong or whether the issue was the means by which alcohol was consumed. For instance, one argument held that beverages such as beer and wine were not as bad as hard liquor because the alcohol content was lower. The counterargument held that all alcohol should be prohibited because it did not matter what the content was as long as alcohol was being abused. Whether one became intoxicated on beer or whiskey was inconsequential. Those in favor of temperance argued that too much alcohol consumption resulted in a man being unable to work, and, thus, unable to care for his family or set a good moral standard.

The Progressive Era

Toward the end of the 19th century, the Progressive movement was coming into power, and it aimed to reform all areas of society. Among the forces opposed by Progressives were the large power of corporations, unfit working and living conditions, and waste and disease in cities. Many reformers also referred to the still-rampant use and abuse of alcohol. Although not all Progressives favored reform in all of these areas, many did, and once again alcohol became a frequent target. Some Progressives joined forces with the temperance societies that had been crusading throughout the 19th century, including the Women's Christian Temperance Union. Many businessmen, although not favoring Progressives' control of the workplace, favored prohibition, desiring to control all aspects of their workers' lives to increase their profits and feeling a sober workforce would result in more profits for the company.

The Eighteenth Amendment and the Era of Prohibition

All of these forces combined to favor a constitutional amendment banning the sale of alcohol or, as it was finally worded "the sale of intoxicating liquors." The Anti-Saloon League, created in 1895, had been pushing for this move for quite some time. Some thought this language would ban only wine and hard liquor, such as whiskey, however, beer was ultimately targeted as well. The Eighteenth Amendment was also helped to fruition by World War I, as many brewers were German, and Germany was considered the main enemy in World War I. Moreover, beer was viewed as wasteful, and its ban was perceived as a simultaneous jab at the Germans and at general waste. Thus, a number of factors brought the Eighteenth Amendment to fruition in 1919. Briefly put, this amendment prohibited the manufacture, sale, and transportation of intoxicating liquors, and it went into effect on January 16, 1920.

The Volstead Act, which enforced the Eighteenth Amendment and defined intoxicating liquors to include beer, was passed the same year as the amendment. The Volstead Act, though, was extremely underfunded. For example, as mentioned earlier, it provided for hiring less than 2,000 agents nationwide to ensure its enforcement. To add to the government's problems, many local law enforcement agents refused to help the federal government enforce the law in any way. One reason was that they opposed Prohibition, sometimes fearing reprisals from organized criminals, or because they were being bribed by those same organized criminals.

Prohibition, once it was generally seen as failing, became a political bone of contention, and many urban Democrats favored its repeal. Rural Democrats, who were often conservative Protestants, had been in favor of Prohibition in the first place, leaving the Democratic Party hopelessly divided over the issue. With the start of the Great Depression in 1929, the money spent on Prohibition was seen as wasted, and many people thought the taxes gained from making liquor legal again would also help the economy. When Franklin D. Roosevelt was elected president in 1932, one of his first acts in 1933 was to legalize the sale of beer (which he accomplished by declaring beer nonintoxicating, as the Eighteenth Amendment only banned the sales of intoxicating liquors). He then helped to push the

New York City deputy police commissioner John A. Leach (right) watches agents pour confiscated liquor into a sewer following a raid during the height of prohibition. (*Library of Congress*)

Twenty-First Amendment, which reversed the Eighteenth, through Congress, and it was quickly ratified by the states.

The one question many ask is that if such a large number of the population was opposed to Prohibition, how did it pass? For instance, the Catholic Church opposed the measure as wine was used in the sacrament of Holy Communion. The one explanation offered is that the Prohibition forces were simply better organized. Temperance societies had existed for at least a century, so they were better prepared for the battle as opposed to those who thought Prohibition was a mistake.

Prohibition failed for a number of reasons. First, it never had the federal monetary backing it needed to be an effective deterrent. Second, local officials often refused to help enforce the laws. Third, and most importantly, it moved the entire alcohol industry underground, offering the lure of huge profits to those willing to supply the product. These bootleggers formed the backbone of strong organized crime networks, sometimes working in collusion, sometimes in competition with another.

The Bootlegging Industry and the Rise of Organized Crime

As noted, with Prohibition came the rise of the illegal alcohol trade. Rum-runners, those who made a career out of transporting or flat-out smuggling liquor from such countries as Canada, found a lucrative business for themselves. Not all rumrunners became gangsters, however; some merely provided the goods that the gangsters would control. Organized crime, run by gangsters, dealt with more than just liquor; such organizations also controlled prostitution, drugs, and politics. Illegal liquor provided them with the funds necessary to control such operations and bribe officials to look the other way.

Rumrunners had a large choice in what kind of drink to trade in, ranging from cheap Caribbean rum from the island of Bimini to the more expensive liquors, like whiskey and beer from Canada, gin from England, and champagne from France. Often, a large ship would carry its goods to just outside U.S. territorial waters, known as the Rum Line, and then transfer its goods to smaller boats, which could more easily outrun the Coast Guard. Although unanticipated, by Prohibition's end this resulted in a Coast Guard better trained to protect the country, and a new group of noncommissioned officers in the Navy, as the former rumrunners proved to be trained in exactly the skills the Navy needed when their Prohibition-era jobs suddenly became defunct.

Al Capone

A wide network of suppliers and distributors was set up, and at the top many individuals became famous, rich, or both. Among the most famous were Al Capone and the gangs of Chicago. Born in New York City, Italian American Al "Scarface" Capone became involved in gangs even before the Prohibition era. He earned the nickname Scarface as a teen, when a knife fight resulted in a deep slash to his cheek.

Capone later married and moved to Chicago, right about at the start of Prohibition. His new boss, Johnny Torrio, quickly promoted him in the ranks, making him second in command and giving him charge of most of the prostitution and bootlegging rackets in Chicago. Indeed, one of Capone's most notorious deeds was the 1924 takeover of the city government of Cicero, Illinois, to give himself and Torrio's gang a safe place to house their operations when Chicago decided to crack down on crime. In 1925, Torrio survived an assassination attempt and decided to turn all of his operations over to Capone and retire.

Capone then built one of the largest crime operations ever and made millions year after year. Besides controlling Cicero, he also managed to control Chicago by intimidating or bribing the police and other city officials. Capone was not the only mobster in Chicago, though, and he was linked to many murders in his attempts to wipe out his rivals.

Indeed, Chicago's gang wars in the 1920s were infamous, and a large part of the image of the 1920s as the era of gangsters and bootleggers derives from organized crime in Chicago. This network stretched over much of the Midwest, including other large cities, such as Detroit. The city was controlled by gangs who ruled different sections of the city and competed for bootlegging rights. The Torrio/Capone gang controlled the city's

Glamorized Images

Movies have often glamorized the role of the gangster in American life. From depictions of real-life criminals such as John Dillinger, Al Capone, and Bonnie and Clyde, the gangster lifestyle was often portrayed as one of fancy suits, high living, and rebellion against the system. Many law enforcement officials, such as the FBI's J. Edgar Hoover, denounced how gangsters were made into heroes on the movie screen.

During the Jazz Age, gangsters started to acquire a certain status in American society.

The image of how gangsters supposedly lived belied the reality of the lifestyle. For every Al Capone who lived a lavish lifestyle there were dozens of street-level hoods who had to fight on a daily basis for their lives and operations.

The other image of the gangster was that of an American businessman. Some gangsters, like Al Capone, would merely argue that they were part of the American Dream. They ran a business operation, providing goods and services to those willing

South Side, and Capone's leadership launched the Chicago Outfit, a well-known organized crime group that maintains operations today in several states. The Little Italy neighborhood was controlled by the six Genna Brothers and their gang, who set up small distilleries in individuals' basements to maximize their liquor-making capacity. Dean Charles (Dion) O'Banion (1892–1924) and his mob controlled the North Side of the city. In 1924, O'Banion died at the hands of Torrio/Capone gunmen, at the orders of the Unione Sicilian. In fact, O'Banion's 1924 murder sparked an escalation in gang wars that lasted until the St. Valentine's Day Massacre in 1929.

After O'Banion's death, the North Side gang was taken over by Earl "Hymie" Weiss (1898–1926) and George Clarence "Bugs" Moran (1891–1957). Moran and Weiss wanted to avenge their leader, and targeted Johnny Torrio. However, Moran's gun misfired during the assassination attempt, leaving Torrio wounded. At this point Torrio handed his empire to Capone and retired to Italy, leaving Capone to continue and expand his operations.

The most well known of the Chicago gangland killings was the St. Valentine's Day Massacre in 1929, in which Capone took aim at Moran. Moran and Capone had already made numerous notorious attempts on each other's lives, including Capone's successful hit on Weiss in 1926, and Moran's attempt on Capone in the same year. The St. Valentine's Day Massacre was supposedly carried out by Capone's lieutenant, Jack "Machine Gun" McGurn (1905–1936), and, although seven were killed, Moran arrived late to the meeting and so was unharmed. Capone escaped any charges in this incident, but it was a blot on his carefully cultivated, positive public image. Moran, in his public outrage, named Capone as the orchestrator of the hit, and lost face and mafia support himself in that to pay for them. Many pointed out that the Wall Street moguls who manipulated the stock market were no better than those who controlled the illegal liquor industry. After all, those who controlled the stock market were not above eliminating their competition. What might have differed was the means to do so. What was the difference between someone who manipulated stock prices to make a fortune while others lost theirs and someone who sold a bottle of whiskey?

No matter how much a high-living lifestyle might have been projected, the true nature of the gangster could not be hidden. Hollywood has not always shown the gangster as a high-living hero; even in the earlier days of gangster epics the violence of the era was portrayed. What was shown was that with muscle and brain one could rise to the top of the crime world. Just as in the corporate world.

way. Moran would ultimately die in jail of lung cancer in 1957 after being arrested for comparatively petty bank raids.

To maintain public support, on the advice of his publicist, Capone allowed himself to be a media figure. He gave funds to the poor and publicly proclaimed his anti-Prohibition stance, a position that was shared by many. He also established soup kitchens during the Great Depression, providing meals to hundreds of hungry people. However, public perception went against Capone after the St. Valentine's Day Massacre and the stock market crash of 1929. Until then, some of his success was fueled by a degree of public support for his activities. Capone was eventually convicted of tax evasion in 1931, and he spent more than a decade in prison. He suffered from syphilis for most of his life, and the disease worsened in prison. After conviction, he was moved to Alcatraz Island, where he had poor access to his network of informants and stoolies (those who would betray their bosses or friends in exchange for favors). He ultimately died in 1947, shortly after his release.

Criminals were involved in a large number of areas, both individually and in various organizations, that have come to be called generally "the mob." Chicago was certainly a bootlegging hub in this era, but it was far from the only center. Indeed, Al Capone got his start in a New York City gang, and the New York crime families controlled more than just bootlegging in the 1920s. Indeed, New York's Five Families—the Genovese, Gambino, Bonanno, Colombo, and Lucchese—all Sicilian in origin, controlled liquor trade in the state and much of the country. However, these families were not just interested in running rum. They were organized criminals who controlled gambling and prostitution rings, loan sharking, and traded in professional killing. Although Prohibition gave the mafia an excellent monetary base, this was by no means its only method of survival.

Al Capone, the son of Neapolitan emigrants, is America's most legendary gangster. In a touch of irony, many Chicagoans during the Great Depression saw Capone as a hero for his running of soup kitchens, helping to feed people, during the economic crisis. (*Library of Congress*)

Masseria, Luciano, and Gang Warfare

Starting in 1920, Joe "The Boss" Masseria (1879–1931) dominated mafia activity. Originally from Sicily, Masseria took control of the Morello (later Genovese) crime family and effectively controlled most territorial rifts for a number of years. His contemporaries included such figures as Charles "Lucky" Luciano (b. Salvatore Lucania, 1897–1962) and Joe Adonis (b. Giuseppe Antonio Doto, 1902–1972). Masseria effectively ran most of the bootlegging and other crime activities in New York, including protection rackets. Unlike Luciano, Masseria was only interested in trusting other Sicilians, and this was one of the things that led to Luciano arranging Masseria's killing in 1931. Luciano desired his own power and used this trust to betray Masseria.

Luciano eventually became famous for forming the National Crime Syndicate after arranging for the killings of Masseria and Salvatore Maranzano (1868–1931), which allied a wide variety of crime groups and tried to prevent warfare between the various crime families. He was ultimately deported to Italy after a prison stay. However, he gained his fame in the Prohibition era for helping to run Joe Adonis's Broadway Mob, along with Frank Costello (b. Francesco Castiglia, 1891–1973). Costello would rise to be the head of the Genovese family for many years.

The Sicilians were the major force in New York's organized crime, but other gangs were sometimes able to gain a toehold. For example, Benjamin "Bugsy" Siegel (b. Siegelbaum, 1906–1947) and Meyer Lansky (b. Majer Suchowlinsky, 1902–1983) were born to Jewish American parents. As teens, they set up protection rackets, requiring a $5 fee from pushcart vendors whose merchandise they would otherwise burn. In 1921, they developed a gang known as the Bugs and Meyer Mob in New York City. Originally, the gang supplied drivers and stolen trucks for bootleggers, but it ultimately became involved in the entire range of gangster-related activities. Indeed, Siegel and Lansky worked with Lucky Luciano on numerous occasions, and the Bugs and Meyer Mob often helped the Broadway Mob protect its alcohol shipments. Siegel became famous for building up commercial Las Vegas in the 1940s, even though he lost money on the venture and was ultimately killed for his failure to turn a profit on the mob's money. Lansky continued to be involved in the mob until the 1960s when he sold off many of his Las Vegas holdings to Howard Hughes and retired.

Though less famous than the Chicago and New York gang members, Cincinnati bootlegger George Remus (1876–1952) was well known in his own right during the Prohibition era. Remus, a German immigrant who arrived in the United States as a child, had no family ties to organized crime networks. He was trained as a lawyer, and, when Prohibition started, Remus decided to get around the law. He bought distilleries, ordered liquor from those distilleries for his own use for medicine (the use of alcohol for medicine was legal at this time even under Prohibition), and then sold this "medicinal" alcohol illegally. He made large sums of money off the sales and used some of the money to throw lavish parties at his home in Price Hill, one of the richer parts of Cincinnati. At more than one party, Remus presented new cars to many of the guests. Remus was eventually convicted of bootlegging and sentenced to two years in jail. After he was released from jail, he was divorced by his wife, who had been liquidating and hiding his assets with the help of a federal prohibition agent who was her lover. Remus shot and killed his wife on the day of the divorce but was acquitted on grounds of temporary insanity. He then moved out of Cincinnati and stayed out of the limelight, avoiding the bootlegging business. Remus was the model for the Jay Gatsby character in F. Scott Fitzgerald's novel *The Great Gatsby*.

Another midwestern city famous for its Prohibition-era gangs was Detroit. The Purple Gang was really a loose confederation of Detroit-area mobsters. The gang originated before World War I on the city's lower east side, where poverty dominated most lives. However, the city's proximity to Canada made bootlegging an appealing activity for the group when Prohibition began. In fact, the gang was far more likely to hijack a shipment being run by another bootlegging organization than to establish its own operations in an area, and many groups had to run their liquor through Detroit to get it out of Canada. The Purple Gang supplied Al Capone's Canadian whiskey as part of its underworld activity. The group's leaders included the four Bernstein Brothers, and the group is generally recognized to have been predominantly Jewish. In addition to its bootlegging activities, the Purple Gang also helped corrupt union leaders keep members in line and quell nonmember complaints during the cleaners and dyers war.

Alcohol Production Outside Organized Crime

Many towns and burgs had their own famous criminals, at least as well known locally as those in the big cities. Much later in the 20th century, the comic strip *Hi and Lois* once touched on this. The eldest son, Chip, was eager to compete with a friend's famous relative, who was on the road crew for the famous rock band Grateful Dead. Chip begged his dad for a famous ancestor. Hi finally remembered that in the 1920s somebody in Lois' family had gotten in trouble with the law for bootlegging, to Chip's great elation.

Indeed, one of the reasons bootlegging thrived throughout the Prohibition era was the country's proliferating opposition to it. While the economy boomed, people wanted to celebrate. When the bottom dropped out of agriculture, people wanted to commiserate. It seemed impossible for many to perform either of these tasks entirely without alcohol. Thus, even as the government and temperance groups lauded Prohibition's benefits, the underground network of anti-Prohibitionists kept on growing. Even some who supported limits on legalized drinking still thought drinking champagne at weddings or keeping a little whiskey on hand could be perfectly acceptable.

Some people went so far as to brew their own moonshine, a name derived because such homegrown brews were typically produced at night (i.e., by the shine of the moon) to reduce the possibility of capture. Much, though by no means all, moonshine was brewed in southern Appalachia before being raced up to Detroit. Such moonshine is often called rotgut becaue of its impurities, and such impurities can have serious implications. People have gone blind, temporarily and permanently. Some even died, for instance, from drinking moonshine with too much methanol. Despite its risks, and the threat of prosecution that still exists, home brewers continue to distill their own hard liquor. Though homemade wine and beer became legal in 1978, moonshine remains off limits, and therefore, perhaps, all the more appealing. Indeed, moonshiners birthed an entirely different industry, when, in the Prohibition era and beyond, runners in fast cars would outrace the law and each other. The roots of NASCAR racing are likely found in rum-running. Indeed, NASCAR driver Lloyd Seay (d.1941) died in a bootlegger dispute.

People found a plethora of ways to make and move alcohol, and some even found novel ways to make and transport relatively safe alcohol. For instance, Vermonter Clive Irwin made alcohol by hiding a still behind the walls of his house. He placed the components for making alcohol in various chambers, closed up the process, and distilled the alcohol at the end. The still was not found in his Burlington home until about 80 years later, well after his death. Many others continued the activities that their families had carried on for years, brewing alcohol in their bathtubs and

Flapper hides a flask in her boot, Washington, D.C., 1922. The speakeasies of Prohibition brought women into the sphere of public consumption. (*Library of Congress*)

basements and in special rural locations. These practices became more popular with the rise of Prohibition. Although some of this alcohol was safe, a great deal of it was not, but generally the aim of those selling it was to make money selling a product they thought was probably safe. They did not intend to be fraudulent. Others did not have this ethical concern, taking advantage of Prohibition to sell anything people would buy, regardless of safety. It should also be noted that some individuals would also drink anything that had the word alcohol in its name, regardless of safety, and so some drank wood alcohol (methyl alcohol) and rubbing alcohol (isopropyl alcohol) rather than drinking alcohol (ethyl alcohol). Many went blind drinking these products, or died from them.

Others made money legally anticipating the end of Prohibition and became famous later for other reasons. Joseph Kennedy Sr., for example, bought up large stocks of alcohol in the early 1930s predicting the repeal of the Eighteenth Amendment. It was perfectly legal to buy wholesale lots of liquor, even before Prohibition's repeal, so Kennedy's actions were well within the law, so long as he did not trade in the liquor to individuals while Prohibition was still in effect. Kennedy then made a tidy sum reselling that alcohol after Prohibition was repealed but before other stocks of alcohol could make their way onto the market.

Battling the Illegal Liquor Trade

As noted, among the problems facing the Volstead Act was that it was underfunded and lacked any real support in many major cities. This caused many police forces to oppose the Volstead Act or at the very least to not want to enforce it. Other police forces were corrupt or intimidated and were sometimes threatened by or paid off by the bootleggers to look the other way. However, a Bureau of Investigation (which would become the Federal Bureau of Investigation [FBI] in 1935) did exist in this era, as did a Bureau of Prohibition. The latter agency was created to employ the 2,000 people whose salaries the Volstead Act could fund. The agency was bounced around as an arm of several federal bureaus, beginning as the Prohibition Unit of the Bureau of Internal Revenue (which became the Internal Revenue Service in 1920). In 1927, the Department of the Treasury made it an independent unit, but it was absorbed by the Department of Justice in 1928, made part of the FBI (then called the Division of Investigation) in 1933, and returned to the Treasury Department in 1935, where it ultimately became the Bureau of Alcohol, Tobacco, and Firearms.

Early in the Prohibition era, the New York City enforcement team of Isidore "Izzy" Einstein (1880–1938) and Moe Smith (d. 1961) earned fame for busting the most speakeasies ever. Between 1920 and 1925, the team arrested 4,932 people, and roughly 4,700 were convicted. They were known for using disguises to trick liquor sellers to sell them drinks before busting a joint. However, they were unpopular with local police, who were being bribed to look the other way by bar owners and gangsters. The pair lost their jobs in 1925, in spite of their many successes, and questions remain about whether they suffered from the Volstead Act's chronic underfunding or a nasty political turn of events.

The most famous member of the Bureau of Prohibition was, by far, Eliot Ness, who was charged with attempting to corner Al Capone on bootlegging charges. Ness joined the Bureau of Prohibition in 1927. He started with a team of 50, but kept reducing its number until, ultimately, he had a group of 11 incorruptible men working for him whose unwavering support of the law earned them the nickname "the Untouchables." Ness ran an extensive wiretapping operation that allowed him, within six months of assuming his position, to seize breweries he estimated to be worth over a million dollars. Capone found Ness to be a serious thorn in the side, and frequent assassination attempts were made. Although no one succeeded in killing Ness, a close friend of his was murdered. However, it was not Ness's unit that ultimately brought about Capone's end, but the other arm of the Bureau of Prohibition working on the Capone case, the tax evasion agents.

Criminal Activities Outside Prohibition

In addition to the celebrated bootlegging gangsters, there were other well-recognized criminals in this era. Indeed, a number of bank robbers and others whose crimes had little to do with Prohibition would become famous in the early 1930s. Several of the most well-known criminals of the 1930s actually launched their careers in the 1920s, even though it would be a few years before their fame eclipsed that of the bootleggers and moonshiners. These individuals were often celebrated because they were seen as part of the overall Roaring Twenties, and they were commemorated in the 1930s as the victory of the common folk over the few remaining rich. Some movies in the 1920s and 1930s even showed criminals in a favorable or neutral light, often painting them as Robin Hood figures who sought financial justice in an unbalanced world. These positive portrayals often alarmed law enforcement officials, such as famed FBI leader J. Edgar Hoover.

Figures like George R. "Machine Gun" Kelly (1895–1954) stand out, as they were famous not just for their Prohibition activities in the 1920s, but also for kidnappings and armed robberies. Kelly was jailed when he was caught bringing liquor onto an Indian reservation in 1928, but he earned an early release for good behavior. Kelly's career finally ended when a kidnapping went awry, leading the FBI to his hideout in 1933. Half of the most famous crime duo in the 1930s, Clyde Barrow (1909–1934), also got his start in the Roaring Twenties. He was arrested once in 1926 (for failure to return a rental car) and again in 1928 (for possession of stolen property), well before he met Bonnie Parker (1910–1934) in 1929, when they began a crime streak of their own, specializing in bank robbery. Immortalized in a 1967 film starring Warren Beatty and Faye Dunaway, Bonnie and Clyde still maintain a certain legendary status despite the reality that they were criminals who were eventually gunned down by law enforcement.

John Dillinger really began his career in prison in 1924. He and a friend robbed a well-known local grocer in their hometown of Brightwood, Indiana. Although the friend was given a light sentence, Dillinger received a 10-year term that left him embittered. He spent his time learning how to be a criminal and, upon his release, formed his own gang and went on bank-robbing sprees until he was murdered by federal agents as he emerged from the Biograph Theater in Chicago. Baby Face Nelson, whose fame came from robbing banks with the Dillinger Gang in the 1930s, began his career working for Al Capone in the 1920s. Nelson was not viewed with the same Robin Hood patina as Dillinger and some others. He was known for his violence, in spite of his dedication to his family.

Pitted against these criminals, at the national level, was the Bureau of Investigation, headed, from 1924, by the famed J. Edgar Hoover. Hoover got his start in the Justice Department during World War I and moved himself into the Enemy Aliens Registration Section in 1919, eventually becoming its head. Thus, from an early period, he saw himself as prosecuting threats to America. In the early 1920s, he moved into what was then called the Bureau of Investigation as its deputy director. In 1924, he was named its acting head, and, in 1925, he took the position permanently, serving until his death in 1972.

During the 1920s, Hoover began his move toward making the bureau the top investigative organization in the country, creating the bureau's "Ten Most Wanted" list in part to draw attention to the agency. He was very successful in trumpeting the agency's success, persuading the news media and entertainment industry to give it favorable treatment, and collecting files of personal information on prominent politicians to convince them to leave the FBI alone. All of these activities began in the 1920s, and many of the gangsters of the 1920s and 1930s, including John Dillinger, were what Hoover used as the agency's springboard to fame.

The Legacy of Jazz Age Crime

The 1920s are remembered as a period of speakeasies, bootleggers, and gangsters. Capone is still proclaimed one of the most famous prisoners in Alcatraz to visitors touring the island. Movies are still made about the gangsters of the period, such as *Bugsy* (another film about a crime figure starring Warren Beatty), which celebrated Bugsy Siegel. The gangsters and bootleggers of the period also continue to influence the public's perception of the 1920s.

One of the main things remembered about the 1920s is the nightlife culture that grew directly out of the bootleggers. People also cite the 1920s in discussions over whether bans on drugs, such as that on marijuana, should be continued. Most people believe "harder" drugs, such as cocaine, should be banned. However, views on some other drugs cause schisms similar to those drawn between the prohibitionists and the anti-Prohibitionists in the 1920s. A sizable percentage of people favor legalizing or decriminalizing marijuana. Many of those who hold this opinion publicly use Prohibition as an example of a failed social experiment, and cite the decreased crime and violence that came after the end of Prohibition as evidence of what would happen if marijuana were legalized. However, others see marijuana as a gateway drug, the use of which often leads to those hard drugs. Those people wholeheartedly support the ban.

The 1920s are also seen as the first modern decade, and in this way the period shapes how we see the present. Thus, the gangsters and bootleggers of the 1920s, and the world in which they moved, continue to shape our understandings of the past and the present. Although the gangsters and bootleggers knew they were flaunting the law, they might argue that they were merely following the American Dream: to make money and live well.

Whether it was the risk in partaking of illegal liquor or the violence that accompanied the trade that gave the Jazz Age the name "Roaring

Twenties," there is no denying the thrill that permeated such activities. Whether one's participation was subtle, such as purchasing a bottle from a local bootlegger, or more overt, such as a gang boss bribing law enforcement officials to look the other way, there was a certain feeling that came with the risk of being caught. This in itself helped make the period "roaring."

References and Further Reading

Kobler, John. *Capone: The Life and World of Al Capone*. New York: Da Capo Press, 2003.

Mordden, Ethan. *That Jazz! An Idiosyncratic Social History of the American Twenties*. New York: G. P. Putnam, 1978.

Perrett, Geoffrey. *America in the Twenties*. New York: Simon and Schuster, 1982.

Rockman, Seth. *Welfare Reform in the Early Republic*. New York: Bedford/St. Martin's, 2003.

Sann, Paul. *The 20s: The Lawless Decade*. New York: Crown, 1957.

Thompson, Neal. *Driving with the Devil: Southern Moonshine, Detroit Wheels, and the Birth of NASCAR*. New York: Crown, 2006.

Jazz Age Evangelism | 4

John H. Barnhill

Origins

Religious freedom was arguably the main basis for the founding of the British colonies. The settlements at such places as the Massachusetts Bay Colony, Rhode Island, and Maryland were supposedly established for religious freedom, although that freedom was not always extended to splinter groups. Maryland was intended to be a haven for Catholics, although in its history there was violent backlash against them. Thus, there is no arguing about the importance of religion in American history. Although the Bill of Rights established the separation of church and state, the influence of evangelism in the United States has always been strong and the presence of Christianity has certainly made its mark.

What made the presence of evangelism so prominent during the Jazz Age? For starters, this was the end of the Victorian era whereby society was expected to adhere to specific values. There was a new sense of openness about how people lived their lives. Couples dated and courted in ways previously seen as improper. The rise of Hollywood promoted sexuality in ways many considered shocking. To many, what they considered traditional values of purity and proper behavior were tantamount. During the Jazz Age, certain evangelists provided that spiritual leadership.

Jazz Age Evangelists

Dwight Moody

Evangelism was not a phenomenon restricted to the Jazz Age alone. The movement, and many of its practitioners, lasted through the 20th century and into the 21st. Evangelism in America predated the United States itself, dating from the first Great Awakening (approximately 1720-1750) and

Dwight Moody was a very popular and effective late 19th-century evangelist. The creator of modern mass evangelism, he preached to audiences of thousands in the United States, Canada, and Great Britain. (*Library of Congress*)

itinerant preachers of personal conversion such as George Whitefield. In style and methods, 20th-century evangelism owed much to the evangelists of the 19th century, especially Dwight L. Moody.

With only a fourth-grade education, this Chicago shoe salesman became the leading religious figure of the Gilded Age. He invented the modern way of evangelism that lasted through the 20th century, including the Jazz Age of the 1920s and 1930s. Moody combined revivalism and the mass media in a four-year campaign that began in Britain in 1873 and then spread to America's cities—Brooklyn, Philadelphia, New York, Chicago, and Boston. He combined prayer and publicity in civic spectacles that the newspapers used to increase circulation. Moody and the press fed off each other, drawing crowds larger than at any earlier time in the cities' histories. Critics complained that the revival was an artificial construct, but Moody justified his approach by saying he preferred advertising to preaching to empty auditoriums. Moody had good business sense. His approach made him an involuntary celebrity, a star made brighter by the media. Moody made evangelism a commercial entertainment of modern proportions.

Billy Sunday, evangelist (1862-1935). (*Library of Congress*)

Billy Sunday

The first of the Jazz Age evangelists, Billy Sunday (1862–1935), built on Moody's success and made evangelism muscular. He used his athletic skills and squeaky clean Christian image in sports and preaching, using sports metaphors in his sermons and incorporating athletic physicality in his revival preaching. He rode the Prohibition movement to the maximum. He altered the image of Christianity as delicate and tame.

Billy Sunday was born in Ames, Iowa, a month before his father died of pneumonia. He and his brother grew up in an orphanage. In 1883, he signed with the Chicago White Stockings and soon gained fame as a baseball player, notably as a speedster, the first to circle the bases in 14 seconds, and a record-setting base stealer. Then he got religion at an 1886 outreach of the Pacific Garden Mission in Chicago and in 1891 began a career that would see him addressing more than 100 million people—without loudspeakers, radio, or television.

Sunday gave up a $400 per month baseball salary (the average American wage was $480 per year) and rejected later offers of $500 a month, even $2,000 a month. He worked at the Young Men's Christian Association (YMCA) for $83 a month and in 1894 became advance man for evangelist J. Wilbur Chapman at $40 a week. Chapman left evangelism in 1896, and Sunday preached his first sermon in 1897. He was ordained a Presbyterian minister in 1903. By 1909, his traveling entourage included his wife, who handled finances and planning, and Homer Rodeheaver, a soloist and song leader. Sunday's greatest moment came in 1917 when a 10-week revival in New York City brought in a $100,000 love offering (which he donated to the Red Cross and other charities) and brought

Evangelists and National Morality

During the Jazz Age, the image and presence of evangelists in the public eye took numerous forms. In 1927, Sinclair Lewis published *Elmer Gantry*, a scathing indictment of religion and religious leaders. Supposedly based on actual people, the book centers on a man who becomes a Pentecostal minister for monetary, and not spiritual, reasons. Although he faces charges of fraud, Gantry survives. This controversial book was banned in some places. To the religious community the book was an outrage, an attempt to discredit its leaders. To the book's supporters, it was merely a true statement of the hypocrisy in organized religion.

Yet despite how Lewis portrayed modern-day evangelism, to those in the movement their work was very real. The national morals were to be protected. Many evangelists scoffed at any criticisms heaped on them because they believed they were following the word of God. No scorn would stop them in their work.

Of course, the biggest confrontation between the religious and secular sectors of society came with the infamous Scopes "Monkey" Trial of 1925 (see chapter on *Reformers, Radicals,*

98,000 conversions. Sunday collapsed while preaching in Des Moines in 1933. At his peak, he turned down a million-dollar movie offer. He believed God had called him to evangelize and remained true to his calling until he died of a heart attack in 1935 at the age of 73.

Billy Sunday's wife, Helen Amelia Thompson Sunday (1868–1957), remained home with the children until 1907, at which time she took over the business and administrative functions and began speaking to women's groups. After his death, she remained active in speaking at youth rallies and raising money for rescue missions and other ministries. She was active in the work of Bob Jones University, Youth for Christ, and Voice of the Andes, a radio station.

Mordecai Ham

Mordecai Ham (1877–1961) converted (or "saved" according to evangelistic terms) more than 300,000 people, including Billy Graham. Ham was born in Kentucky to a family that traced its lineage back through eight generations of Baptist preachers. Surrounded by faith, he knew from age eight that he was saved, and at age nine that he would be a preacher. Not until 1900 did he answer the call, studying and preaching in neighborhood churches, including one once pastored by his grandfather, until 1901, at which time his revival success was such that he became an itinerant evangelist, first in Kentucky, and then throughout the South. His approach was to take on the hardest case in town, convert him or her, and let the efficacy of his message bring the "lesser" sinners to his revivals. Like Moody and other evangelists, he let the spirit take over when he preached. He and Socialists). At heart was whether the teaching of Darwin's theory of evolution should be banned from public school classrooms in favor of teaching the Biblical view of creation alone. To the religious community, defending their faith was paramount. The academic community—many of whom were in fact Christians themselves— saw the ban on teaching evolution as a step backward into the Dark Ages.

The religious community was also very active in keeping an eye on Hollywood. As the Victorian-era values concerning sexuality evaporated, so did the restraints on the entertainment industry to keep its depictions in check. But with the participation of numerous ministers and other religious leaders, film censorship became acceptable as such leaders sat on review boards. Any romantic scenes were regulated. Lovers who kissed on screen had to do so with closed mouths. Although some forms of sexuality, such as in films depicting Greek and Roman times, often showed some scantily clad women, many religious leaders kept an eye on Hollywood's output to ensure that American morals were not being corrupted.

faced his share of threats for his stance in favor of Prohibition and, later, from atheists. After more than 30 years on the road, in 1940 he began broadcasting over a 40-station radio network.

Aimee Semple McPherson

Aimee Semple McPherson (1890–1944) was born Beth Kennedy near Ingersoll, Ontario, Canada, to a Methodist father and a Salvation Army mother. She renamed herself Aimee Elizabeth Kennedy. As a teenager she became a Pentecostal after hearing preacher Robert Semple, whom she married at age 17 and followed to China. Robert died two years later. After a bout of appendicitis at age 23, Aimee decided to become a minister, claiming that a voice had given her the choice of dying or entering the ministry. Then she married Harold McPherson, a businessman. Together the McPhersons traveled North America in their "gospel" car, covered with religious slogans and Bible verses. In 1917, Aimee began publishing *The Bridal Call*. Aimee began drawing crowds, and even a quiet divorce failed to slow the increase in her popularity. Between 1918 and 1923, she was a traveling evangelist. In 1919, revival meetings in Los Angeles made her famous. In 1922, she launched her first overseas tour to Australia. By 1923, she was preaching at the 5,300-seat Angelus Temple. From the temple in 1924 she began the first American Christian radio broadcasts. One tour that lasted 150 days required her to deliver 336 sermons and to travel 15,000 miles. The audiences exceeded 2 million people.

McPherson's services included parades, bands, speaking in tongues—pageantry and entertainment for Christians repelled by the offerings of

Itinerant evangelist Aimee Semple McPherson was a shining star in the religious revival of the early 20th century. (*Library of Congress*)

nearby Hollywood. She sometimes dressed in costume to match the theme of her sermon. McPherson called her movement the Foursquare. Taken from the Bible, Foursquare included Christ as Savior, Baptizer with the Holy Spirit, the Great Physician, and imminent King.

All was going well until Sister Aimee disappeared in 1926. Reemerging 39 days later, she claimed she had been kidnapped for a $500,000 ransom. Law enforcement was skeptical, but the district attorney declined to prosecute McPherson on charges of adultery and perjury. Seemingly, she had been in Carmel, California, with her married lover. Subsequently, she liberalized her appearance—bobbing her hair and wearing short skirts—and began dancing and drinking, in the process provoking her entire 300-member choir to resign. With time and the Great Depression the scandal faded. The Angelus Temple began providing food, clothing, and other items to needy families. McPherson married and divorced in the early 1930s, but the war years were otherwise quiet. In 1944, McPherson preached to a crowd of 10,000 in Oakland and died the next day of kidney failure and a barbiturate overdose, probably accidental although speculation about suicide arose.

McPherson was the prototype of the modern woman televangelists. She was the first woman to receive a Federal Communications Commission (FCC) license. Her preaching was heard by millions over 45 radio stations. She wrote half a dozen books, 180 songs, and seven operas. She innovatively incorporated elements of vaudeville and Hollywood into her preaching, and she incorporated social ministry and a Bible college to train Pentecostal ministers, missionaries, and evangelists. The International

Church of the Foursquare Gospel remains strong today, with 24,000 churches in 99 countries and 2.8 million members worldwide.

William Simmons

The 1920s religious fervor was part of the Jazz Age excess that resulted from disillusionment with World War I. William Simmons, insurance salesman and founder of the Ku Klux Klan, was an evangelist. Mattie Howard, blue-eyed beauty turned gangster's moll and almost Hollywood starlet (had she avoided incarceration), spent eight years in the penitentiary and after sliding back into crime finally saw the light, got religion, and became an evangelist. Frank Buchman focused his crusade on the Ivy League, where he converted first the elite leaders, publicized their conversions, and then brought in the lesser lights; Buchman had an unnatural preoccupation with his followers' sex lives that led to his being banned from Princeton and elsewhere. Sam Small, Sam Scott, and Sam Jones were active conservative, dry preachers of the era. Emile Coué wrote *Self-Mastery Through Conscious Autosuggestion* but his legacy is the phrase "Every day in every way I'm getting better and better." Father Divine in Harlem preached communal living and interracial harmony. Billy Sunday denounced alcohol, liberalism, and science, and Aimee McPherson dressed like an angel, made her sermons into dramatic productions, baptized 150 at a time, and had a "miracle room" for those healed by her hands.

Uldine Utley

Uldine Utley, little remembered today, inspired a Broadway play, *Bless You, Sister*. Utley (1912–1995) had been a protégé of Dr. John Roach Straton in the mid-1920s. At first she was a Baptist but became a Methodist in 1929. Utley was known as "the Garbo of the Pulpit" and was known to display herself in a bathing suit. Straton began pastoring Calvary Baptist Church in New York City in 1918. At the time he had a national reputation as a strict fundamentalist, proclaiming biblical inerrancy and literalism and decrying the moral decline of Christian civilization, particularly the hellish city of New York. In 1926, he encountered Utley, aged 14, at the Florida Bible Conference. A feature in the April issue of *American Magazine* estimated that Utley had brought 10,000 souls, mostly men, to Christ. Straton arranged an East Coast evangelism tour that in the fall brought Utley to New York for four weeks, initially at Calvary but finally before 10,000 people at Madison Square Garden.

Straton's actions concerning the presence of women in the evangelist movement alienated his fellow Baptists who did not believe women should preach. A heavy-handed leadership style and suspected financial irregularities led to a decline in his career in the years before his death in 1929. As for Utley, she grew up. Without Straton promoting her and the novelty of precocity, she faded. By 1920, the Methodist Episcopal Church allowed women ministers to preach, baptize, and wed, although it rarely gave them churches to pastor. In 1935, 23-year-old Uldine Utley enrolled in the Association of Methodist Women Preachers. Her last moment in the limelight was ordination in the Methodist Church. She married in 1938, had a subsequent mental collapse, and spent the rest of her life in California mental institutions, dying in 1995.

Daniel Paul Rader

Evangelist Daniel Paul Rader (1879–1935) was less famous, less notorious, than Aimee Semple McPherson or Billy Sunday, but he provided a strong legacy and was an example of those who brought continuity and stability to evangelism. Rader was born in Denver, Colorado, the son of a Methodist missionary. He began preaching around 1895. He returned to Denver, where he attended the University of Denver, the University of Colorado, and Central College, Missouri, between 1897 and 1901, earning a reputation as a football player and boxer at Colorado and coaching in Missouri. Several coaching stints later he became an ordained minister in 1904, taking his first pastorate in Boston in that year. He left the ministry to promote boxing in 1909 but returned in 1912. In 1914, he began his evangelistic career as an itinerant in Ohio, moving quickly to the nondenominational Moody Church in Chicago.

In 1921, Rader had been pastor of Moody Church for seven years. He was also president of the Christian and Missionary Alliance (C&MA) denomination and traveled extensively to preach. Moody Church was proudly independent, and its board began worrying that the C&MA influence might be getting too strong. Rader left Moody, intending to hold a tent revival under a prefabricated steel structure in New York City. The deal fell through so he set up the Big Steel Tent in Chicago, spread the word through handbills and radio, and drew capacity crowds of more than 4,000 through the summer. Then he decided to make the Big Steel Tent permanent. Forced to choose between the C&MA and the tabernacle that replaced the steel tent, he chose the tabernacle. He established it with no members, no governing board, and no denomination. Services were held Sunday afternoons so people could attend after church. Rader began preaching in the tabernacle in 1922.

Rader preached not only at the tabernacle and on the radio but also on the street, at Thanksgiving men's only meetings, at summer camps, at foreign missions, at evangelistic campaigns, and at other churches in a visiting role. He was more subdued than Billy Sunday, using less slang and acrobatics and more stories from everyday life. His themes were God's love, the need for all to face up to sin and accept Christ, and the obligation of Christians to put their faith to work in the world.

Rader's use of media   Radio was new in 1922. The first amateur broadcast aimed at a wide audience was in 1919. When a local radio station needed to fill airtime, Rader jumped at the opportunity. For three years he occasionally broadcast music and preached for various Chicago stations before signing with WHT in 1925. The WHT programs attracted music lovers, teens, children, sports fans, and others. When CBS picked up the broadcasts, the audience swelled into the hundreds of thousands. Rader's pathbreaking use of radio influenced others, including Clarence Jones, "the father of missionary radio."

Rader was also important as a precursor of Youth for Christ, AWANA, and other youth ministries. His staff included Clarence Jones and Lance Latham, who were encouraged by Rader to bring in children who had never been inside a church before. They used clubs, radio programs, and summer programs with catchy slogans, games, and music.

In 1932, Rader implemented a program of grassroots evangelism by forming small clubs for men and women to meet and study the Christian faith and evangelism. These were the World Wide Christian Courier clubs, incorporating Bible studies and elements of fraternal orders but emphasizing proselytizing and witnessing. Rader's ministry collapsed in 1933, so the clubs were largely stillborn. The ideas and methods are seen in many ministries today.

Chicago Gospel Tabernacle   Part of Rader's use of mass media was the creation of the Chicago Gospel Tabernacle. In a very effective use of radio, gospel programming began in 1922. This was not limited to the use of the airwaves alone, for the tabernacle also promoted conferences and various social programs. The tabernacle had come far from its humble origins in a small wooden building.

Rader traveled around the world twice. Additionally, tabernacle mission work included conferences and support of missionaries through the world. Among the 150 missionaries Rader's efforts sponsored were his sister, three daughters, and others, and future missionaries received their initial impetus at the tabernacle.

The tabernacle itself was unimposing, as it was initially only a temporary building. It was 170 by 170 feet, and wood and tile walls replaced the initial canvas. It had a platform large enough for the choir and two pianos, wooden pews, and coal stoves for winter heat. Two sides were lined with offices and activity rooms. Later, a cafeteria was added. Like modern megachurches, the tabernacle had a large congregation, many of whom had no history in traditional congregations. The attraction was a charismatic preacher who worked with his staff to identify the interests and needs of the congregants. Small groups and special programs provided fellowship. Outreach and missionary programs built on the internal programs. Among the programs was the tabernacle's pantry, which fed many during the Depression.

When Rader lost his primary financial supporter, who suffered financial blows during the Depression, he was unable to cover his mortgage. At the same time the radio ministry began losing money. His California Tabernacle was a financial liability, and Rader got trapped in California by a court order barring him from leaving until its debt was paid. Finally back in Chicago, Rader assumed the tabernacle's debt, left it, and declared bankruptcy, saving the tabernacle, which continued as a traditional church until the late 1970s. Rader continued to evangelize until his death in 1938.

Influencing future evangelists People Rader influenced include Peter Deyneka Sr., evangelist to eastern Europe; Merrill Dunlop, Christian musician and evangelist; and Charles Fuller, founder of the Fuller Theological Seminary and an extremely prominent radio evangelist in his own right. He also influenced Torrey Johnson, first president of Youth for Christ and evangelist; Clarence Jones, founder of missionary radio station HCJB in Quito, Ecuador; Lance Latham, founder of AWANA; and others.

Although Rader preferred nondenominationalism, and Utley switched denominations, for some Jazz Age evangelists, the Pentecostal denomination provided a stabilizing influence. The Assemblies of God evangelists were examples of strong Pentecostal stability. Although Pentecostalism dates from 1901, the heyday of Pentecostal evangelism was the 1920s and 1930s. These were the years when Pentecostal churches grew rapidly nationwide, Pentecostal evangelists were preaching in storefronts, skating rinks, brush arbors, garages—to small groups and in citywide crusades. Aimee Semple McPherson was an Assemblies of God evangelist from 1919 to 1922. She brought many independent Pentecostal churches into the Assemblies of God during those years.

Smith Wigglesworth

Another Assemblies of God evangelist was English-born Smith Wigglesworth (1859–1947), the "Apostle of Faith." Born a nominal Methodist of religiously indifferent parents, he was born again at age eight and reputedly had the power to convert others at that early age. In his teens he was active in the Salvation Army, where he met his wife, Polly. They ran a mission together for more than 20 years. Although he was a powerful man, he inevitably had to interrupt his sermons within two or three minutes because he began crying. Polly handled much of the preaching. Then, in 1907, he received the gift of tongues and his evangelistic career began.

From his beginnings as an illiterate plumber, Wigglesworth became a faith healer, a charismatic theologian, and an evangelist. He also became the author of *Ever-increasing Faith*, which sold more than 100,000 copies, as well as works on tongues and other gifts of the Holy Spirit. His wife of 31 years, Polly, taught him to read. After she died in 1913, he traveled and preached in the United States between 1914 and 1935. Wigglesworth was one of the most prominent of the early Pentecostal evangelists and among the first to attract large audiences to it.

Morris Plotts

Morris Plotts (1906–1997) was six foot four inches tall, a dynamic presence. Plotts became a minister at age 19 in Nebraska. He married Neva Holdiman in 1928, and the two jointly pastored a Methodist Church. Dissatisfied spiritually, the Plottses finally came to Pentecostalism in 1932. That launched a ministry that would last for decades. Plotts set the pattern in 1933.

While in Sharon, Iowa, Plotts began evangelizing the nearby town of Montezuma. The times and the neighbors were hostile to Pentecostalism, so it took little time for Plotts's long and loud tent services to provoke the Montezumans. Arrested for creating a public nuisance, Plotts continued to hold services from his jail cell. He attracted hundreds to the jail, and steel bars barely slowed the baptisms in the Holy Spirit, the bringing of souls to salvation, and the healings of the ill and lame. Hundreds, and sometimes as many as 1,000, attended his meetings at New Sharon. People would drive more than 100 miles to hear him, and many were saved and baptized in the nearby river. Plotts had greater tasks in store: becoming evangelist to the world, especially East Africa. By the time he retired in 1989, he had formed many churches throughout the world, traveled more than 2 million miles, preached 10,500 times in 3,367 different locations, and raised about $83.5 million for mission work.

Ethel Musick

Ethel Musick began traveling with a Sister Tomson before setting out on her own as a church planter and a teenage evangelist. When she married, she began taking her husband with her. Their children were rootless, lacking a permanent home, as was common for Pentecostal evangelists in the 1920s. Ethel Musick established six new churches and built five new church buildings in only 18 months.

Charles Price

Another English transplant was Charles Price (1887–1947). Born and educated in England, Price emigrated to Canada, then to Washington, where he converted and began working at a Free Methodist Mission, eventually becoming a Methodist minister with liberal leanings. Later he became a Congregationalist. After 12 years as a Congregationalist minister, he was pastoring a church in Lodi, California, when he heard Aimee Semple McPherson in San Jose. He quickly fell under her influence, began speaking in tongues, and converted. Returned to Lodi, he began a revival, causing denominational leaders concern. Price left the Congregationalists, opened the Lodi Bethel Temple, and began working as an itinerant evangelist in Oregon and British Columbia. Over three weeks in 1923 he preached before 250,000 and healed many. Among those healed that year were Lorne Fox and his family. Fox and his sister became evangelists shortly thereafter. Price's ministry expanded through Canada and the American Midwest. In 1926, he began publishing *Golden Grain*, a magazine that included personal testimonies of healing and miracles. When his lawyer absconded with all his money in 1928, Price lost his temple but continued preaching in his "Kanvas Kathedral." Continuing to travel, he claimed 35,000 conversions in 1928 alone. He remained active during the Depression, spreading his ministry to England, Europe, and the Middle East as well as the United States. By 1939, he estimated that he had traveled more than a million miles since he began evangelistic work in 1922.

He continued to travel through World War II until he retired in 1945. He died in 1947. Although not formally affiliated with any denomination, Price had a special relationship with the Assemblies of God. As well as evangelizing, he wrote several books, taught at Southern California Bible College, and preached at many churches.

Robert Reynolds Jones

Robert Reynolds Jones (1883–1968), better known as Bob Jones Sr., was born in Alabama. He converted at age 11, served as Sunday school superintendent at 12, and became an ordained Methodist minister at age 15. He began his evangelism in the Alabama cotton fields, brush arbors, and country churches. From small beginnings he became an internationally known evangelist, rated by Billy Sunday as the greatest of all time. His meetings drew up to 10,000 people, and he converted thousands each campaign. By the time he was 40 he had converted 300,000 people and preached 12,000 sermons to some 15 million people. He is best remembered as a pioneer in Christian education. He founded Bob Jones University in 1927. His grave is on the campus.

The African American Community

The Jazz Age was also a pivotal era for the black church. During the 1910s and 1920s, several black leaders founded new religious movements. These "black gods of the metropolis" included Prophet Cherry of the black Judaism movement in Philadelphia; Noble Drew Ali of the black Muslim Moorish Science Temple in Newark; Elder Lightfoot Solomon Michaux, founder of the Gospel Spreading Church of God; Father Divine of the Universal Peace Mission Movement in Harlem; and Daddy Grace. The most famous were Grace and Divine.

Sweet Daddy Grace

Charles Manuel "Sweet Daddy" Grace (1881–1960) founded the United House of Prayer for All People, known as one of the most extreme charismatic sects in the United States. Born Marceline Manuel DaGraca on the Portuguese island of Brava, Cape Verde, he moved with his family to Massachusetts at the turn of the century. Early on he worked as a cranberry picker, dishwasher, and peddler of patent medicines. He Americanized his name during this time. Although baptized Roman Catholic, he was drawn to Protestantism, particularly the holiness movement. He tried several times to start a church but was removed from a Nazarene pulpit and failed to attract a following during his "Gospel Car" travels through the South. Finally, in 1919, at Wareham, Massachusetts, he opened his first House of Prayer.

Bishop Grace operated as a virtual one-man show. Grace had churches in both the South and the North, from Florida to New York. The movement was not schismatic; rather, Grace developed it himself. Most

African American preacher Daddy Grace, in Arab dress, with arms raised, and image of Christ in top left corner, Harlem. (*Library of Congress*)

members were in the economically depressed black ghettoes. To these people he offered self-improvement, upward mobility, and respectability. About 25 percent of the followers were church officers, reinforcing the sense of importance and dignity. Grace was a healer and miracle worker and, to many believers, God incarnate. Grace and others, including Father Divine, changed the face of the American black church.

Father Divine

Father Divine (1880–1965), born George Baker near Savannah, Georgia, moved to Harlem in 1915 after years of itinerant preaching in the South. He became one of Harlem's largest landlords and became wealthy through restaurants, grocery stores, and other businesses. As Reverend Major Jealous Divine, he established the Peace Mission movement, the largest black ghetto religious movement, during the Depression. Relocated to Sayville, New York, the movement was integrated by the mid-1920s, and an initial membership of 40–50 grew as his sermons attracted busloads of curiosity seekers. Rallies in the 1930s routinely brought out 5,000 to 10,000 people. In 1931, police arrested hundreds of his followers for disturbing the peace and arrested Divine himself for running a disorderly establishment. Divine

Religious leader Father Divine holds a parade to celebrate the aquisition of a new communal dwelling which he calls Heavens, New York, New York, July 31, 1938. (*Bettmann/ Corbis*)

was found guilty. While Divine was in jail, the otherwise healthy judge died unexpectedly. Reportedly, Divine said, "I hated to do it."

Divine provided food, clothing, shelter, jobs, and a charismatic message. He established economic cooperatives, organized political moves against racism and lynching, and provided a foundation for the modern church-driven civil rights movement. His health and influence waned in the 1940s. After his first wife died, he married a white Canadian woman in 1946. In the 1950s, a follower donated Woodmont, a 32-room Philadelphia mansion on a 73-acre estate. Divine began going into seclusion periodically in about 1955, and his wife became the public voice of the movement. Peace Movement members were independent, self-supporting, nonviolent, and celibate.

Women in the Evangelist Movement

The Pentecostal churches were dominated by women, even as they took their message to the streets to bring in the converts that allowed the churches to proliferate. Among the most powerful of the street evangelists were Katie Nubin and her daughter, Rosetta Tharpe, who were gifted at the passionate music needed to hold the attention of a street audience. Tharpe's career would last into the 1950s. As recording technology improved, sanctified evangelists took their music to the studio. Arizona Dranes, with her Okeh recordings of the late 1920s, was a trailblazer for gospel music. As black recordings became commercially viable, in 1925 Columbia Records began recording black preachers. These recordings rivaled blues records into the early 1930s. In the 1930s, gospel evangelism moved into the Baptist and Methodist churches, led by Sallie Martin and Thomas A. Dorsey of Chicago's Pilgrim Baptist Church. Martin was important in establishing a network of gospel groups throughout the United States, and Dorsey was the major writer of gospel songs.

Music in Evangelism

Music was also the calling of the guitar evangelists, blues performers who crossed over into Pentecostal-Holiness music. Guitar evangelists included such names as E. W. Clayborn and the Reverend Charlie Jackson, among others. Most notable was "Blind" Willie Johnson. Johnson was one of the greatest slide or bottleneck guitarists ever. He used a pocketknife as his slide. His music incorporated blues and sacred styles, but most of his lyrics were clearly spiritual. Born in 1897 near Brenham, Texas (though other sources say either Marlin or Temple, Texas, in 1902), by the time he was five he lived in Marlin. It was in Marlin that he told his father he wanted to be a preacher and where he made a guitar out of a cigar box. Johnson was not born blind but was blinded by lye at age seven during a dispute between his father and stepmother, most likely by the stepmother. At age 12 his father put him on the streets to earn money with his 12-string and deep voice. Later he became a preacher but continued playing on the streets of north Texas. When he married at age 25, he and his wife, Angeline, performed blues together. Between 1927 and 1930 he recorded 30 sides for Columbia Records. According to legend, he nearly started a riot in New Orleans by performing "If I Had My Way I'd Tear the Building Down" in front of the courthouse. More likely, he was arrested because police were worried about the incendiary title. Although Johnson was one of Columbia's most popular makers of race records, Johnson was poor through his life. He never recorded again after 1930, spending the 1930s and 1940s back on the streets of Texas, and at the end he was preaching and singing on the streets of Beaumont. His house burned in 1945 (other sources say 1947 or 1949); with nowhere else to go, he lived in the ruins, sleeping on a wet bed until he caught pneumonia and died.

Late in the Jazz Age, blues evangelist Roma Wilson (1910–) began his career. Born in Hickory Flat, Mississippi, Wilson took up the harmonica at age 13. By 18 he was an ordained Pentecostal minister. He and his partner, the guitar evangelist Reverend Leon Pinson, became itinerant evangelists on the north Mississippi church circuit. Wilson had his greatest success in the 1940s, when he and his children—sons on harmonica, daughter on guitar—performed on Detroit's Hastings Street. His recordings date from 1948, but he did not receive national recognition until the 1990s. The total number of traveling harmonica-evangelists never exceeded 200 during their peak years.

Black evangelism also created gospel music, a marked departure from traditional black sacred music, which at the turn of the century rested heavily on the mainstream (white) European tradition. Black services at the time were reserved, in the white fashion, and black sacred music, such as that of the Fisk Jubilee Singers, was consecrated, sanitized, and sedate. The Pentecostal-Holiness movement growing in the black church changed that. It led to the creation of sanctified churches where the new gospel music found a home. The new music was emotional, relied heavily on call and response, incorporated dance and song, and encouraged moaning, repetition and revision, foot stomping, and hand clapping. It was a musical equivalent to the holy dance and speaking in tongues.

Catholicism in the Jazz Age

Evangelism during the Jazz Age was not restricted to the Holiness Pentecostals. One of the most controversial evangelists was a Catholic, Father Charles Edward Coughlin (1891–1979.) Born in Hamilton, Ontario, Canada, and educated at St. Michael's College and St. Basil's Seminary, Coughlin was ordained in 1916. Coughlin was strongly influenced by Pope Leo XIII's encyclical, *On the Condition of the Working Class*, which called for sweeping reforms to counter socialism. Coughlin assisted at several parishes around Detroit before receiving the new Shrine of the Little Flower Church in Royal Oak in 1926. The new parish had only 25 families, but Coughlin's preaching soon generated the need for a larger church to hold 600 people. He began weekly radio broadcasts on October 3, 1926. Originally intended as a children's program, the broadcast shifted to adult topics such as social reform, causing the Ku Klux Klan to plant a blazing cross on his lawn. Undeterred, Coughlin persisted, and by 1930, CBS had taken up his increasingly popular program, giving him a national audience. Coughlin preached against the Soviet Union, socialism, easy divorce, and the decline of family values. He advocated a living wage and old age insurance, and he spoke against the concentration of wealth and the corruption of industrialists.

Coughlin attacked both left and right and, when asked by CBS in 1931 to tone down his rhetoric, he refused and lost his contract. He set up his own radio network, which grew to more than 30 stations. His complete radio discourses, published in 1933, sold over a million copies. Initially a supporter of Franklin Roosevelt, Coughlin turned on the president and the New Deal and in 1934 formed the National Union of Social Justice. By then his weekly radio audience had reached 30 million. He also published *Social Justice Weekly*. Coughlin had a mellow voice that was almost irresistible.

Coughlin began working with the era's radicals—Huey Long, Francis Townsend, Gerald L. K. Smith, Milo Reno, and Floyd B. Olson—to unseat Roosevelt in 1936, but Long, the designated candidate, was assassinated, and the party chose William Lemke, who was buried in the Roosevelt landslide. Coughlin replaced the National Union of Social Justice with the Christian Front and became strongly anticommunist and isolationist. Moving

Perhaps the most widely heard anti-Semite of the pre-war period was Father Charles E. Coughlin, a Michigan-based Roman Catholic cleric, whose extremely popular 1930s radio program routinely attracted up to 40 million listeners. After 1938 Coughlin added in increasingly vicious anti-Semitic comments to his already strident programs. (*Library of Congress*)

sharply to the right, he defended Nazism and became outspokenly anti-Jewish. Barred from the airwaves and the mail during World War II and threatened with defrocking by his archbishop, he retired in 1966 but continued writing anticommunist pamphlets until his death on October 27, 1979.

Outsiders in Evangelism

Doc Springer

Another quirky sort was Curtis Howe "Doc" Springer (1896–1996). Although best known for his purchase of the Zzyzx Hot Springs resort in 1944, where his miracle cures would earn him the title, "king of the quacks," he had his beginnings in the Jazz Age as a radio evangelist, Methodist minister, and medical doctor. During World War I Springer taught boxing in the army. After the war he worked at an academy in Florida and married Mary Louise Berkebile, who convinced him that Pennsylvania was the place to build a health resort. In 1931, he opened Haven of Rest in Maple Glen, Pennsylvania. In the 1930s he began his radio evangelism at KDKA in Pittsburgh. With a mix of charisma and fast talking, he brought in guests at no charge, offered free college to youngsters who were willing to work on his rabbit farm, and, inevitably, encountered financial woes that led to loss of the resort for nonpayment of taxes in 1937. After that he was quiet until he built Zzyzx in 1944 on land he did not own and put in a hotel, church, radio station, and airstrip, and eventually began selling house lots. By the 1970s he was in trouble with the Food and Drug Administration for false advertising, the American Medical Association as a quack, the Internal Revenue Service (IRS) as a tax evader, and the Bureau of Land Management for misusing government land. He died in Las Vegas in 1986.

John R. Brinkley

John R. Brinkley (1885–1941) was on the fringes of the evangelist list. Born John Romulus Brinkley, the only son of a country doctor and his wife in Beta, North Carolina, Brinkley was an orphan by age 10. An aunt reared him until he left home with an elementary education and began working as a railroad telegrapher. He attended Bennett Medical College in Chicago and Eclectic Medical College in Kansas City. Although he never graduated, he got a medical license in Arkansas and several questionable diplomas. Under state reciprocal agreements, his Arkansas license qualified him in Kansas, where he began transplanting goat gonads in 1917. The proceeds from his procedure for sexually rejuvenating aged men provided him with the means to build and operate KFKB (Kansas' First, Kansas' Best) radio. He was known as a radio evangelist but was more specifically a huckster and medical quack. He provided entertainment and ads for his secret cures. The medical community convinced the state to revoke his medical and radio licenses, so he ran a write-in campaign for governor in 1930, getting almost 30 percent of the vote. He tried to run twice again but got only 30 percent of the vote and failed both times. He then moved to Del Rio, Texas, opening station XERA, Villa Acuna, Coahuila, and became a specialist in prostate problems and goat glands. At one point he was extremely wealthy but eventually lost his radio station and his business. He died in San Antonio, penniless, after legal problems with the IRS and the U.S. Postal Service, malpractice suits by patients, and medical problems including three heart attacks and an amputation due to poor circulation. Before his death he planned to become a big-time preacher.

Herbert W. Armstrong

Herbert W. Armstrong (1892–1986) was born a Quaker in Des Moines, Iowa. He married Loma Dillon in 1917. For the next decade he was largely disinterested in religion, caring more about his business. Loma Armstrong became familiar with the doctrine of the Church of God–7th Day (COG-7th Day) in 1927 while they were living in Oregon. She told Herbert they were celebrating the Sabbath on the first rather than the seventh day of the week. Armstrong had time on his hands because business was slumping, so he researched the matter, intending to prove his wife wrong but finding that she was right. After this introduction to Sabbatarianism, Armstrong became a COG-7th Day minister in 1927. He began his radio evangelism in 1934, the Radio Church of God. That same year in Eugene, Oregon, he began producing *The Plain Truth.* In 1938, the COG-7th Day church stripped him of his license because he was teaching that Jewish feast days applied to the COG-7th Day. Armstrong kept his church and radio ministry and began preaching that Armageddon was imminent. After World War II he opened Ambassador College, a Bible school in Pasadena, California, to train ministers who would build churches for Armstrong. The Radio Church of God became the Worldwide Church of God in 1968, the church split in 1974, and Armstrong removed his son, Garner Ted, from the fellowship in 1978. Garner Ted formed his own church, the Church of God International, in Tyler, Texas. By then Armstrong was declaring that he was God's apostle for the final days. His church went into receivership in 1979 until California could investigate allegations of financial abuse by church leaders. Armstrong died in 1986.

Gerald Lyman Kenneth Smith

Gerald Lyman Kenneth Smith (1898–1976) was born in rural Wisconsin. At age 12 he became a Disciples of Christ minister in Indiana. In 1928, he moved to Louisiana for his wife's health. In Shreveport he pastored a church and had a radio program, where he spoke on behalf of the unions and other social justice causes. He gained fame and influence largely because he was, as H. L. Mencken said, a superior speaker to even William Jennings Bryan. Smith was a devoted follower of Huey Long and entered politics during Long's administration as Louisiana governor. Smith and Long together developed the "'share our wealth" program. When Long died, Smith thought Franklin Roosevelt had ordered the assassination to keep Long from running for president in 1936. Smith hated Roosevelt and joined with Coughlin and others in the 1936 campaign to oust Roosevelt. When Roosevelt won reelection in 1936, Smith formed the Committee of One Million, a crusade against the imminent takeover of the United States by communists. In the midst of the Depression, the possibility seemed real, and Smith had backing from some congressmen and industrialists such as Horace Dodge.

Smith was a prolific fund-raiser. He used radio, direct mail, book distribution, and personal appearances. He lacked organizational skills to sustain a movement that was characterized by paranoia and demagoguery. Smith was anti-Semitic and isolationist, and in 1942 he blamed Jews for his failure to get the Republican senatorial nomination in Michigan. In 1943, he formed the America First Party to save white Christian America. He also claimed that Jesus was a non-Jewish blue-eyed blond, claimed Hitler was persecuted by the Jews, and denied the Holocaust. By 1944, he was on the fringe and getting fringier with each racist, anti-Semitic, white supremacist word. He spent his final 15 years in Eureka Springs, Arkansas, building a 70-foot-high Christ of the Ozarks, an amphitheater, and a Bible museum.

Outside the Mold

Cora Fauss

Not all evangelists became famous, important, rich, or influential. Most worked in real, not relative, obscurity, doing what they thought God had called them to do. Typical was Cora Fauss.

Cora Fauss (1907–2003) was born in Hatfield, Arkansas, a premature two-pound baby with little chance of surviving. Fortunately, she did survive, and she grew up in a typical Pentecostal family—rural, working poor, and extremely religious. Her family moved to Eufala, Oklahoma, when she was three, and to Dustin, Oklahoma, when she was four or five. When she was nine, she had her first experience of God calling her to be saved. Her mother told her she had to wait until she was 12, so Cora got saved at age 13. As she told it, she went to the altar and tried to pray. Having no success, she thought she should sing a song, "I'm Glad I Have Salvation in My Heart." Jesus took that song and gave her a new one. She was saved, but she was not yet feeling the spirit. That is, she was not yet speaking in tongues. She was still a Baptist and seeking a closer connection with Jesus.

During a Fourth of July revival at an all-night meeting, her mother and father got the gift. Cora habitually prayed every day when tending the family cows. One day while taking water to her brothers who were working in the fields, she was praying and suddenly began speaking in tongues. When she got to her brothers she could not speak in English.

Many Baptists at the time were hostile to Pentecostals. When the church asked all who spoke in tongues to leave, Cora and her family left for a brush arbor revival 10 miles down the road. They invited the evangelist to their town. In those days it seemed everyone was an evangelist—whether trained itinerant or church member feeling inspiration. Cora began working revivals and by age 16 got her license to preach. She held her first revival that year. At age 18 she began pioneering in western Oklahoma, holding open-air revivals and meeting in homes and raising money to open Pentecostal churches. In 1926, she began traveling with Ethel Musick. While with Musick in 1926–1927, she met her husband, Milton Fauss. They spent the rest of their lives moving from one church to another, mostly in Texas but also in Kansas, Missouri, and Oklahoma. They never got rich, but they never gave up. He died in 1984 and she died in 2003.

Jazz Age evangelism was a diverse movement with a few celebrities, a few charlatans, and a lot of feverishly devoted Pentecostals. Its practitioners built on the work of those who had gone before and incorporated tools—radio and a touch of Hollywood flamboyance—that matched the spirit of the age. Jazz Age evangelism laid the foundation for those to follow—Bob Jones Jr., Garner Ted Armstrong, Billy Graham, Benny Hinn, and many others.

References and Further Reading

Billy Graham Center Archives, Wheaton College. Jazz Age Evangelism, text only version.

Canipe, Lee, "The Unlikely Argument of a Baptist Fundamentalist: John Roach Straton's Defense of Women in the Pulpit." *Baptist History and Heritage,* Spring 2005. Available at http://www.findarticles.com/p/articles/mi_m0NXG/is_2_40/ai_n15922366.

Davis, James O. "The Historical Role of the Assemblies of God Evangelist." *Enrichment Journal,* Fall 1999. Available at http://www.ag.org/enrichmentjournal/199904/124_evangelists.cfm.

Epstein, Daniel Mark. *Sister Aimee: The Life of Aimee Semple McPherson.* New York: Harcourt, 1994.

Evensen, Bruce J. *D. L. Moody and the Rise of Modern Mass Evangelism.* New York: Oxford University Press, 2003.

Grammer, Lydia. "Father Divine, New Religious Movements." 2000. Available at http://religiousmovements.lib.virginia.edu/nrms/Fatherd.html.

Jeansonne, Glen. *Gerald LK Smith—Minister of Hate.* New Haven, CT: Yale University Press, 1988.

Johnson, R. K. "Evangelist Bob Jones, Sr. Biographical Sketch." Available at http://www.tks.org/BioOfBobJonesSr.htm.

Kansas State Historical Society. "John R. Brinkley, A Kansas Portrait." 2006. Available at http://www.kshs.org/portraits/brinkley_john.htm.

Lee, R. Alton. *The Bizarre Careers of John R. Brinkley.* Lexington: University Press of Kentucky, 2002.

Mangin, John. "Gods of the Metropolis: The Rise and Decline of the Black Independent Church." *The Next American City,* Issue 3, October 2003. Available at http://www.americancity.org/article.php?id_article=61.

Orange, A. "The 'First Century Christian Fellowship' Campus Crusade in the 1920s." *The Religious Roots of Alcoholics Anonymous and the Twelve Steps.* Available at www.orange-papers.org/orange-rroot150.html.

Consumers | 5

Susan Ferentinos

One January day in 1929, a woman in New York gave vent to her desires for luxury. Writing in her journal, she exclaimed, "After reading the society section in the Sunday papers, I almost go mad. I'd give *anything* to be rich enough to go to boarding school. Sometimes I almost go wild wanting it. Oh, gee! To be wealthy—Oh, to be wealthy!" (Diary, 27 January 1929, Radcliffe Institute, Collection 92-M10). This woman was not alone. During the Jazz Age, Americans gained a heightened awareness of what money could buy. Material goods beckoned as never before, promising to provide happiness and fulfillment through consumption. Commercial entertainment venues represented an easy escape into a world of fun and fancy. And dominant cultural values shifted steadily away from prizing hard work and thrift toward embracing leisure and novelty. Such changes produced a cultural revolution that still reverberates in the 21st century. Indeed, many historians identify the 1920s as the start of the modern era in the United States, when the values and structure of the culture we know today became established and entrenched. In many ways, these changes revolved around the way Americans interact with goods and services, and so the modern values that emerged in the 1920s are often referred to collectively as "consumer culture."

The Rise of Consumer Culture

Consumer culture refers to much more than simply an economic system based on consumer goods, instead of, say, raw materials. Rather, this economic system brought with it a slew of changes to the larger society, affecting ideas about selfhood, gender, morality, religion, education, class, and the family, to name but a few examples. Many historians describe this transformation as a shift from a producer culture, where people's worth was determined by what they could produce, to a consumer culture, where people were judged by their ability to consume. The older moral order cherished frugality and self-control, and the newer value system embraced immediate gratification and the satisfaction of desires. Novelty and innovation were prized, and in many ways, style came to matter more than substance.

Numerous factors coalesced to launch these changes, and many involved a changing economy. In the late 19th century, federal laws supported the creation of huge corporations, which in turn controlled much of the nation's capital. Such wealth supported the rise of improved modes of production and transportation, and these in turn facilitated a national (as opposed to local) market for goods. In the early 20th century, the increased ability of businesses to produce and distribute goods meant they needed to locate more customers. Their efforts to woo consumers led to many of the messages that eventually became an integral part of consumer culture.

Another economic factor influencing consumer culture was the shift in the work experience of many Americans. The rise of large corporations and factories meant increasing numbers of people worked for someone else, rather than working for themselves as farmers, artisans, or owners of small businesses. Working for someone else was a difficult transition for many men, who had been raised in an era when the ideal of the "self-made man" was the standard trope of success. In the new work environment, one seemed to have less control over one's destiny, but this loss of autonomy could be counteracted by exercising agency in the realm of consumption. People could exert control and become who they wanted to be through the skillful purchase of the right products. Likewise, as the white-collar professions grew, the older producer ethic, which valued people by what they produced, no longer made sense when so much of the population was not *producing* anything, but was instead selling, advertising, accounting, or managing. Consumption, on the other hand, was an arena open to everyone and so became the new universe in which to judge a person's value.

The rise of consumer culture also contributed to a change in morals. The new worldview provided challenges to Victorian morality, which had stressed restraint and chastity. In contrast, the culture of the 1920s disparaged delayed gratification and reified pleasure. The impact could be felt in both the public's approach to commodities and the approach to sexual ethics. Sexual taboos became less stringent, and the country experienced what many have described as the first sexual revolution.

Consumer Culture as Mass Culture

Before World War I, the United States was very much divided into different regional cultures. A country this geographically vast, economically varied, and ethnically diverse simply was not all that cohesive, until consumption became a unifying feature. So, in many ways, consumer

Billboard advertising Endicott-Johnson shoes, showing man displaying shoes, 1923. (*Library of Congress*)

culture became America's first mass culture. National companies, national advertising, chain stores, and popular culture (such as movies, magazines, and broadcast radio) distributed on a mass scale—all of these things created a common set of experiences for people throughout the country. And the values of consumer culture enforced a mass culture by creating a shared ethic to unite everyone.

One of the many ways in which consumer culture contributed to mass culture was by creating a "democracy of desire." Although class distinctions remained a facet of American culture, consumer goods provided a site in which everyone, regardless of class, could be equal in their desire to acquire the luxury offered by the consumer age. This was a significant change. In previous eras, class determined even what a person could hope and dream. In the consumer age, however, department stores, advertisers, and the manufacturers of consumer goods conspired to create a vision of the world where luxury was attainable, regardless of one's station at birth. Public amusements reinforced this trend. There, at the amusement parks, vaudeville shows, and moving picture houses, people of all backgrounds could mingle and share a common role as consumers of entertainment. As such, these venues provided a fantasyland where a changing social order could be temporarily resolved.

Sadly, this lessening of class distinctions amid the creation of a mass culture was not as far reaching as it might have been. For although it provided a means to bridge the differences between the working class and those who were more comfortable, consumer culture excluded many—most notably nonwhites—from its invitation to the good life. Indeed, some have argued that the unifying force of consumer culture in fact rested on the exclusion of other races from its promises. Advertising appealed to whites of all classes, but often this appeal was based on the denigration or mocking of other races. In a similar vein, the popular culture portrayed on radio, film, and vaudeville stages often relied on racial stereotypes for its humor. By systematically demeaning people of color, consumer culture promised privilege and entitlement to whites, regardless of class. As a result, poor whites were able to envision themselves as part of a society with access to consumer luxury. In this way, consumer culture lessened class tension while at the same time exacerbating racial discrimination.

Aspects of Consumer Culture

Leisure

Along with the shift from a producer culture to a consumer culture came a corresponding shift from a traditional work ethic, which valued hard labor and diligence, to an ethic of leisure, where one's ability to partake in the good life of luxury and amusement mattered most. One consequence of this transition was the increasing availability of commercial leisure activities. Sports fields, dance halls, and moving picture houses sprang up in urban areas in the early years of the 20th century and had spread to nearly all parts of the country by the 1930s. In the 1920s, various trends in leisure activities swept the country. Dance marathons, crossword puzzles, and mah-jongg all became popular during this era. Young people, in particular, responded enthusiastically to the appeal of these ventures, and their embrace of commercial amusements moved social life away from the family home and into the public realm. As a result, young people had greater opportunity to meet friends whom their parents did not know and to engage in a greater range of sexual exploration. These activities illustrate the far-reaching cultural impacts of consumption, which spread far beyond the economic realm to affect nearly all aspects of American life. At the same time, this new generation came of age with the expectation that a significant portion of one's income would be spent on leisure, rather than saved. In this way, new cultural values became entrenched.

Around World War I, feature-length moving pictures became popular, and movies became a key component of commercial leisure during the Jazz Age. The first talkie, a film with audible dialogue, appeared in 1927. Before then, films were silent, and dialogue was written on the screen in between acted scenes. For this first generation of feature-length moviegoers, however, the technology was good enough, and thousands of people flocked daily to movie theaters in large cities. Indeed, by the late 1920s, 95 million movie tickets were sold each *week*. Such popularity led to larger and larger theaters with increasingly elaborate architecture. Indeed, many of these buildings truly deserved the title of "movie palace," which is what the largest and most ornate were called. Such theaters could host thousands of people in one evening. For instance, the Rialto Theater in Joliet, Illinois, could accommodate 2,800 moviegoers, and a young man in Minneapolis boasted to his rural relatives that his local movie house, the Minnesota Theatre, had 4,500 seats and was seven stories high. Such elaborate venues made moviegoing an event; people went to the movie theater for more than just to see the films. They went to indulge fantasies of glamour and luxury made newly available to them through the lure of consumer culture.

Appearance

The cult of the first impression created heightened pressure to be neat, clean, and attractive in the Jazz Age. Whereas an earlier era had determined that character was a person's most important attribute, the standards of the Jazz Age insisted that appearance was the chief point on which a person would be judged. For women especially, this message was driven home by the increasingly common display of the female body, in movies, beauty pageants, and swimsuit contests, all of which became popular in this era. Alongside these changing standards, advertising provided a steady stream of consumer goods to help Americans improve and stylize their appearance.

To begin with, ready-made clothing became a practical option for the middle class during the 1920s. In previous eras, clothes were individually made and tailored to fit the specific measurements of the wearer. Women's and children's clothes were most often made at home, although those who could afford it often hired dressmakers to produce more formal outfits. Mass-produced clothing, to be sold off the rack, began growing in popularity with the expansion of the garment industry in the late 19th century and first decades of the 20th century. Urban department stores became popular at the same time, allowing for a convenient place to purchase such clothing. But buying clothes in such a fashion was an unpredictable process until World War I. During the war, the federal government created standardized clothing sizes to enable efficient and inexpensive manufacture of soldiers' uniforms. The concept of standardized sizes made buying ready-made clothes more appealing.

At the same time, advances in the advertising industry allowed mass producers of clothing to better sell their wares to a national audience. Advertising gave Jazz Age consumers a taste for fashion and introduced them to ideals they could aspire to by purchasing the right type of clothes. An example of this trend is found in the "Arrow Man" of the 1910s and 1920s. The collars of men's shirts used to be detachable to allow for frequent washing. In the 19th century, these collars were stiff and cumbersome, but Arrow brand collars introduced a more comfortable alternative. The company sold the new style through an advertising campaign that featured men who epitomized the new masculinity of the Jazz Age: stylish, efficient, modern. Customers bought the clothing to achieve the desired image. In this way, Americans in the 1920s came to believe one's consumer choices were an indicator of personality. And what better way to quickly convey information about oneself than through appearance?

Control of appearance through the purchase of consumer goods also contributed to an explosion in the cosmetics industry in the 1920s. Before 1920, only two cosmetic companies in the United States had sufficient sales to pay federal income tax; by 1928, more than 18,000 cosmetic companies paid taxes. Such growth was fueled mostly by female consumers, who responded to the emphasis on looks and style by purchasing a vast array of products aimed at enhancing their beauty. This behavior was encouraged by most mainstream women's magazines, which depended on advertising money for their profits. In 1929, fully one-fifth of advertising in four popular women's magazines was devoted to cosmetic products. One young woman described the pressure to beautify when she wrote in her diary in 1928: "I have been reading an artical [sic] on beauty plus cosmetics. It moved me so I long to purchase all the cleansing creams and astringent lotions, and vanishing concoctions and shades of beauty mud, and rouges and perfumes and powders on the market" (Beth Twiggar Diary, Next Day [after March 14, 1928], Goff Papers, Radcliffe Institute).

This quotation points to another aspect of the consumer age: fear of inadequacy. Advertising in this era, particularly advertising for cosmetics and toiletries, introduced a slew of potential embarrassments that could be remedied through the use of advertised products. Over and over, consumers were warned about the social humiliation awaiting those who fell victim to bad breath, body odor, or a rough complexion. In a time of changing social relations, when success depended on making a good impression, Jazz Age consumers were ready to be alerted to these problems through "scare-copy" advertising, and they were willing to spend millions of dollars to remedy the problems with consumer goods.

Consumer Culture in the Home

Consumer culture introduced the concept of style into American culture as it had never existed before, not only in personal appearance but in home furnishing as well. Certainly, those with the financial means to decorate their homes tastefully and elegantly had always done so, but generally speaking, in previous eras, home furnishings were intended to be timeless. In the consumer culture, however, novelty and modernity took on ever-greater importance. One's house could now be stylish or out of style, and in a world where first impressions mattered, most American families with disposable income chose to allow consumer values into their home. During the Jazz Age, the middle-class American family lived in a stylishly decorated home, owned a number of electric appliances, and ate meals prepared with at least some processed food.

Home ownership increased in the 1920s, and by the end of the decade a greater percentage of Americans owned their homes than at any other time before the post–World War II housing boom of the 1940s and 1950s. The Sears & Roebuck Company, whose business empire was based on mail-order sales, began offering ready-made kit houses in 1916. These kits provided plans and precut building supplies in one simple package, designed so customers could assemble the houses themselves, in just a few days. Although the Sears & Roebuck Company was not the first to offer such kit homes, it was the largest dealer in the 1920s, reaching 324 homes sold in a month by mid-decade.

As more people lived in homes they owned, and as popular culture introduced new standards of style, home decorating became more of a national pastime. For example, before the Jazz Age, talking about indoor bathrooms in houses had been a source of embarrassment, eliciting little thought until needed. In the 1920s, however, bathrooms became showcases

It seems as if anything and everything was available from the Sears catalog, including homes. (*Library of Congress*)

of style. Supply companies introduced colored fixtures and art deco designs, and colored bath towels became a trend. In a similar vein, there emerged numerous commercial magazines devoted to interior decorating. *Better Homes and Gardens* began publication in the early 1920s, and *House Beautiful,* which had been in existence since the turn of the century, introduced an annual book in the mid-1920s to showcase the latest trends in home decor.

One of the most significant changes in American homes of the World War I era was the new availability of electricity. By 1930, two-thirds of American homes had electricity, and this technology combined with consumer culture to produce a steady stream of electric devices for the home. Although electric refrigerators and stoves were not embraced on a mass scale until after the Jazz Age, other appliances—such as vacuum cleaners, clothes irons, electric mixers, and rudimentary washing machines—were in wide use during this era. The spread of these products coincided with a trend away from the use of hired domestic servants among the middle class, but ironically, the new inventions did not make up for the loss of extra hands. As consumer goods enabled more thorough cleaning, standards of hygiene rose higher, and the loss of domestic servants meant middle-class women actually ended up spending more hours a week cleaning. This development provides one example of a situation where the reality of the consumer age failed to live up to its promise.

One final area of home life that was revolutionized in the early 20th century was food. As Americans adjusted to the idea of buying what they had previously made or done without, habits of food preparation changed. Store-bought bread, canned and frozen vegetables, and condensed soups were just some of the processed food that came into common use during the Jazz Age. This shift toward convenience food was aided by the trend away from domestic servants, improved shipping methods, technology such as quick-freezing, and advertising campaigns that convinced American housewives of the quality of such goods. One advertising campaign by General Mills created a fictional homemaker named Betty Crocker to tout the company's wares by sharing recipes and making serving suggestions. Strategies such as this one linked processed foods with traditional feminine caretaking, easing the transition of consumer values into the most intimate areas of domestic life.

Americans opened their homes to consumer values in the 1920s, and as a result, the rhythms of family life changed, as middle-class women spent more time cleaning with electric appliances, families ate more processed food, and electric lights and radio changed the way people spent their evenings. Another consumer good that had a significant impact on family life was the automobile.

Automobiles

In discussing the lasting impacts of the 1920s on American culture, one could do worse than give automobiles the coveted place at the top of the list, for it was during the Jazz Age that the automobile became an integral part of America, setting Americans on a course that is still being following more or less unquestionably.

Automobiles had been available in the United States since the end of the 19th century, but it was not until the 1920s that they became a staple of middle-class America. In 1919, there were 6.7 million cars in this country; 10 years later that figure had more than quadrupled to 27 million. This surge can be explained in large part by the efforts of two early figures in the automobile industry: Henry Ford and Alfred P. Sloan. Henry Ford, founder of the Ford Motor Company, revolutionized manufacturing by introducing the assembly line in the 1910s, significantly expanding the number of autos that could be manufactured in a given day. Ford was also a pioneer in providing benefits to his workers. He believed in making sure his employees were content, were well cared for, and had enough money to purchase consumer items. As such, Ford set a precedent that the laborers of America would be able to take part in consumer culture as consumers, not just manufacturers, although it is worth noting that despite Ford's innovations in this area, he remained a staunch opponent of unionization, a movement aimed at ensuring these benefits for all workers.

Ford created the technical means by which enough automobiles could be produced to meet demand during the 1920s, but his rival at General Motors, Alfred P. Sloan, was instrumental in creating that demand. Sloan's first innovation was to offer different makes of car to denote different price and status levels. Thus, under Sloan's direction, Chevrolet emerged as an accessible auto for working people, marked by a relatively low market price and the absence of frills. Meanwhile, Cadillac became the General Motors brand that signified refinement, class, and disposable wealth. Likewise, while Ford was busy building automobiles to last, Sloan realized that the market for first-time car owners would eventually stagnate. To offset this reality, he set about refining the idea of cars as status symbols. Within this way of thinking, novelty and the latest design were assets many customers were willing to invest in. Thus, Sloan introduced the yearly model and succeeded in equating car models with social status in 1920s America.

Yet the automobile had an impact in American culture beyond simply marketing and production strategies. The popularization of this mode of transportation influenced many other aspects of the economy, as related industries such as oil, rubber, and steel expanded accordingly. In addition, automobile travel supported the service industry by fostering growth in hotels, restaurants, gas stations, and tourist attractions. People also needed proper places to drive their autos, and as a result the miles of roads in the United States more than doubled between 1920 and 1929. Finally, cars brought changes to social life. Families became less dependent on each other, as autos enabled family members to live more autonomous lives. In a similar vein, cars enabled young people to date and court in privacy, away from the prying eyes of kin. As such, automobiles contributed to the revolution in morals that occurred in the Jazz Age and raised the concerns of many a guardian of morals. In the words of one, "Traveling round the country in an auto, young people practically are invisible. They are not seen by their parents, their family, or their neighbors, perhaps not by anybody that they know. They are off in an exciting adventure in a world of their own, perhaps a fairy land, but not a very safe land for them to play in" (Lee 1932).

Despite the array of wonders available to consumers during the Jazz Age, not all Americans experienced consumer culture in the same ways. Generally, when advertisers envisioned the "average" consumer, they thought of white, native-born, urban men and women. Those who did not match that criteria were largely ignored, and thus their experience of consumer culture depended more on their own determination to take part.

African American Consumers

The United States after World War I was a place marked by racism and segregation, and African Americans were largely excluded from participation in the larger culture. White-owned businesses often refused their patronage, movie palaces and vaudeville shows restricted them to the worst seats, and discrimination in jobs and education denied them the potential of earning the money required to purchase consumer goods. Nevertheless, African Americans did engage with consumption; the circumstances of that engagement simply varied from what was perceived as the (white) norm.

With regard to public amusements, African Americans occupied a strange position. Many commercial entertainment venues refused to admit black patrons, while at the same time depending on black performers to entertain their white audiences. The very jazz music that gave the era its name originated as an African American art form. Likewise, movies and vaudeville shows often relied on racial stereotypes of African Americans—performed by black actors or whites in blackface—for their humor. The racial caricatures so prominent in mass entertainment, combined with racist admittance policies, inspired many African American entrepreneurs to open alternative sites of public amusement, specifically catering to an African American clientele. Black jazz clubs, in fact, became one of the few places where white and black Americans intermingled in the 1920s, as visiting black-owned clubs became popular among white bohemians, a practice known tellingly as "slumming." However, economic restraints limited the number and quality of such venues.

Generally speaking, advertising in the 1920s followed a similar pattern. Businesses with a white customer base did not also seek to reach African Americans through advertising. However, African American characters appeared regularly in advertising to whites, most often in the role of servant. For instance, an ad for Drano drain cleaner featured an African American bathroom attendant grinning at a white businessman at a sink over the headline, "Yes, suh, Boss. I keeps 'em moving with Drano." In many cases, advertising campaigns aimed at whites showcased fictitious African American trademark figures, such as Aunt Jemima or Rastus, the Cream of Wheat chef (*Saturday Evening Post*, May 9, 1931, reproduced in Marchand 1985, 126). There is some evidence that despite these demeaning images, African Americans were more likely to choose national brands when making purchasing decisions, probably because buying products from national companies allowed them to bypass local suppliers, with whose exclusionary practices blacks were well acquainted.

As with commercial entertainment venues, African American–owned manufacturing sprang up to satisfy the consumer desires of African Americans that were not being met. This was a particularly common practice in the toiletry industry, where black-owned businesses offered special products to meet the cosmetic needs of their customer base. In the 1920s, African American women could choose from Nile Queen cosmetics, High Brown soap, or the toiletries of the Madame CJ Walker Company, all of which were specifically designed for African Americans by black entrepreneurs.

Consumers in the Country

Although the racism of the 1920s no doubt played the largest role affecting African Americans' interaction with consumer culture, the fact that so many lived in rural areas was also an influence. Black or white, rural Americans experienced consumption in distinctive ways.

Many observers saw 1920 as a watershed year in the development of the United States. According to the national census, in that year for the first time more Americans lived in urban areas than on farms. The nation, it seemed had moved once and for all away from its agrarian roots. Nevertheless, this statistic can be misleading; at this time, an "urban" area was defined as any place with more than 2,500 people. Had the census used the more reasonable definition of areas of 25,000 or more residents, just a little more than a third of Americans (36 precent) would have been classified as "urban," only slightly more than those who lived on farms (30 percent). To be sure, a sizable portion of the population still lived in rural areas and small towns during the Jazz Age.

In the country, the temptations of consumer culture were not so close at hand. Public amusements were often miles away, a simple visit to a department store could require a special trip to the nearest city, and the peer culture that judged people by the goods they purchased was not as ever-present as in the close confines of an urban area. In fact, many rural areas did not even have electricity until well after the 1920s. For instance, as late as 1935, 92 percent of school children in Breathitt County, Kentucky, lived without this luxury.

And yet, rural residents were certainly aware of the cultural transformations taking place. Magazines arriving by mail and traveling movie shows that came to rural areas and projected films onto the sides of buildings gave rural residents a taste of the glamorous world of consumption. And for some, particularly young people, the discrepancy between country living and the lifestyle shown in popular culture could be frustrating. One young woman living in a small farm town in Wisconsin complained to her big-city cousin: "We have not a Vitaphone [to show talking pictures] as yet. You see we live in a one horse town which can't afford every thing right away. . . . There isn't much to do around here except to go to church, shows and dances and those are the only really [sic] excitment [sic] around here to attend" (Letter, Irma Grantin to Alice Miller, May 3, 1929, Rabus Scrapbooks).

Radio offered another vehicle by which folks in the country learned consumer values. A radio was one consumer good many farm families invested in, so as to keep current on weather forecasts and crop prices. Once purchased, however, the radio could keep a farm wife company during the isolation of daily housekeeping, as she listened to shows sponsored by various corporations. Furthermore, the large rural audience for radio deserves much of the credit for the popularization of country music on the airwaves during the 1920s.

The development of mail-order catalogs, most notably Sears & Roebuck and Montgomery Ward, in the late 19th century had offered farm dwellers a means of accessing manufactured goods, and in the 1920s this continued to be a major means by which rural Americans participated in consumer culture. Finally, the automobile offered farmers the opportunity to reduce some of the burden of farm work and the isolation of rural life.

In 1920, in fact, families on farms were more likely than urban households to own an auto.

Immigrants

To be sure, the rise of the consumer age played out differently in rural areas than it did in urban areas. But even within the city there were variations. Urban immigrants were another group who experienced consumption in unique ways. The years preceding the Jazz Age, 1890–1915, saw a huge influx of immigrants from Southern and Eastern Europe, an average of a million a year. World War I curtailed much of this relocation, and by the early 1920s Congress was taking steps to staunch the flow of the foreign-born. The National Origins Act (1921) and the Johnson-Reed Act (1924) greatly restricted the number of immigrants allowed to enter the country in a given year.

Yet even though immigration was restricted during the Jazz Age, there remained huge numbers of Americans in the 1920s who were foreign born. In addition, many of those who arrived in the United States before World War I faced challenges in this decade from their children, who had grown up straddling the two worlds of their ethnic communities and the American mainstream. For many immigrant families, consumption provided the site upon which to act out this conflict. For younger immigrants and the children of older immigrants, participating in consumer culture became a means by which they could claim their status as Americans, because at this time consumption lay in such contrast to the values of the Old World. Particularly for young women, adopting fashionable, American-style clothing marked them as modern and showed their allegiance in the battle between tradition and innovation. The same was true of those who partook of American popular culture, such as movies and public amusements.

Such an embrace of the American consumer ethic was not without conflict. Many older immigrants, perhaps rightly, interpreted this behavior as a rejection of their countries of origin and so clung stubbornly to an anti-consumption ethic. One 18-year-old daughter of Hungarian immigrants captured the competing views of the immigrant family when she said of her parents, "They don't believe in makeup, short dresses, fancy styles, curled hair, etc. . . . You can't go to clubs, you can't have your own opinions—for crying outloud [sic], what does he want us to do, pack up and go to his village in Hungary to live?" (Interview with Irene, Hungarian, YWCA Ms 59). The equation of consumer values with Americanism extended beyond immigrant communities as well. Numerous reform agencies devoted to serving immigrant populations taught shopping skills as a means of Americanizing the foreign-born.

Convincing People to Buy

The Development of a Mass Market

In the years preceding the Jazz Age, the beginnings of a national market began to emerge. New industrial practices, such as Henry Ford's assembly

Fashion show at the WIls Shop, a store specializing in corsets, brassieres, hats, and bonnets, Washington, DC, ca. 1921. The changes in women's fashions during the Jazz Age were seen as both liberating and controversial. (*Library of Congress*)

line, led to increased production, which in turn created the need for more customers. Improved distribution channels—transportation, chain stores, and mail-order operations—allowed manufacturers to reach a wider territory of consumers. And a nationally based popular culture—disseminated by magazines and, later, radio—enabled advertising to reach potential customers in all regions of the country.

These years also saw the development of brand-name products. As manufacturing companies grew and diversified the goods they offered, they began giving specific names to individual products. For instance, the toiletry manufacturer Procter & Gamble produced a mild, white soap, which it named Ivory Soap. Branding helped distinguish one company's wares from another's through distinctive names and packaging. It also offered customers the assurance of consistent quality. When shoppers asked their grocer for crackers, they took their chances; when they asked specifically for Uneeda Biscuits, they knew what they were getting.

Although a mass market already existed by World War I, the means by which manufacturers reached consumers improved dramatically during the Jazz Age. New trends in advertising, the development of market research and segmentation, and the wholesale acceptance of consumer credit acted together to convince Americans to consume as never before.

The Opportunity to Participate in the New Consumer Culture

The Jazz Age certainly saw an increase in conspicuous consumption by leaps and bounds. Although there were two periods of recession during the 1920s, people saw their rates of disposable income rise by about 1 percent per year, and they had easier access to credit. This does not mean, however, that the middle classes were becoming richer; rather, while disposable income rose somewhat, so did prices. Real income among the middle classes did not keep pace.

The problem for manufacturers was how to get the working classes to buy their products. New advertising techniques would be the answer. Although advertising was hardly a new idea, during the Jazz Age consumers were enticed to buy certain items in order to feel that their lives, and status, could and would be improved through the use of certain products. As World War I was over, and conserving resources was no longer an issue, encouraging people to buy was not a chore. In an interesting note, most of those who

Advertising

In the 1920s, the advertising industry reached new levels of sophistication, which played a crucial role in the establishment of consumer culture. Advertising was more than just the vehicle through which people learned about a specific product; it also schooled Americans on the values of the consumer age. Within the world of 1920s advertising, one's social status depended on the goods one purchased. Style was as important as function, and people were judged by the products they used. Eventually, these scenarios became true in the real world as well.

Originally, manufacturers simply placed notices advertising their wares in the back of publications, along the lines of modern-day classified ads. In the late 19th century, publications began integrating advertisements with articles, and as a result, advertising became more visual. In response to the greater demands of creating this type of material, specialized agencies began to appear. After 1890, more and more manufacturers hired out the work of writing ad copy to these advertising agents. As production increased and a mass market developed in the early 20th century, the need for sophisticated advertising became more pressing. The potential of advertising to reach, and even create, an audience of prospective consumers became even more obvious during World War I, when the government used artfully done public service announcements to educate citizens about their responsibilities during wartime. The need to rely on these announcements, which mimicked advertisements, for information taught the public to pay attention to this type of message.

The advertising industry blossomed during the Jazz Age, and many of the aspects of advertising that we take for granted today began during this period. Advertisements became more visually appealing, as they incorporated more color, a deco style (a neoclassical, decorative style), and, in the made purchases were women, but most advertising designers were men. Even into contemporary times, advertisers try to lead consumers to believe that buying and using their products will make them more appealing to the opposite sex, provide better representation among one's friends, land them a better job, or provide them with a higher status in overall society.

Although some people might not have had immediate access to the cash necessary to participate in the new mass consumption during the Jazz Age, help was readily available. As mentioned, the Ford Motor Company provided installment plans for those who wished to purchase a car. Large retailers, such as Chicago's famous Marshall Field's, provided credit to its customers. The idea of "buy now, pay later" was enticing. Whether these items were actually necessities was not the issue; the ability to attain them was.

late 1920s, photographs. Advertising copy became less factual and more emotional, as advertisers began to adapt the study of psychology to the purpose of selling products. And in a changing culture, where appearance suddenly seemed to matter more than character, advertising offered consumers a leg up in the contest for social success by promising style.

Before the 1920s, the dominant form of advertising relied on what was known as "Reason-Why" copy, so called because it provided readers with factual information about the product, supplying the "reason why" it should be purchased. This style remained common in the 1920s as well, particularly in advertising to men or advertising involving a technological product. For instance, a 1927 ad for Zenith radios stated, "Musical tone is a delicate and elusive thing—only such fine precision as Zenith builds into radio can catch all the subtle and intricate shadings of voice or instrument" (Jacobson 2001).

However, during this decade, a new approach to advertising became dominant: the emotional appeal. Rather than targeting consumers' rationality, emotional-appeal advertising spoke to their desires—for popularity, romance, and status. Ad after ad promised social success in exchange for purchasing a given product, as when an advertisement for Palmolive soap began with the headline "The Prettiest Girl in Her Set" and continued, "Everywhere a beautiful complexion is regarded as woman's chief charm. And now *every* woman may have a clear, wholesome skin . . . clear, attractive." Ads during this time also presented the flip side of social success; for the unwary, humiliation lurked around every corner, and only the use of an advertised product could prevent such a fate. These ads tapped into people's social anxiety, such as when an advertisement for Amolin deodorant powder announced, "Society Simply *Won't* Stand for Indelicate Women!" The emotional appeal extended beyond the social realm as well; some advertisements simply created positive associations with a product by invoking images of tranquil home life or by linking their goods with glamour and luxury (Marchand 1985, 208–217).

The Development of Market Research

The growing sophistication of the advertising industry can be explained in large part by the sector's acceptance of psychology as a tool for selling products. Increasingly, advertisers came to believe that purchasing decisions were not always rational and that appeals to the deeper psychological desires of consumers could boost sales. These developments were possible in part because of a concurrent expansion of the social sciences, including psychology, that took place in the early 20th century. In addition to the use of psychology in advertising, the social sciences influenced American business by providing the tools to better adapt advertising messages to specific audiences.

The social sciences—sociology, anthropology, psychology—introduced the concept that human mysteries could be revealed by systematic research, much as the more traditional scientific research of biology and chemistry could uncover mysteries of the natural world. For advertisers, research modeled after the social sciences promised to illuminate why people bought some products and not others. In 1915, for example, one of the largest and most influential advertising agencies of the early 20th century, the J. Walter Thompson Company, established a research department and staffed it with prominent social scientists. This department pioneered studies into consumer motivation and habits, allowing the agency to hone its advertising messages.

Market research gave businesspeople the information they needed to reach their desired audience, and this in turn led to market segmentation, dividing the mass market into categories to better target the most likely customers. In the 1920s, market segmentation had begun, but it was still quite rudimentary by today's standards. Mostly, manufacturers hoped to reach the wealthiest segments of society, because they were most likely to have disposable income. As such, much of the market research in this era focused on the habits of the white, native-born middle class: what they read (to determine appropriate venues for ads), where they lived, and how they shopped. For example, in the mid-1920s, when the J. Walter Thompson Company wanted to learn more about the potential customers of one of its clients, Woodbury's soap, the agency sent questionnaires only to students of Vassar, an elite women's college, and to debutantes in four cities on the East Coast. It was not until the late 1920s that some industries, such as car manufacturers, began to move beyond the basic segmentation of the market by gender and income level to more nuanced categories like age and region.

The Availability of Consumer Credit

The 1920s also saw a revolution in consumer credit. The purchase of home appliances and automobiles simply would have been out of reach of most

American families had they been required to pay cash for such items, as they had in earlier eras. But in the 1920s, new options were available. Americans could purchase big-ticket items on installment, paying a portion of the total cost each month until the entire amount was paid off. Installment plans originally developed in the 19th century, but until about the mid-1910s they carried a stigma of poverty; they were something only poor people used. This attitude changed in the Jazz Age, however, due in large part to the adoption of installment plans by the automobile industry. The first automobile financing company emerged in 1913, but it was not until 1919 that buying automobiles on credit became common. That year, General Motors, one of the major auto manufacturers, established an independent finance company, the General Motors Acceptance Corporation, to help customers afford the purchase of an auto. The system took off, and by 1924, nearly three out of every four new cars purchased in the United States were bought on credit. The trend toward installment lending enabled the transformation of cars from a luxury item for the very rich, to a regular facet of middle-class family life. The success of financing in the automobile industry inspired other industries to adopt similar strategies, enabling families in the 1920s to "finance the American dream," by using credit to purchase durable goods.

Conclusion

America's Jazz Age sparkled with the lure of new temptations. Commercial entertainments taught the masses to dream of luxury and escape. Fashion trends and cosmetics offered average citizens the possibility of becoming beauty queens. Homes were transformed into showcases of style and convenience, and automobiles, once the toys of the rich, were suddenly available to almost all. Consumer culture was a means by which African Americans fought for inclusion in the American dream, rural towns were linked to urban culture, and immigrants signaled their assimilation. All this potential and possibility wreaked profound change. To be sure, Americans' idea of the basic necessities of life expanded; they embraced leisure and learned to judge people by the things they bought. But the effects of the consumer revolution went still further. Movies, vaudeville, and national chain stores created a mass culture that ultimately smothered regional variations. The availability of commercial entertainment changed courtship patterns and family social life. The spread of automobiles changed the American landscape, as cities sprawled and distances could be traveled with ever-greater speed. In many ways, trends that began in the 1920s set the country on a course it continues to follow, for it marked the beginning of the consumer era.

References and Further Reading

Ad*Access. In Duke University Rare Book, Manuscript, and Special Collections Library. Availalable at http://scriptorium.lib.duke.edu/adaccess.

Calder, Lendol Glen. *Financing the American Dream: A Cultural History of Consumer Credit*. Princeton, NJ: Princeton University Press, 1999.

Collection 92-M10. "Diary." 1929. Schlesinger Library, Radcliffe Institute, Harvard University, Cambridge, MA.

Glickman, Lawrence B. *A Living Wage: American Workers and the Making of Consumer Society*. Ithaca, NY: Cornell University Press, 1997.

Goff, Beth Twiggar. "Papers." Schlesinger Library, Radcliffe Institute, Harvard University, Cambridge, MA, 1920–1994.

Hill, Daniel Delis. *Advertising to the American Woman, 1900–1999*. Columbus: Ohio State University Press, 2002.

Jacobson, Lisa. "Manly Boys and Enterprising Dreamers: Business Ideology and the Construction of the Boy Consumer, 1910–1930." *Enterprise & Society* 2 (2001): 225–258.

Kern-Foxworth, Marilyn. *Aunt Jemima, Uncle Ben, and Rastus: Blacks in Advertising, Yesterday, Today, and Tomorrow, Contributions in Afro-American and African Studies, No. 168*. Westport, CT: Greenwood Press, 1994.

Laird, Pamela Walker. *Advertising Progress: American Business and the Rise of Consumer Marketing*. Baltimore: Johns Hopkins University Press, 1998.

Lears, T. J. Jackson. *Fables of Abundance: A Cultural History of Advertising in America*. New York: Basic Books, 1994.

Lee, Joseph. "Graded Recreation and Social Hygiene." In *ASHA*. Minneapolis, MN, 1932.

Marchand, Roland. *Advertising the American Dream: Making Way for Modernity, 1920–1940*. Berkeley: University of California Press, 1985.

Olney, Martha L. *Buy Now, Pay Later: Advertising, Credit, and Consumer Durables in the 1920s*. Chapel Hill: University of North Carolina Press, 1991.

Rabus, Alice Miller. "Scrapbooks." Three boxes. Minnesota Historical Society, St. Paul, MN, 1920–1957.

Sivulka, Juliann. *Soap, Sex, and Cigarettes: A Cultural History of American Advertising*. Belmont, CA: Wadsworth Publishing, 1998.

Sivulka, Juliann. *Stronger Than Dirt: A Cultural History of Advertising Personal Hygiene in America, 1875–1940*. Amherst, NY: Humanity Books, 2001.

Spurlock, John C., and Cynthia A. Magistro. *New and Improved: The Transformation of American Women's Emotional Culture*. New York: New York University Press, 1998.

Strasser, Susan. *Satisfaction Guaranteed: The Making of the American Mass Market*. New York: Pantheon Books, 1989.

Turbin, Carole. "Collars and Consumers: Changing Images of American Manliness and Business." In *Beauty and Business: Commerce, Gender, and Culture in Modern America*, edited by Philip Scranton, 87–108. New York: Routledge, 2001.

YWCA National Board. Archives, Ms 59. Sophia Smith Collection, Smith College. Northampton, MA, 1889–1959.

Musicians and Entertainers | 6

Kurt Gartner

The 1920s were years of tremendous change and creative growth for musicians and entertainers. Jazz, which was becoming the first musical art form of U.S. origin, pervaded other forms of expression, such as dance, theater, and film and became a reflection of the cultural assimilations and dichotomies of the period. Jazz was a conduit of common experience for people of disparate cultural, economic, and racial backgrounds. This essay reflects neither an attempt to present in-depth studies of artists nor an effort to provide an exhaustive list of entertainers of the decade. Rather, it is a snapshot—a cross-section of the entertainment scene of the day.

Because jazz music was first played in the bordellos and bars of New Orleans, moralists of the day labeled jazz alternatively as a disease or "the devil's music" and used equally critical terms in an effort to quell its growth in popularity. The moralists' political power was very real; it led to Prohibition and other legal actions against enterprises associated with various forms of entertainment in the Jazz Age. In stark relief to this aspect of the social climate of the 1920s was the attitude of the younger generation, who experienced the euphoria of the end of World War I, sustained economic prosperity, and an increased focus on individuality and women's rights. This generation wanted to be entertained. The sense of jazz as a forbidden form of entertainment only added to its mystique and appeal. By 1922, the market was becoming saturated with recordings by the Original Dixieland Jazz Band (the first commercially recorded jazz group), pianist James P. Johnson, and Mamie Johnson, the first commercially recorded African American singer who codified the 12-bar blues form with her 1920 recording of Perry Bradford's "Crazy Blues" (over time, blues became a major component of the musical vocabulary of jazz musicians).

Some authors have referred to the "casual racism" of the period; however, the racism was far from casual for the African American artists who performed in segregated nightclubs around the country. Typically, these entertainers could only enter such clubs to perform and had to enter through secondary building entrances. Of course, these artists faced a host of additional barriers. Despite these severe limitations, nightclubs and the like represented the few venues in which it was socially acceptable for blacks and whites to interact. Arguably, jazz musicians were ahead of the social curve in terms of integration, as they began to perform in integrated ensembles decades before African American athletes were integrated in professional sports or African American students were integrated in public schools. As for the music, jazz itself was euphoric in the 1920s, and it gave audiences exactly the sensation they were seeking.

Defining Jazz of the Period

The term "jazz" is rather broad. Its origin and meaning have been subjected to retrospective scrutiny and parsing by scholars, musicians, and critics. The term may have originated among traveling minstrels; it may have African or Arabic origins as a slang term describing the sex act; or it may have roots in the French verb *jaser,* connoting engagement in animated dialogue. Several well-known musicians have rejected the term outright. For example, the formidable composer and bandleader Edward Kennedy "Duke" Ellington (1899–1974) believed his music transcended the term "jazz." Like the music itself, the term is probably not attributable to a single event, person, or place. The term was codified in 1917 through several newspaper articles and the seminal recordings of the Original Dixieland Jazz Band. For the purpose of this essay, one should note the primary stylistic and cultural connotations of jazz in the 1920s.

Despite the inherent problems with the term, historians have developed a working definition of jazz based on the following general principles, which should apply to the music of the 1920s:

1. It features improvisation, a composition that is created extemporaneously, during performance. This facet of jazz, when applied in ensemble settings, necessitates a balance between elements that are prearranged (written) with those that are created spontaneously based on the evolving tradition and the current musical moment (unwritten).

2. It includes a rhythmic sense called "swing," which has several components. Melodic lines are generally played in rhythmic subdivisions of three per beat; the first note of each beat is two subdivisions in length, and the second note occupies the remaining subdivision's note length. This rhythmic approach creates the "loping," often lyrical melodic line against the steady time-keeping of the rhythm section. Ragtime, the immediate predecessor of jazz music, typically included two subdivisions per beat rather than three, creating a markedly different feeling in listeners. Additionally, the swing feeling includes a great deal of syncopation, or rhythmic stresses that fall between the regular beats of the music—those to which you might tap your foot. (Giddins 1998; Tirro 1993)

Jazz originated as a musically democratic style in that it was based on collective improvisation. In this style, individual wind players such as

Along with contemporaries such as Louis Armstrong, Duke Ellington was a jazz pioneer who influenced musicians for decades. (*Library of Congress*)

cornet (a brass instrument very similar to the trumpet), clarinet, and trombone simultaneously performed melodies and countermelodies, with the primary melody generally carried by the cornetist. Although each melody or countermelody may have sounded satisfactory on its own, its mystique lay in its relationship with the other "voices" or instrumental melodies. The "rhythm section," comprising a bass voice (such as tuba or string bass), a chording instrument (such as banjo, piano, or, later, guitar), and drum set or "trap set" (originally assembled from various military and concert drums and "contraptions"), provided the rhythmic and harmonic foundation of the ensemble. This ensemble structure led to the prominence of the "combo" (a truncated form of "combination") and later the big band, with even greater complements of wind and rhythm section players.

Although certain combos were often identified with their leaders, audiences expected strong group performances. For example, Ferdinand Joseph Lamothe "Jelly Roll" Morton (1890–1941), the self-proclaimed inventor of jazz, was an exceptional pianist and highly capable solo performer. During the 1920s, he performed with several groups, and was leading the Red Hot Peppers by mid-decade. Joseph "King" Oliver (1885–1938), one of the most prominent cornetists of the Jazz Age, was closely

Marriage Made in Heaven? Radio and Jazz

The Jazz Age was an important time for artistic development in the United States. From writers to musicians to filmmakers, the Jazz Age witnessed a flourishing of cultural pursuits across the artistic spectrum, all of which left influences into contemporary times. But what would modern entertainment be without the radio?

Radio networks arose during the Jazz Age. By the end of the Jazz Age, commercial radio broadcasting was off and running. Music was the dominant format on most radio stations. Classical music was the preferred form at first, but halfway through the Jazz Age, jazz music was found on the airwaves.

Along with the craze over radios came a craving for modern dance, especially to jazz music. As noted in many places, there were some objections to both the music and the dance styles. Regardless of how some might have reacted, many across the nation embraced this

associated with his bands, including his Creole Jazz Band, which recorded hallmark sessions in the early 1920s. Although the limitations of recording technology affected the balance of the ensemble, the interaction of the wind players and the style of the soloists are studied to this day.

The swing feeling and syncopation of jazz may be created by a single performer, particularly if the performer is an extraordinary pianist. James Price Johnson (1894–1955) demonstrated both syncopation and swing feeling in his recordings. His 1921 composition "Carolina Shout" is a prime example and remains one of his best-known works. Johnson played the sequential, swinging melody with his right hand. The swing feeling is intensified by its juxtaposition with Johnson's left-hand accompaniment, which generally keeps steady time. Additionally, this recording includes a sophisticated example of polyrhythm, another rhythmic concept of jazz performance. Basically, polyrhythms are different rhythms that are played at the same time, creating a feeling of musical tension. While a polyrhythm is "in progress," it may be difficult for the listener to reconcile the rhythms, either individually or collectively. In "Carolina Shout," for example, Johnson played phrases in which right and left hands implied two-beat and three-beat meters, respectively. As his right hand played a melody implying a "1–2, 1–2" feeling, his left hand actually played "1–2–3, 1–2–3" groupings, creating rhythmic tension until he rhythmically "resolved" the two lines.

Jazz Beyond the Delta

During the 1920s, jazz was commercial music. Its popularity soared as the means of its transmission improved. From its original venues—the streets and saloons of New Orleans—jazz spread across the nation via traveling tent shows, riverboats, and trains, which brought musicians to the cities of new form of entertainment. The popularity of dance halls is undeniable, and people of all ages flocked to these halls as a way to spend an evening. With the popularity of dance halls came the growth of dance lessons, although many dancers merely copied what they saw on the movie screen and elsewhere. Dance marathons became a fad, with couples competing to see who could endure hours of nonstop dancing. Specific dances gained notoriety during the Jazz Age, such as the Charleston, the fox trot, and the Lindy Hop.

Although it is hard to nail down the one dominant form of popular entertainment in the Jazz Age, it is true that different forms of art were often combined, from music to movies to dance. Listening to jazz on the radio or in a club, coupled by watching dances on the movie screen or by fellow dancers, all came together to provide hours of fun for those who chose to participate.

the north. The exodus of African Americans—musicians, in particular— was hastened by several factors. Storyville, the New Orleans district in which prostitution was legalized, was a hub of popular music from its opening in 1898. In response to increasing pressure from puritanical elements of society, the federal government officially shut down Storyville in 1917. The Eighteenth Amendment, ratified in 1919, banned the production and sale of alcohol in the United States, effectively closing many of the remaining venues in which jazz was heard. The rise of organized crime and the availability of alcohol in Chicago made this city the new center of jazz entertainment in the 1920s.

Technology facilitated the growing prominence of jazz. Mechanical and electronic reproductions of performances became available nationally through player piano scrolls, published sheet music, radio broadcasts, and wax cylinder (later, phonograph) recordings. In fact, the inception and development of jazz music closely parallels the chronology of the development of audio recording and mass reproduction techniques. Of course, access to early recordings provides ample opportunities for present-day research and enjoyment. Access to these recordings in the 1920s allowed musicians to study and influence each other's performances with greatly reduced barriers of time, distance, and stigmas of racial prejudice.

Chicago Jazz

During the 1920s, Chicago was as much a *place* for jazz as a style of jazz. Another term for music of this period is "hot" jazz. The frenetic urban lifestyle led to several critical developments of jazz music. Based on New Orleans jazz—brought north by New Orleans musicians—Chicago jazz was regarded as a more energetic type of music, based in part on a faster tempo and a more streamlined ensemble texture. The textural aspect appealed to audiences' taste for featured soloists rather than the "group improvisation" of New Orleans jazz. The evidence supporting the argument that Chicago jazz was generally faster in tempo is not incontrovertible. Much of the evidence is based upon a limited library of recordings, which may have been subject to technical flaws in reproduction. These flaws may have rendered the playback of recorded music at a faster rate than that of the original performances (In addition to tempo, this technical flaw would also raise the pitch level of such recordings).

Undeniable, however, is the fact that many soloist-based groups emerged from Chicago jazz of the 1920s. Furthermore, Chicago was a musical training ground for more white musicians who embraced the jazz style. One famous example of homegrown Chicago jazz artists was the Austin High Gang, a group of musicians, most of whom attended Chicago's Austin High School. This and subsequent groups came to represent and influence the Chicago style of jazz through their performance practices and choices of instruments used. Notable names of this movement include clarinetists Frank Teschemacher, Mezz Mezzrow, Pee Wee Russell, and Benny Goodman; saxophonist Bud Freeman; cornetists Jimmy McPartland and Muggsy Spanier; trumpeter Wingy Manone; banjo and guitar players Dick McParland and Eddie Condon; pianist and bassist Jim Lanigan; pianists Dave North, Art Hodes, and Joe Sullivan; drummers Dave Tough, George Wettling, and Gene Krupa. While these white musicians were performing on the city's North Side, formidable musicians—many transplanted from New Orleans—performed on the South Side. Important South Side musicians included Louis Armstrong, Lovie Austin, Johnny Dodds, Freddie Keppard, Jimmie Noone, and Joe Oliver.

The New York Scene

Throughout the 1920s, New York City had a vibrant, diverse musical scene that reflected the popularity of jazz. During Prohibition, New York had many speakeasies where jazz music could be heard. (Like those in Chicago, many of the New York establishments had connections with organized crime.) Also, many vaudeville theaters featured popular music and dance. The popularity of public (amateur) dancing associated with jazz was on the rise, and various ballroom orchestras catered to black and white audiences. Jazz found its way into social gatherings of a more informal nature, as a central aspect of Harlem's famous rent parties. And, like the developing assembly-line technique of producing automobiles, composers of New York's Tin Pan Alley "manufactured" popular music (influenced by jazz) at a fantastic rate.

"Stride" Piano Style

Many demographic and musical factors led to the development of jazz piano performance in the 1920s. Seeking work and a better life, hundreds of thousands of African Americans migrated to industrial cities of the North. Inadequate housing and opportunistic landlords led to extreme overcrowding and overcharging of black tenants in these cities, particularly New York. To raise funds, many tenants organized rent parties, in which they charged admission for guests to gather, socialize, consume alcohol, and enjoy live music. Because of space and other considerations, the piano became an instrument of choice at many of these parties, which served as a sort of training ground for many New York pianists, including Willie "The Lion" Smith and Fats Waller. One of the originators of the stride style was the aforementioned James P. Johnson. Like many of his contemporaries, Johnson was a capable ragtime player who was also classically trained. He generated the striding characteristic of his music with his left hand, which provided a complete accompaniment—a bass line on downbeats and full chords on upbeats.

While maintaining the syncopated rhythmic quality of ragtime, Johnson played with a greater sense of swing than ragtime players did. Furthermore, his classical training allowed him to play in a virtuosic manner, inventing complicated polyrhythms and harmonic relationships at fast tempi and using the full range of the piano keyboard. At rent parties or at the dance halls of New York's Hell's Kitchen, Johnson was quite capable of holding his own in "cutting contests," competitive displays of virtuosity among jazz musicians. The stride piano innovations of Johnson and others came to be known collectively as the "Harlem School."

New York Big Bands

Based on the definition of jazz offered earlier, one may draw stylistic distinctions between the performance practices of various New York big bands that emerged in the 1920s. Among the developing ensembles were big bands that featured improvisation and the hard-edged syncopation commonly associated with the jazz of the period. Additionally, there were many genteel dance orchestras and bands that played popular music in a less frenetic manner that was primarily *imitative* of the jazz style—arguably, the first examples of "light jazz." Of these two types of ensembles, the former typically played the dance halls of Harlem, and the latter performed in the relative formality of upscale hotel ballrooms. To a degree, these distinctive stylistic approaches illustrate the European and African traditions that make up jazz. In general, African music and dance include a greater emphasis on improvisation and incorporation of syncopation like that which is found in jazz. The European musical tradition includes an emphasis on closed formal structure and the dominance of wind and string instruments in ensemble settings.

Perhaps the most representative examples of big bands and dance bands of New York in the 1920s were those led by Duke Ellington and Paul Whiteman (1890–1967), respectively. Occupying a stylistic middle ground were groups such as the one led by Fletcher Henderson (1897–1952). While Ellington's work led to the swing style of the 1930s, Whiteman helped to establish the concept of "symphonic jazz" and solidified the important place of the "crooner" in the dance band for an entire generation.

Paul Whiteman (shown here in 1960), an enormously successful bandleader in the 1920s and 1930s, pioneered a symphonic approach to dance music and created the "band show" format still in use today. He hired and encouraged many fine instrumentalists and vocalists and through his efforts helped jazz gain popular attention and acceptance. (*Library of Congress*)

Duke Ellington began to study piano during his childhood in Washington, D.C., and was playing professionally at the age of 27. During 1923–1927, he began to develop his compositional and arranging style as well as his professional relationships in New York through his work with Elmer Snowden's Washingtonians. Also, he continued to hone his significant skills as a pianist, playing various venues, including the rent parties of Harlem. Several members of the Washingtonians stayed with Ellington when he formed his own group, which gradually grew in size.

By 1927, Ellington was leading a 12-piece group at New York's famous Cotton Club, where he and trumpeter James "Bubber" Miley introduced audiences to their examples of "jungle style" jazz. This particular style includes extensive use of tom-toms by the drummer; unusual instrumental sounds, such as growling effects by the wind players; and exotic scales and harmonies. Ellington recorded several tunes in this style, including "East Saint Louis Toodle-oo" (1926), "The Mooche" (1928), and "Jungle Nights in Harlem" (1930). This was but one phase of Ellington's stylistic evolution, which later included extended compositions, film scores, and liturgical music. Ellington's band was remarkably stable, retaining many members for years, even decades. This allowed Ellington to compose and arrange in a particularly individual way, exploiting the specific talents of each player in the group. Additionally, the group toured extensively for many years, bringing Ellington's musical influence to bear through direct contact with audiences as well as through recordings. Ellington directed the band until his death in 1974, whereupon his son, Mercer, began to lead the band.

Paul Whiteman's background was quite different from that of Ellington. Born in Colorado, Whiteman studied viola and performed with the Denver Symphony Orchestra and, later, the San Francisco Symphony Orchestra. After a stint as a navy bandleader during World War I, Whiteman led bands in San Francisco, Los Angeles, and Atlantic City, New Jersey, before settling in New York. By the mid-1920s, he was widely known in the United States and was touring on an international scale. With the momentum of his great popularity, Whiteman embarked on tours featuring works he commissioned from several U.S. composers. The first such commissioned work was George Gershwin's *Rhapsody in Blue*. Whiteman's other projects included live radio broadcasts, performances in feature films, and composition of Broadway musical scores.

Whiteman dominated the dance band scene of the 1920s, and his ensemble became a sort of staging ground for band members launching careers as bandleaders or featured artists. Notable among the entertainers who performed with Whiteman were Jimmy and Tommy Dorsey, who became formidable bandleaders in their own right, and singers such as Bing Crosby, one of Whiteman's Rhythm Boys. Although dance bands did not place a great emphasis on improvisation, they did not exclude jazz soloists entirely. Whiteman's group had several improvising soloists at various times, including Bix Beiderbecke, cornet; Frankie Trumbauer, saxophone; Joe Venuti, violin; and Jack Teagarden, trombone. Other groups followed or paralleled Whiteman's approach to arranging and ensemble sound. Notable among these were the orchestras of Guy Lombardo and Lawrence Welk.

Tin Pan Alley: Portraits of Two Cornetists

Musicians of the 1920s came from widely varied backgrounds. The following biographical sketches are included to offer some finer granularity to this snapshot of the period's entertainment scene. The sketches are of two cornet players who were contemporaries. Louis Armstrong was an artist whose name is strongly identified with jazz and its development. He was an African American musician, born in impoverished conditions in New Orleans, who transformed the very idiom of jazz performance while transmitting his art on a global scale through live and recorded performances. At the age of 70, he died with his reputation as an artist and his legacy as an entertainer firmly intact.

Bix Beiderbecke, only two years younger than Armstrong, was born into a white, middle-class family in Iowa. He learned his craft through listening and performing on nearby riverboats, studying recordings of the greats—Armstrong, in particular—and traveling to various cities to perform with many jazz groups. An alcoholic, Beiderbecke died at the age of 28, still essentially unknown. Although their professional paths crossed, the individual stories of Armstrong and Beiderbecke are quite different, and shed light on the ubiquitous quality of jazz throughout the United States.

Louis Armstrong was one of the 20th century's most important jazz innovators and performers. (*Library of Congress*)

Louis Armstrong

Louis "Satchmo" Armstrong (1901–1971), the jazz cornetist, singer, and composer whose innovations were already apparent in the 1920s, had a profound influence on the style, composition, and performance techniques of subsequent generations of musicians. Armstrong spent his childhood in poverty in New Orleans, assimilating the music of churches, dance halls, and saloons. After a period of performing as a street musician and being arrested for delinquency, Armstrong was befriended by Joe "King" Oliver, one of the fathers of jazz and a popular New Orleans musician of the period. Oliver, like many New Orleans musicians, moved to Chicago in the 1920s. Oliver's move afforded Armstrong the opportunity to replace him in Kid Ory's band in New Orleans. Within four years, Oliver summoned Armstrong to Chicago to play second cornet for Oliver's Creole Jazz Band.

Armstrong spent much of his time in Chicago during the 1920s. He performed on many early recordings with Oliver but became increasingly motivated to find a better artistic outlet for his individual style. With the encouragement of his wife, Lillian Hardin, who was Oliver's pianist, Armstrong left Chicago and the Creole Jazz Band in 1924 to perform in New York with Fletcher Henderson. Although the format of the larger band was restraining on the whole, Armstrong was able to develop his individual style through improvised solos.

By 1925, Armstrong had returned to Chicago, where he embarked on his career as a soloist and bandleader. The power, virtuosity, and fluency of his improvisation were unprecedented and dominated the collectively improvised polyphony of New Orleans–style jazz. Gradually, Armstrong's ensembles evolved into the role of accompanist, complementing his virtuosic solo style. This stylistic progression is evident in Armstrong's most famous recordings of the second half of the decade. "Big Butter and Egg Man" (1926), "Potato Head Blues," and "Struttin' with Some Barbeque" (1927) were conceived in the New Orleans style. "Weather Bird and West End Blues" (1928) had a smaller group format, featuring pianist Earl Hines. By 1929, Armstrong had settled on a big band format, which he retained well into the 1940s.

In addition to developing a soloist-based texture of jazz music, Armstrong played a role in standardizing other aspects of musical style. He was involved in the trend among musicians to move from cornet to trumpet as the standard "high brass" voice of the ensemble. His lyrical improvisations were marked by a relaxed sense of independence from underlying rhythms, innovative use of timbre (tone), and a conspicuous lack of clichéd phrase endings. He developed a personal style of scat singing, in which he improvised musical lines with series of syllables that imitate instrumental sounds more than intelligible words. He advanced the integration of blues style into jazz, through his instrumental and vocal performances. Through his arrangements, Armstrong influenced the trend away from the two-beat feeling of the jazz of the 1920s, setting the stage for swing music of the 1930s with its four-beat feeling.

(Leon) Bix Beiderbecke

Cornetist Bix Beiderbecke (1903–1931), a contemporary of Louis Armstrong, was a significant innovator of improvisatory methods in his own right. Furthermore, he imitated African American musicians in his formative years, subsequently blending these and other influences into his individual style. This developmental method became a trend among white musicians of the decade, supported by the increased access to jazz music through recordings, radio, and live performances. Arguably, he was the first white jazz musician to be respected—and ultimately imitated—by African American jazz musicians.

Musicians performing on riverboats that traveled up and down the Mississippi River delivered jazz sounds to Beiderbecke, who lived in a port city during his youth. Beiderbecke studied classical piano from an early age, but he was continually frustrated by his inability to read music, possibly the result of a learning disability. Taken by the sounds of jazz, he abandoned formal piano study, and by his high school years he had begun to study Original Dixieland Jazz Band recordings. Also during this time, he learned of Louis Armstrong and began to perform publicly. He developed a self-taught method of playing cornet, including an unconventional approach to "fingering," or pressing certain combinations of valve

Portrait of Bix Beider-
becke, jazz cornetist
and composer of the
late 1920s who had a
significant impact on
the history of music
before his death at
the age of 28. (*Bett-
mann/Corbis*)

The girls see him
play, have heard
of him, Florence
is taken with him?

keys to play desired pitches on the instrument. Like many white, midwestern parents, Beiderbecke's parents strongly disapproved of his jazz studies.

In 1921, his parents enrolled him in the Lake Forest Military Academy,
north of Chicago. If they had sent him to Lake Forest to reduce his exposure to jazz, Beiderbecke's parents had committed a grave error. Beiderbecke spent much of his time in Chicago listening to jazz, and he was
expelled from the academy before the end of the school year. In 1922, he
remained in Chicago, where he often heard King Oliver's Rhythm Kings.
Subsequently, he performed in Chicago, New York, and St. Louis with various groups, including the Wolverines, Frankie Trumbauer's groups, and

the Paul Whiteman King of Jazz Orchestra, in which he developed his limited skill in reading music.

Certainly, Beiderbecke's life was shortened by his severe alcoholism. By 1929, he returned to his hometown of Davenport to recover, but the recovery was never complete. In 1930, he returned to New York to play limited engagements with the likes of the Dorsey Brothers and Benny Goodman. In 1931, he died of pneumonia and complications brought about by cirrhosis of the liver.

Beiderbecke's individual style was marked by a variety of technical peculiarities and diverse musical interests. As noted, he was a self-taught cornetist. His unique fingering technique yielded unusual timbres, as different valve combinations produce different balances of overtones that make up the cornet's overall sound. Furthermore, he continued to play cornet—an instrument with "mellow" timbrel characteristics—in a time when the trumpet, a much "brighter" sounding instrument, was becoming the instrument of choice among most brass players. Although he lacked some of the more typical tone production techniques that had been all but standardized by Louis Armstrong, Beiderbecke was acutely aware of intonation, the ability to purposely play in (or out of) tune. He used a refined approach to intonation to shape his melodic lines, creating tension and repose relative to the harmonic underpinnings of the ensemble.

Finally, Beiderbecke was a devotee of the classical music of contemporary composers, particularly the French composer, Claude Debussy. In studying and imitating the sounds of Debussy's piano works, Beiderbecke became familiar with certain compositional techniques that became part of his personal jazz lexicon. He incorporated elements of Debussy's extended harmonies and unusual scales into his own playing. Incidentally, Debussy's style of composition was commonly referred to as "impressionism," a term rejected by Debussy himself. Although Beiderbecke had abandoned the formal study of piano, he continued to play piano and use it as a compositional tool throughout his career. Although he apparently did not notate them, he composed and recorded several pieces for piano. These pieces reflect Debussy's influence in style and title, but they also include rhythmic elements of jazz and ragtime. A prime example of this body of work is Beiderbecke's "In a Mist," recorded in 1927.

Beiderbecke and Armstrong were not mutually exclusive characters. They admired each other's work and were known to have heard each other's playing, albeit surreptitiously, in segregated clubs. Although Armstrong was by far the better-known and more influential musician, the study of both artists reveals the importance of individual experience and its influence on musical style.

Jazz and Popular Dance

Early jazz music had both aesthetic and functional appeal. It was dance music that inspired motions reflecting the general euphoria and celebration of youth that was common to the period. Like jazz music, dance styles were uniquely American combinations of African and European influences—namely, improvisation in context of defined form, and in solo, couples, and group contexts. Two notable dance styles of the 1920s were the Charleston and the Lindy Hop. The Charleston had its origins in an African American folk dance of Charleston, South Carolina. The dance style was elevated to national prominence through "Charleston," the closing number of the first act of *Runnin' Wild*, a two-act musical comedy that opened on October 29, 1923, at the New Colonial Theater on Broadway. New York–based "stride" pianist James P. Johnson composed the music for this show. The Lindy Hop, named after Charles Lindbergh's transatlantic flight of 1927, became a primary attraction of dance halls such as the Savoy in Harlem. This couple's dance included both closed position and breakaway moves and was further developed by Frankie Manning of the dance troupe, Whitey's Lindy Hoppers. The style was transmitted and documented by Manning in several films produced in the 1930s.

However, with these new dances also came new charges of racism in jazz music. During the 1920s, young people were going out unchaperoned more and more frequently, especially aided by the increased use of the automobile. Gone were the Victorian era codes of behavior while courting whereby young couples had some form of escort or chaperone for their social activities. With the rise of the automobile age, people, both young and old alike, could go out together at night in ways never considered before, away from the watchful eyes of some sort of guardian.

Once in these clubs people were engaging in their new dances. In what would foreshadow the racism that accompanied the early years of rock music, jazz music, as noted, would be called the "devil's music." Moreover, since a goodly number of jazz musicians were African American, some segments of white America believed whites were being "brought down to the level of the Negro" through what they saw as wild gesturing to "jungle music." When accompanied by the changes in women's fashions during the 1920s, whereby women were showing more of their legs due to the fact that skirt lengths and dress hemlines were becoming shorter all the time, more conservative elements of society feared that blacks were using jazz music to seduce white women. And, when these young and impressionable couples left the clubs in a "riled up state," and were traveling alone in their automobiles, sexual immorality might possibly ensue. Again, such charges would also be made during the 1950s and early 1960s as rock music began to pervade the land.

Jazz in the Modern Age

Jazz remains a popular form of music to this day. As with any other art form, it has gone through numerous changes, but the center focus remains the same. Many major metropolitan cities have what is often referred to as a "smooth jazz" radio station that performs quite well in the Arbitron ratings, although many believe this new smooth jazz style is not really jazz at all. Documentary filmmaker Ken Burns produced a series on jazz, and clubs and concert halls continue to be filled with audiences devoted to the music. Many college music departments have their own jazz bands that often perform in collegiate competitions. Many jazz artists have a soft spot for the holiday season and record jazz versions of classic Christmas tunes.

As with many other artists working in different mediums, jazz artists took full advantage of the time period in which they lived, giving the 1920s its name, "the Jazz Age," and creating an art form that is truly American in origin. While other musical forms have come and gone out of style, jazz is one style that continues to endure no matter what the time period may be.

References and Further Reading

Dicaire, David. *Jazz Musicians of the Early Years, to 1945.* Jefferson, NC: McFarland and Company, 2003.

Ewen, David. *The Life and Death of Tin Pan Alley: The Golden Age of American Popular Music.* New York: Funk and Wagnalls Company, 1964.

Forte, Allen. *The American Popular Ballad of the Golden Era, 1924–1950.* Princeton, NJ: Princeton University Press, 1995.

Gabbard, Krin. *Jammin' at the Margins: Jazz and the American Cinema.* Chicago: University of Chicago Press, 1996.

Giddins, Gary. *Visions of Jazz: The First Century.* New York: Oxford University Press, 1998.

"Popular and Social Dance." 2006. Microsoft Encarta Online Encyclopedia. http://encarta.msn.com.

Tirro, Frank. *Jazz: A History.* New York: Norton and Company, 1993.

Waller, Maurice, and Anthony Calabrese. *Fats Waller.* New York: Macmillan Publishing Company, 1977.

Wondrick, David. *Stomp and Swerve: American Music Gets Hot, 1843–1924.* Chicago: A Cappella, 2003.

Immigrants and Nativists | 7

Mitchell Newton-Matza

The Jazz Age is remembered for the many innovations, creations, and changes it brought to American society. From artistic endeavors to cultural changes, and to innovations in business and industry, there was certainly a discernable change in American life. Although not all of these changes were openly embraced by the whole of society, there was a new expression of what it meant to be an American. But, as Americans were expressing themselves in newer ways, many wondered if the presence of the foreign born in the country would have a negative impact.

Although the United States was built on and by immigration, there was an ever-growing mistrust of immigrants. The United States boasted a strong, unique culture, and many began to fear what foreign-born groups might do to alter that culture. The country was not concerning itself with taking on the troubles of the world and retreated into isolationism. Once again, the presence, and continued influx, of immigrant groups was seen as a problem. Many native-born Americans questioned whether these new residents were willing to become American and fully embrace American ideals.

Americanism

What exactly makes one an "American?" Is it being native born? Can anyone achieve American nationalism? If so, can a naturalized citizen be just as American as a native-born citizen? Is being American a state of mind or a legal formality? And, if a person embraces Americanism, does that mean renouncing one's ethnic heritage for the sake of the new citizenship, or can one's ethnic heritage be incorporated into American society? During the Jazz Age, the issue of immigration once again became a prominent national issue.

Physical examinations of immigrants at Ellis Island, New York, 1923. These examinations were usually unsanitary, with medical instruments being used over and over without being cleaned after each patient. First class passengers were not subject to these exams. (*National Archives*)

Many studies of the Jazz Age allude to the increase of nativism and ideological intolerance across the nation. The call for immigration restriction was on the rise, and several nativist groups, most notably the Ku Klux Klan, terrorized the foreign population, not to mention numerous native-born groups, such as African Americans. Several authors label the 1920s as a decade of tribalism and xenophobia. As one clergyman of the era remarked, "If we are to have an American civilization we must assimilate the stream of newcomers. If we do not assimilate them they will adulterate us with an admixture of old world morals" (Quoted in Dinnerstein and Reimers 1975, 70). This racism and xenophobia were not shared by all. Though recognizing the tribalism of the Jazz Age period, John Higham writes that "as early as the late 1920s, a decline of racism in intellectual circles set in" (Higham 1975, 58). As with any groupings of people, it is impossible to gauge what everyone was thinking. Nevertheless, during the Jazz Age, there was a vigorous debate about what American values were, and what it would take to preserve them.

The idea of Americanism was anything but new. In 1890, the U.S. Census announced that the frontier was closed. The United States had reached the end of the continent; all that was needed was to fill in the gaps. Three years later, the famed historian Frederick Jackson Turner presented his paper "The Significance of the Frontier in American History." In his frontier thesis, Turner examined what helped to produce the unique American culture. After all, virtually everything that created American society was brought from elsewhere. The U.S. legal system was based on

Historian Frederick Jackson Turner presented his provocative essay, "The Significance of the Frontier in American History," in 1893 at a meeting of the American Historical Association. The essay opened up a new period in the interpretation of American history. (*Library of Congress*)

British common law, the dominant English language spoken was not native to the continent, and the dominant Christian religion originated and was developed in the Eastern Hemisphere. Even the capitalist economic system was brought from the Old World.

Yet somehow Americans were a unique stock. Where did this come from? Turner said the frontier was what made Americans so unique. The constant settling and resettling of the frontier helped create and develop the American character. Although Turner's thesis lost its impact over time, the frontier thesis remains an interesting interpretation of American culture and is still discussed in classrooms today.

But what was the diversity of American culture in 1893, when Turner first presented his paper? The huge influx of newer groups into American society, such as those from Eastern and Southern Europe, Mexico, and parts of Asia, were either just beginning or still some time away. Many

The Sense of Being an American

In the movie *Stripes* (1981), Bill Murray's character, John Winger, contemplates what it means to be an American. Winger, besides referring to Americans as "mutts," makes the pronounced statement that "our forefathers were kicked out of every decent country." In the earliest settlements in North America, although some members of the so-called nobility might have made the trek, the settlement of America was not made by the upper classes but by the middle classes and lower classes (who had their own hierarchy, such as the Puritan society).

Where and when did the idea of being an "American" first come about? During the earliest years of American history, most settlers had no intentions of staying permanently. The idea was to live for a time in the New World, make a mark, and then return to their homeland.

During the Jazz Age, the idea about what it meant to be an American was hotly debated. Many feared foreigners and any ideas they might bring into the country. Catholicism was hated, as were those who practiced the religion. Many immigrants were from overwhelmingly Catholic countries, such as Poland. There were calls to stem the tide of new immigrants, especially those

groups who had arrived in America before this time, such as the Irish and Chinese, were kept on the sidelines. African Americans, although not an immigrant group per se (for immigration implies a voluntary decision to enter a new country, as opposed to the slave heritage), had other concerns, such as fighting the oppressive racist Jim Crow laws of the South. What concerned some aspects of American society was preserving so-called American traditions and values. Blacks had already been part of American society for centuries and were thus expected to maintain native values. The new influx of immigrants from parts of the world not previously seen in such large numbers gave many Americans reason to believe their society was being threatened by the presence of what they viewed as inferior people.

Isolationism

Just as America was coming out of the World War I era and entering the Jazz Age, the country entered a period of isolationism. The United States turned inward and in the process turned its back on external problems. To be certain, although diplomatic ties with other countries were anything but broken, the country was not going to concern itself with world problems, especially those that had brought about World War I. Rather, America's first and foremost concern would be itself. With this renewed sense of self-preservation came the renewed notions of protecting American culture, values, and traditions. To do so, the role of the immigrant in American society was once again a major issue.

considered to be inferior. This generally meant people from Central and Eastern Europe. But in both cases one of the major reasons for discrimination was religion, and not just against Catholics, for the Jewish population was also lumped into that group. For those opposed to these groups, the argument was that the newly arriving people had no intentions of embracing American culture.

The idea of Americanism went beyond race, ethnicity, and religion. Political views were also suspect. To embrace any sort of radical ideology, such as communism and socialism, was considered extremely anti-American. Not only were these "foreign" ideologies, but the very foundations of these beliefs went far beyond traditional American values. A true American would never advocate the overthrow of the government for the sake of a foreign ideology.

So what does it mean to be an American? Is the country a melting pot where everything meshes together or a salad bowl where distinct portions are identifiable? The drive to restrict immigration during the Jazz Age clearly indicates the former.

Early Nativism

The debate about the issue of immigration, or, for that matter, the response to the introduction of any foreign ideas, went back to the early years of U.S. history. The colony of Maryland, for example, was supposed to have been established as a Catholic haven in an overwhelmingly Protestant colonial nation. That idea was not completely fulfilled as numerous violent attacks on Catholics took place during early colonial years because many thought the Catholic religion was detrimental to society. Even during the American Revolution, some Americans were opposed to France's help during their struggle. Being that France was an overwhelmingly Catholic country, many were afraid the French would force the United States to convert to Catholicism. During the first Age of Reform (ca. 1820–1860) and during the Progressive Era (ca.1890–1920), which ended just as the Jazz Age was beginning, protecting American culture from foreign influence was a major concern.

This drive toward nativism took place in both the social and political arenas. In the area of politics, the Know-Nothing Party, which arose during the 1850s, took on the issue of immigration. This movement had an anti-Catholic tone, as the large numbers of Irish who were entering the nation at the time were overwhelmingly Catholic. Many believed the pope would try to undermine American culture and turn the population into one of "idol worshippers." The name "Know-Nothing" supposedly came about because when members were asked about their organization, they merely said "I know nothing." The Know-Nothing Party would come to naught, especially as they were not addressing the major issues of the day, such as slavery.

During the Civil War, recent U.S. immigrants felt no reason to join the army and fight for either side, because they did not feel fully incorporated into American society. At the end of the Civil War, immigration began to rise again, especially in response to the need for labor, which had been a common concern since the earliest years of U.S. history. This need for labor carried on into the post–Civil War years as the Industrial Revolution achieved monumental proportions in the United States. The Office of the Commissioner of Immigration was established in 1864 to bring in contract laborers, usually for a period not to exceed 12 months. The southern states were especially interested in hiring European workers, mostly to supplant black workers.

Changing Face of Immigration

From the end of the Civil War to the start of World War I, newer immigrant groups were arriving into the country. Before this time, the predominant groups tended to come from England, Germany, and Scandinavia. The Burlingame Treaty of 1868 permitted the entry of Chinese laborers, especially to work on the railroads, but strong anti-Chinese sentiment on the West Coast caused the treaty to be reworked in 1880. Although Chinese laborers were not forbidden to enter the United States at first, an 1882 law—known as the Chinese exclusionary laws—did just that, prohibiting such workers for a 10-year period. Chinese immigration was not officially permitted until 1943.

The Japanese faced a similar situation in the early 1900s. The Japanese and Korean Exclusion League formed on the West Coast, and in San Francisco separate public schools were required for the Japanese, Korean, and Chinese. In a so-called gentleman's agreement between the United States and Japan, the latter country agreed to put a voluntary cap on emigrating workers. The state of California took things a step further when it limited the right of Japanese to own and/or lease farm lands.

The group that especially alarmed mainstream American society was the new influx of people from Eastern and Southern Europe. Large numbers of people began to arrive from places such as Russia, Poland (although Poland did not exist as an independent country at this time), Austria-Hungary, and Italy. The largest U.S. cities, such as Chicago and New York, absorbed the bulk of these immigrant populations. On the eve of World War I, nearly 75 percent of immigrants came from Eastern and Southern Europe.

What must be noted, however, was that the United States was not always the first choice of settlement for these immigrants. Countries such as Brazil and Argentina were major sources of competition for this new European labor source. Although there was an outward opposition to mass immigration in the United States, many welcomed the newcomers, especially the owners of industry. Capitalist industry has always looked for ways to minimize expenses and maximize profits, and employees have always borne the brunt of what employers would do to cut costs. With the advent of the Industrial Revolution and with the increased use of unskilled over skilled labor as machines became more important than craft skills, finding ways to pay workers as little as possible became a stronger focus than ever. Immigrant workers fit that role perfectly as they could be paid the absolute bare minimum.

When women and children entered the workforce, employers were able to pay them at a rate far lower than that of men. As the new wave of immigration came into the United States, so did a new way of increasing profits. Although native-born women and children may have had no legal rights, and no true access to the legal system for protection, recently arrived immigrants were especially treasured by employers. Not only were immigrants paid less than anyone else, but they had even fewer legal protections, something easily exploitable by employers who felt no compunction about complying with any sort of government labor laws.

Xenophobia

With these new groups, however, came a new wave of prejudice. The use of cheap immigrant labor was already a major issue for those wishing to restrict immigration, for it was argued that jobs were being taken away from good native-born citizens. Rather than blaming the employers who hired this cheap form of labor, people were angry at those who sought to make a better living than what was available elsewhere. This prejudice also came in the form of religious hatred. Many in this new immigration wave were Jews escaping persecution in such places as Russia, and others were Catholic. With that, deep-rooted biases were again brought to the surface.

In addition, many believed immigrants were stupid, criminal minded, dirty, and they bred like rabbits. Immigrants were accused of adhering to antiquated Old World ways. They were also accused of turning what was said to be decent housing into filthy slums. Immigrants were said to be sleeping as many as 20 or more in apartments meant for five. This was sometimes true, for many families, desperate for rent and food survival, did overload living arrangements. But what was usually not mentioned was how some landlords preyed on immigrant's circumstances to squeeze every dime they could out of their tenants while providing little, if any, services conducive to any form of clean living.

Immigration Concerns in the Early 20th Century

Naturally, immigration slowed to a trickle during the World War I years. During the war years, a bill concerning literacy tests for immigrants resurfaced. Such bills were not new, for such legislation was proposed during the presidential administrations of Grover Cleveland and William Howard Taft, both of whom exercised their veto power over the measures. President Woodrow Wilson vetoed another such bill twice, but a Congressional override in 1917 made it mandatory for immigrants over 16 years of age to be able to read between 30 and 80 standard words in English or another language. Then, in 1918, as World War I was in its final year and the Jazz Age was just beginning, Congress passed a measure forbidding entry to any immigrants who were anarchist, as well as any other person who advocated the overthrow of the government. A 1920 law allowed for the deportation of any such person described in the previous law. Many argued that it was necessary to pass such laws, for a country has the right to protect itself.

At the start of the Jazz Age, the issues of radicalism and immigration were once again tied. Russia saw two revolutions in 1917. The first revolution in March rid the country of the Romanov dynasty; the second revolution in November saw the Bolsheviks seize control. In the United States, the year 1919 held significance. The Socialist Party expelled the segment of its party who supported the Bolshevik Revolution. In the immediate wake of this action two new parties were formed, the Communist Labor Party and the Communist Party, both of which vied for recognition by the Soviet Union, though recognition was refused until the two groups coalesced.

Also in 1919 were the infamous Palmer raids, led by the Department of Justice under A. Mitchell Palmer. These were a series of mass arrests against political and labor agitators (see chapter on *Reformers, Radicals and Socialists* for more). Noncitizens were subjected to deportation. Although the legality of these raids is still highly questioned, scores of foreigners were deported. In December 1919, the infamous "Soviet Ark" (in actuality the USS *Buford*) sailed, deporting 294 people to Russia, including the famed anarchist Emma Goldman. Many saw these raids as valid, however. The ideas of communism, socialism, and anarchism were not American ideas, so they must come from the foreign born (this idea actually stretches back into the 19th century). Much of mainstream America believed the foreign-born population were clearly trying to undermine American society. The federal government responded to both of these notions by taking strong measures against any potential undesirable elements attempting to enter the country.

Congressional Legislation

In 1921 came the Emergency Quota Act. In what would be a precursor to a similar law a few years later, the federal government limited the number of immigrants to the United States. Using the 1910 census as its gauge, the number of any particular nationality allowed into the United States was limited to 3 percent of the group's existing population according to the 1910 census; a cap was set at 357,000, thereby reducing immigration by about two-thirds.

To many Americans, the Emergency Quota Act was not enough. For one, using the 1910 census was seen as a mistake. There was already a sizable Eastern and Southern European population in the United States at that time, so the baseline was too high. What good was being accomplished? Even President Calvin Coolidge wanted America to "be kept American." This Americanism did not include these new European immigrants who were now making a strong mark on society.

Congress answered the call for more stringent legislation in 1924. Known by two names—the National Origins Act or the Johnson-Reed Act—this federal legislation took stern measures against the new European groups, as well as Asians. Congressman Albert Johnson and Senator David Reed worked together to create this law, which established restrictions that, with some future modifications, would be in force until 1952. Although the law passed with few problems, there was some vociferous opposition, most notably from Congressman Emanuel Celler, who battled the law for years.

In taking the 1921 law a step further, the Johnson-Reed Act severely limited immigration to 2 percent of any particular group's U.S. population according to the 1890 census, and a cap was placed at 150,000. The restrictions were especially aimed at the newer European groups as their presence in the United States was nowhere near as strong as it became during the 20th century. The legislation worked well: immigration from these so-called less desirables fell to a trickle. The Johnson-Reed Act was set to last until June 30, 1927. In 1927 the law was extended, with some additional creative mathematics to keep the cap at 150,000, although strong opposition delayed it from taking effect until 1929.

Besides people from Eastern and Southern Europe, Asians also felt the sting of the immigration restrictions. Although Coolidge was opposed to the move, Congress got rid of the gentleman's agreement with Japan. Potential Japanese immigrants now found themselves excluded, just as the Chinese were. The Japanese had previously been denied citizenship through a U.S. Supreme Court decision, and the new law barred any immigration from those ineligible for citizenship. Asian Indians also found themselves prohibited from entering the country, even as laborers.

However, people from other countries, most notably Canada and Mexico, were not excluded from entering the United States. Mexicans did not have a particularly easy time entering the country—they were subjected to visas and a head tax—but it was easier than what their immigrant counterparts from Europe and Asia were facing. One reason for this lax policy was, again, the need for labor, especially in the southwestern farm areas, an area in which many Mexicans preferred to settle.

Americanization Programs

Immigration into the United States was clamped in regards to specific groups, but another issue remained: What should be done with those already in the country? With such a strong foreign-born population, ignoring their presence was not an option. Both recent immigrants, and even first- and second-generation immigrants, needed to be incorporated into American society in some fashion. Many nativists felt that if immigrants were not educated about what it meant to be an American, their foreign ways could corrupt the nation.

Americanization programs, both public and private, were hardly new. People such as Jane Addams and her Hull House in Chicago provided programs for native and foreign-born people to receive education and training as a way to function in American society. Compulsory education for children became public policy, again, for both native and foreign born. Topics such as civics were taught. To promoters of the school system, this was a way of helping people understand how the American system worked, something all of society should know. Detractors wondered if people were really being taught how American civics operated, or if they were merely being indoctrinatated so they would be good, docile citizens who would not question the system.

Many Americanization programs were sponsored by employers. As with other programs, teaching English and American civics to immigrant workers would help them become better citizens and better workers. Many employers hoped to break down barriers that hindered effective communication and interaction. Some employers encouraged foreign-born workers to become U.S. citizens and believed their programs would help them achieve that goal. Furthermore, by helping foreign-born workers to learn English, better workplace safety could be taught, cutting down on the chance of injury and death and keeping an experienced workforce in place.

As with the criticism against compulsory education, however, what some employers were trying to accomplish was called into question. Although many did have the best intentions toward their immigrant employees, others sought to enforce conformity to so-called traditional American values. Foreign-born workers were told to abandon the customs and traditions of their heritage. And, as with programs in the public sector, any sort of radicalism was vigorously discouraged (see the American Education Week controversy in the chapter *Reformers, Radicals and Socialists* for more). Workers who rocked the boat would not keep their jobs for very long.

For many immigrants there were benefits to retaining their cherished heritage while becoming part of American life. Learning English and the American political system meant one could understand the nuances of American society and learn to work with, and benefit from, the system. There was no reason to abandon their traditions and customs in the privacy of their own homes or while associating with others of their particular group. The Old and New Worlds could be easily combined.

Government Concerns and Involvement

The call for Americanization programs was becoming pronounced in several government agencies during the Jazz Age. One person interested in this area was the secretary of labor, James John Davis. In 1923, Davis published an article commemorating Education Week (see chapter on *Reformers, Radicals and Socialists* for more). A man much committed to both immigration restriction and citizenship training, Davis wrote that "Education is the backbone of American supremacy; it is the lifeblood which keeps the energies of a people directed toward a better and fuller enjoyment of the inalienable rights of mankind . . . The duty [of education] which devolved upon every citizen [was] to assist in making Americanism mean no less than was the anticipation of the founders of the republic" (Davis Papers 1923).

As already seen, within the government there was concern over the current immigrant population. The Americanization programs of the Bureau of Education were supported, although indirectly, by other agencies. Davis, himself an immigrant from Wales, corresponded with the American Legion about proper Americanization. In an August 21, 1923, letter to L. B. Schwellenbach, editor of the *Washington State Legionnaire*, Davis wrote: "It is true that there is no possible process that can be devised for turning aliens into Americans by machinery. For Americanism is not a matter of the head, not an operation of the mind and will, but of the soul." In an address to the American Legion on October 15, 1923, Davis proclaimed: "I would admit to America only the alien who is able and willing to accept American customs, American ideals, American institutions, and who can contribute something to the advancement of our civilization" (Davis Papers 1923). Nativist groups welcomed this additional government support. Davis further claimed that "what kind of American can be made out of the individual whose first experience of America come through defiance of her laws, and evasion of her authority? An American must be for America against all the world" (Davis Papers 1923).

The Bureau of Education had been involved in Americanization programs for a long time before the Jazz Age (see chapter on *Reformers, Radicals and Socialists* for more on the formation of the Bureau of Education). The bureau sponsored conferences, printed posters and publications, and actually competed with other government agencies over Americanization programs. One such competition took place in 1916 with the Bureau of Naturalization. Although the Bureau of Naturalization thought it had the obligation to Americanize, the Bureau of Education thought it was better qualified. As John McClymer writes, "neither bureau would consider working with the other save in terms of cooptation, and their brief attempt to coordinate fizzled in [the] argument over publicity" (McClymer 1978, 28). From that point forward, both departments would jealously guard their programs, publicly ignoring the Americanization efforts of the others.

In 1920, the commissioner of education was P. P. Claxton. Appointed in 1911, Claxton vigorously believed in immigrant education. In 1914, the Bureau of Education began a nationwide inquiry into immigrant education, and in 1915, Claxton supported "Americanization Day." He proposed that the school system participate in and sponsor various programs, activities and speeches, because he believed a strong school system was the best way to Americanize.

The competition between the bureaus of education and naturalization did not abate. In the meantime, Americanization efforts continued in the public and private sectors. For years the Young Women's Christian Association (YWCA) conducted Americanization programs with its Ballard School and International Institute, teaching courses ranging from mathematics and language to household skills. In 1919, when the Jazz Age was still very young, Edith L. Jardine, general secretary of the YWCA, wrote an article titled "Ideals of the International Institute for Foreign Born Women

Italian immigrants listen intently to their Labor Department instructor who is teaching them English and citizenship in Newark, New Jersey, in the 1920s. Language, cultural, and economic barriers limited the participation and success of new immigrants in standardized testing. (*Library of Congress*)

in New York City," published by that organization in *The W*. In it, Jardine wrote "Immigration may wax and wane, but surely such work as the International Institute carries on what will always be needed in order to bring closer together for mutual benefit the women of all races who meet and commingle in this country" (New York Senate Report 1920).

The Bureau of Education continued to have an edge over other agencies when it came to Americanization programs. Though Claxton believed in Americanization efforts, he saw that without a properly maintained school system such efforts would come to nothing. In 1916, he wrote that "Within the last two years the people of the country have become conscious of the special need for more adequate provision for preparing for American life and possible citizenship the large number of persons who came to this country from southern and eastern European countries" (Report of the Commissioner of Education for the Year Ended June 30, 1917, Office of Education Papers, National Archives).

Maintaining Old World Identities

For many immigrant groups, although learning the American way of life would help them to survive in the new environment, they were anything but helpless. Many arriving immigrants had contacts in the new country who could help them secure a job, find living quarters, and become acclimatized to the United States. Others received help by settling in areas with others from their particular ethnic group.

Immigrant groups maintained their own enclaves within American society. Although they learned English, and how the U.S. system operated, ethnic and racial groups also maintained their cherished institutions through social, religious, and educational organizations. Many groups, such as Italians and Jews, even had their own entertainment venues, which kept them in close touch with their homeland. The Academy Award–winning film *The Godfather Part II* depicted one such theater as the Sicilian immigrant Vito Corleone watched a show that included a character reading a letter from home that his mother was dead.

The problems faced by the Jewish race over the centuries have been innumerable. From biblical times into modern times, Jews encountered obstacles that were threatening, and devastating, to their lives and livelihood. In the 19th century, European Jews began to journey to America in larger numbers. Here many Jews hoped to escape the harsh treatment they were continuously subjected to in their European homelands. But as with some of the other immigrants many native-born Americans wished to exclude, some Jews brought with them radical ideas of how they would change the world. The Jewish radicals in America, most notably the socialists, hoped to inspire unity, especially among the Jewish race.

The issue of immigration divided many members of the Socialist Party. Many Jews did not want restricted immigration, for the problems facing their relatives in the homeland at least had a solution in America. Morris Hillquit, the noted Jewish socialist and attorney, walked a fine line here. To maintain support, he could not advocate exclusionary policies. Yet he warned against the use of immigrants as strikebreakers and cheap labor (in many ways he was referring to the use of Asians, but he also included Europeans). But Jewish immigrants, though eager to support American socialism, were not about to give up their spiritual roots. As Paul Buhle points out, "Jews lacked the illusion of a happier homeland waiting for their return" (Buhle 1987, 83). What they had was their heritage—and the opportunities of America. According to Buhle, this was of the reasons immigrant Jews supported the political aspirations of the famed socialist Eugene V. Debs; he was the "fitting totem of their own unique Americanization, fusion of age-old messianic hope and egalitarian political-economic promise" (Buhle 1987, 82).

The Ku Klux Klan

While the government was attempting to deal with the immigration issue and immigrant population, other segments of American society were taking more stringent action. To them, there was more than one danger involved with immigrants—old or new. The less desirable people entering the country were bad enough with their Old World ways. What was also a threat to cherished American values were the ideas foreigners were bringing with them, be they political or religious. The one group who embodied hatred toward any sort of anti-American sentiment was none other than the Ku Klux Klan.

Early Klan History

The Klan's history goes back to the immediate post–Civil War years. Formed in 1866 in Pulaski, Tennessee, the Klan from the start promoted the idea of white supremacy in America. This meant a white Anglo-Saxon Protestant society. The first grand wizard of the Klan was the former Confederate general Nathan Bedford Forrest. At first, the major target of the Klan was the former slave population. The post–Civil War amendments to the Constitution—the Thirteenth, Fourteenth, and Fifteenth amendments—not only prohibited slavery but also granted citizenship and voting rights to black Americans. To the Klan this was an abomination. The group was not above using terrorism to keep African Americans subjugated to white control, including outright murder, something that many in the legal system did not concern themselves with solving, or preventing. The Klan also victimized the lower-class white population. The former plantation owners, who previously held strong political power, feared losing this power to the poorer whites, the freed slaves, or both. That was something to be countered.

The Klan effectively used terror and intimidation during the post–Civil War years. With the controversial presidential election of 1876, in which Rutherford B. Hayes gained the White House, part of the deal between the Republicans and Democrats was that Hayes would end Reconstruction, especially by withdrawing U.S. troops from the South. This left the black population at the mercy of groups like the Klan. But as Reconstruction ended, so did the influence of the Klan. The group faded into relative obscurity.

Ever since its inception, the Klan was depicted in both positive and negative ways in popular culture. Thomas Dixon Jr.'s novels *The Leopard's Spots* (1902) and *The Clansman* (1905), for example, reminded many of the Klan's former strong presence. In 1915, the famous Hollywood director D. W. Griffith turned *The Clansman* into one of the most controversial, and yet highly praised films of all time, *Birth of a Nation*. From a filmmaking standpoint, it was a monumental achievement. In terms of its positive portrayal of the Klan and highly negative portrayals of African Americans, the film still generates immense controversy. Blacks were portrayed as drunkards, childlike, and ignorant, and black men were depicted as preying on the virtues of decent white women. Griffith was severely chastised for his film. Even his black housekeeper, who named her son after the director, left his employment. He tried to counter the images in *Birth of a Nation* by his follow-up film *Intolerance*.

The Rebirth of the Klan

Besides the overall controversy of the film, *Birth of a Nation* also inadvertently sponsored the birth of a new Klan through the efforts of William

Simmons. Simmons was a former traveling evangelist Methodist preacher who sold memberships to fraternal organizations. Simmons saw the potential of a Klan revival. As David Kyvig points out, Simmons "seized the opportunity presented by the film's appearance to create a new Klan in which he could sell memberships, costumes, and life insurance" (Kyvig 2004, 166). The Klan was revived during a cross-burning ceremony at Stone Mountain, Georgia, in November, 1915.

With an updated Klan came an updated agenda. African Americans were still a major target, but so were any other segments of Americans deemed undesirable, including Catholics, Jews, and, of course, immigrants. The Klan did not limit itself merely to ethnic and religious groups; even certain native-born Americans were suspect. Leftist thought, whether real or imagined, was also denounced by the Klan. Communists, labor leaders, pacifists, anti-Prohibition advocates, and even those who believed in birth control and Darwinism were suspect. Furthermore, the Klan kept a tight watch on its own communities. Those who were not thought to be living proper American behavior, even Klan members, found themselves feeling their wrath. As Kathleen Drowne and Patrick Huber point out, the Klan "also pledged their devotion to protecting the American family, and meted out vigilante justice to bootleggers, wife-beaters, adulterers, and other perceived threats to their communities" (Drowne and Huber 2004, 10).

It is difficult to ascertain the precise number of people who joined the Klan, but by the middle of 1920 there were about several thousand members. By 1924, that number had grown to between 4 and 6 million members, although some sources estimate the number at around 2 million nationwide. One reason for the leap in membership was the efforts of very aggressive and persuasive recruiters. Simmons used the talents of Edward Clarke and Elizabeth Tyler, providing them with an incentive by promising them a high percentage of the initial membership dues collected as a form of commission.

Klan Influence

What must be kept in mind is that the new Klan was not just a localized rural organization in the southern states. Klan membership, as noted, was nationwide, and extended to urban centers like Detroit and Chicago. In some states, such as Indiana, Texas, and Oklahoma, the Klan had considerable political power. The Klan had a powerful presence in the North and the South. For instance, each of Indiana's 92 counties had a Klan chapter. Membership was also open to women. The Women of the Ku Klux Klan had as many as 500,000 members.

If the Klan had an overall reputation as a racist society, why did so many people join? Were all the members in favor of racial, religious, and intellectual purity (or enforced conformity)? Did all members necessarily feel hatred toward blacks, Catholics, and Jews? What was especially marketed to potential Klan members was the protection of America from those who would undermine their treasured institutions. In terms of the country's black citizens, the Klan preyed on fears that intermarriage with whites would pollute white bloodlines. Catholics were believed to have unwavering allegiance to the pope, a foreigner. Jews, who, like Catholics, had already suffered years of persecution, were thought to be greedy and would enlist the "negro race" to help subjugate the world. Left-wing thinking, such as sexual freedom, unsupervised gender interaction, and even political thought whereby absolute social equality was espoused, were all thought to be against traditional American values. Coupled with the continued immigration of peoples from such places as Asia and Eastern and Southern Europe, America had a right to protect itself. The Klan portrayed itself as promoting and selling America, not bigotry.

In addition to engaging in political action, the Klan held parades, dinners, picnics, and various social activities, such as spelling bees. To some members the bigotry embodied in Klan ideology meant little; for them it was an organization that enabled them to mingle with others in their communities. Even if they were aware of any Klan violence, many members had no desire to participate.

As with the previous incarnation of the Klan, the newer version was not above violence to enforce its thinking upon others. Black Americans were lynched for the flimsiest of reasons, including not being out of town at sundown. A Catholic priest was murdered on his own doorstep. Any sort of lawbreakers, or those who practiced a less than desirable lifestyle, might find themselves on the receiving end of a flogging, or perhaps tarred and feathered. The legal system provided little, if any, relief from Klan attacks, especially in the South. Going to the local sheriff for justice from the Klan was often worthless, for that very sheriff might be the local Klan leader. What must be noted was that these attacks were not limited to the South, but, like Klan membership, were nationwide. Even if a sheriff did investigate a Klan-initiated crime, finding witnesses was a near impossibility.

Images of the Klan in Radical Literature

Given all the violence with which the Klan is usually associated, how did some members view their participation in such an organization? Perhaps part of the answer can be found in a work of historical fiction, *The Flivver King* (1937), by the famed socialist writer Upton Sinclair. In this book Sinclair constructs a fictional story around actual historical people and events. Sinclair is honest about his book being a work of historical fiction, yet he makes it clear that when he discusses specific people and events, he draws from the record.

The Flivver King tells the story of Abner Shutt, a man whose life revolves around the evolution of Henry Ford and his car-making empire. Shutt befriends Ford while the latter is first perfecting his automobile in an old shed. When Ford rises as an industrial giant, Shutt remains part of the organization, although his importance to Ford quickly fades as Shutt becomes merely another employee. Shutt even names one of his children Henry, after his beloved boss. Whatever Henry Ford believes, Shutt believes.

As part of the historical portion of the book, Sinclair relates how the Ford Company began printing anti-Semitic articles in the *Dearborn Independent*, a newspaper purchased for the company, which ran from 1920 to 1927. In the pages of the *Independent* Ford began to publish defamatory comments about the Jewish population, especially drawing from a supposed document called *The Protocols of the Elders of Zion*, which outlined how the Jewish race was going to take over the world. Shutt reads these articles and accepts every word. He even suspects those who point out that the *Protocols* contain untrue and inconsistent arguments. In the book, as in real life, Ford actually wrote nothing for the *Independent*. How much he knew about the paper's contents is unsure. Ford issued an apology, which was accepted, and the paper eventually shut down.

But all this comes together for Shutt when Klan representatives approach him for membership after finding his name on a list of *Independent* subscribers. Shutt willingly joins the Klan, especially after being told how that group protects American society from the "Negro insurrection," as well as "Jews, Catholics, Reds, and other alien enemies." Shutt is asked to keep his eyes open for traitors against the country, with stern action being threatened against such agitators. Shutt attends the nighttime cross burnings, and "when those fires had died down, Abner went away assured that Protestant Gentile American civilization was safe" (Sinclair 1937, 58). Although Shutt's participation in, and enthusiasm for, the Klan fades, he joins because he is certain the changes taking place in American society are not for the best. As for the actual *Protocols*, any authenticity in its writing and dissemination has been thoroughly discredited.

Backlash

The Klan itself experienced a sharp decline during the Jazz Age. Although it enjoyed some political power, for the most part the group did not achieve widespread power. Anti-Klan forces began to gain momentum. Even as early 1924, the Klan took numerous hits from foes who fought against their bigotry and violence. In the North, such as in New Jersey, people had violent confrontations with the Klan, and Klan members would flee the scene.

People called for anti-Klan legislation, and soon corruption within the organization came to light. Many Klan leaders were pocketing membership funds, and many of their violent actions were being investigated and protested. The House Rules Committee held hearings about the Klan. Hiram Evans managed to oust Simmons from power. Clarke and Tyler left the organization, membership plummeted, and by the end of the Jazz Age the estimated Klan population had dropped to a mere 10,000. Although the Klan lasted into contemporary times, and continued acts of violence against African Americans, its influence is virtually negligible.

Deep-Rooted Prejudices against Native-Born Citizens

During the Jazz Age, there were two separate elections that dealt with nativist ideals: one was more pronounced than the other, but both involved native-born candidates. In 1920, the famous socialist labor leader, and failed politician, Eugene V. Debs ran for president from a Georgia penitentiary. Debs, born in Terre Haute, Indiana, made his first real mark on the nation when he helped lead the Pullman Strike of 1894, an action that briefly shut down the nation's railroad system. In 1912, he ran for president on the Socialist Party ticket, and garnered an impressive 6 percent of the American vote.

In 1920, however, Debs was in a federal prison for violating the notorious Espionage and Sedition Acts of World War I. Briefly put, these acts suppressed any form of speech or communication that might potentially harm the war effort. Debs's antiwar remarks in Ohio prompted his conviction. Despite his prison sentence, he still ran for president, and came in third place, after James Cox, the Democratic candidate. But what makes this interesting is that during the Jazz Age, as noted, any form of radical ideology was considered anathema to American society. Debs actually placed higher in the total vote count than more "American" political parties, such as the Chicago-based Farmer-Labor Party.

In the 1928 election, strong anti-Catholic sentiments played a part in the continued dominance of the Republicans in the White House. Riding high off of the supposed prosperity of the 1920s, the Republicans nominated Herbert Hoover. The Democrats nominated Alfred E. Smith of New York. Besides the fact that the Republicans were riding a wave of popularity, Smith's albatross was that he was Catholic. Once again, the old fears that the pope would take over the country should a Catholic be elected president rose to the surface. What added fuel to the fire was that Smith's parents were immigrants, despite the fact he was native born.

Smith was not entirely unloved. He presented a counterpoint to the nativism that haunted the Jazz Age. Smith had considerable support in many areas of the country, not mention that he sided with anti-Prohibition forces. But those who opposed Smith were very well prepared for the fight, especially the leaders of Protestant America. Some proclaimed that a vote for Smith would be to support Satan himself. Hoover trounced Smith in the electoral college, and the Republicans maintained their strength in both houses of Congress.

Conclusion

Again, the question of what it means to be American arises. Is being American a form of purity? People have used the phrases "melting pot" and "salad bowl" to describe American society. Whether one image is more true than the other, or if the truth is a combination of the two, the idea of purity remains. Was remaining pure to one's roots just as important as maintaining the purity of the new country? For many nativists there was no plurality in American society, only the preservation of cherished ideals. But what ideals were in fact treasured across American society? What was a cherished American tradition? Even among the native born, this was unclear. Even those who could claim generation upon generation of ancestors in America knew that although some customs remained, others were changed with time.

As stated earlier, there was still a strong sense of tribalism in the Jazz Age. Sometimes it was an "us vs. them" sort of situation; at other times there were nods of respect. But is this sense of tribalism unique to this specific period of American history? Of course not. Even the smallest study of American history reveals the many voices that helped shaped the country, stretching all the way back to the first permanent settlement of Jamestown in 1607.

So where did the notion of *Americanism* come about? To be sure, certain institutions became more pronounced than others during the first crucial years (even centuries), such as the notions of a democratic society, the dominance of the Protestant religions, the cherished belief in capitalism and private enterprise, and the idea that Americans knew how to take care of themselves. Were these notions in fact true, as stated by Turner in the frontier thesis? Perhaps, but was Turner taking pluralism into account? Even from Jamestown all the way to 1893, when Turner presented his paper, most people who settled America may have come from a select few places—such as England, Germany, France, and Scandinavia—but each of these countries had its own cultures, traditions, and nuances.

Even at the start of the American Revolution, many people living in America still identified with their native land, no matter how many generations removed from that land they might have been. As stated earlier, Turner himself recognized that our initial institutions were brought over from the Old World, yet the United States evolved into a unique land. Turner's ideas were presented at a crucial juncture in American history when many new people were entering the country. One can only wonder what he might say now.

With the term *Americanism* comes an implication, albeit often subtle, of a sense of conformity on some level. The notion of unity is seen on both the Left and the Right. Nor is it unavoidable. It has been said that modern times has seen the triumph of pluralism. After examining the role of immigrants and nativism in American history, it can be argued that this triumph occurred long ago.

References and Further Reading

Buhle, Paul. *Marxism in the United States*. London: Verso, 1987.

Davis, James John. Papers. Library of Congress. Manuscript Collections. Washington, DC.

Dinnerstein, Leonard, and David M. Reimers. *Ethnic Americans: A History of Immigration and Assimilation*. New York: Harper and Row, 1975.

Drowne, Kathleen, and Patrick Huber. *The 1920s*. Westport, CT: Greenwood Press, 2004.

Higham, John. *Send These to Me: Jews and Other Immigrants in Urban America*. New York: Antheum, 1975.

Kellen, Stuart A. *The Roaring Twenties*. San Diego: Greenhaven Press, 2002.

Kraut, Alan. *The Huddled Masses*. Arlington Heights, IL: Harlan Davidson, 1982.

Kyvig, David E. *Daily Life in the United States, 1920–1940*. Chicago: Ivan R. Dee, 2002.

McClymer, John. "The Federal Government and the Americanization Movement, 1915–1924." *Prologue* 10 (Spring 1978): 23–41.

National Archives. Records of the Office of Education. Record Group 12. Entry 6, Historical File. Washington, D.C.

Olneck, Michael R., and Marvin Lazerson. "The School Achievement of Immigrant Children, 1900–1930." *History of Education Quarterly* (Fall 1969): 524–543.

Perrett, Geoffrey. *America in the Twenties*. New York: Simon and Schuster, 1982.

Report of the Joint Legislative Committee Investigating Seditious Activities, Filed April 24, 1920, in the Senate of the State of New York. *Revolutionary Radicalism: Its History, Purpose and Tactics*. Volumes 3–4.

"Revolutionary Radicalism." Report of the Joint Legislative Committee Investigating Seditious Activities. Senate of the State of New York. Part II, Volume II (1920).

Sinclair, Upton. *The Flivver King*. 1937. Reprint, Chicago: Chicago H. Kerr, 1987.

Zolberg, Aristide. *A Nation by Design: Immigration Policy in the Fashioning of America*. Cambridge, MA: Harvard University Press, 2006.

Reformers, Radicals, and Socialists | 8

Mitchell Newton-Matza

Historians generally place the start of the Progressive Era around the year 1890, but the landslide election of Warren G. Harding to the presidency in 1920 marked its end. After President Woodrow Wilson's two terms in office, the country turned away from Wilsonian Democracy to a seemingly more conservative era. The change in political alignment from the Democratic to the Republican Party did in fact start the country in a new direction, but this direction took many paths.

On the eve of the Jazz Age, the year 1917 signaled hope for many, fear in others. While still in the grip of World War I, Russia experienced two revolutions in 1917: the March revolution, which eliminated the Romanov dynasty currently under Czar Nicholas II, and the November revolution, where the Bolsheviks, under Vladimir Lenin, seized control of the country. This sent shock waves around the world, for many believed such a revolution was then possible in their own country.

For radicals and reformers, it appeared as if the times were becoming more dangerous than ever. When World War I broke out, many did in fact see it as a justification of Marxist thought. Many in the radical community believed the working classes would refuse to fight in what they saw as a capitalist war and would rise up against their governments. At the same time, governments feared that such uprisings would take place and were growing increasing suspicious of potentially traitorous activities. On March 25, 1918, just as the Jazz Age was beginning, California congressman Julius Kahn exclaimed, "When a seditious or traitorous voice is raised here, I hope the law will reach out and grasp the speaker. I hope that we shall have a few prompt hangings" (*New York Times* March 25, 1918). Kahn's statement reflects its period.

The Radical Identity

What did it really mean to be a radical, reformer, or, for that matter, a socialist during the Jazz Age? Did one need to meet specific qualifications? When one considers the plethora of mainstream activities during this time, one might think a person would have to be truly outrageous to be considered a radical. The Jazz Age was not an isolated period; it was born out of the post–World War I era, in which antiquated Victorian era values were no longer the norm. As American society began to reevaluate, refine, redefine, and even defend, traditional values, it was not always easy for some to know where they stood.

To understand this, one must think of the terms *culture* and *counterculture*. Culture is typically considered to refer to "the customary beliefs, social forms and material traits of a racial, religious or social group." Although certain characteristics may come into being instantaneously and become part of the dominant thought, cultures take years to develop and are always changing.

Counterculture refers to "a group or movement which can be seen as opposing

The Red Scare

World War I began in 1914 for the European nations, but the United States did not become actively involved until 1917. The American entry into World War I met with mixed reactions within the country and some fear of internal dissent. Two of the methods used to deal with the fear were the Espionage Act of 1917 and the Sedition Act of 1918 (generally referred to together as the Espionage and Sedition Acts). The Espionage Act allowed the government to imprison and/or fine those convicted of disloyalty and obstructing the conduct of the draft, whether by word or deed. The following year, amended sections became the Sedition Act, which allowed people to be prosecuted for "writing, printing, or uttering profane or abusive language about the government, the Constitution, the flag, or the armed forces, or tending to curtail production" (McDonald 1986, 118). Writer and radical Max Eastman remembers that "This elemental hysteria was whipped up by public officials and prominent citizens as well as the press. The country was advised to mob, whip, shoot and kill all dissenters" (Eastman 1964, 29).

The autumn of 1919 would begin the Palmer raids, led by the Department of Justice under A. Mitchell Palmer. This series of mass arrests against political and labor agitators led to deportation for those who were not American citizens. Raids were carried out in no less than 33 cities, and 2,700 people were arrested. Although the validity of the search and arrest warrants was debated, it did not prevent the deportations or incarcerations. Many victims of the raids had committed no crimes, but they were suspect because of their beliefs and/or ethnic backgrounds. Adding fuel to the fire, postal workers discovered no less than 34 mail bombs addressed to or subverting the dominant culture." During the Jazz Age this includes the political outsiders, artists, writers, musicians, and even the young girls who bobbed their hair, wore short skirts, and danced to jazz music. Polite society frowned on certain forms of thought and behavior, believing the old ways were the best.

But when examining those considered to be part of the counterculture, one must consider the word *intentions*. Certain counterculture members did indeed engage in open activities with the sole purpose of garnering attention and upsetting others, but many others were merely trying to live their lives as they saw fit. Many believed their activities were going to benefit society by improving, not overturning, it.

The difference between "traditional" and "radical" is usually defined by those who are dominant in any particular culture. During the Jazz Age, which was coping with the sweeping changes in society brought about by World War I, it was not always easy to know which label a person might fit.

government officials. In December 1919, the infamous Soviet Ark (in actuality the USS *Buford*) sailed, deporting 294 people to Russia, including the anarchist Emma Goldman. The Palmer raids were suspended in May 1920.

Labor Strife Hits the Country

The great strike wave of 1919 took place early in the Jazz Age. Not even a full two years after the revolutions in Russia during 1917, these mass strikes frightened mainstream American society; many believed the American way of life would come to an end if swift action were not taken. The intentions of those who participated varied. Some wanted to replace the existing order, while others merely wanted to improve upon it. Regardless, the fears of a Bolshevik revolution in the United States, coming straight on the heels of victory in World War I, were very real. With one-fifth of the workforce on strike at the beginning of the Jazz Age, about 4 million workers thought these fears were justified.

Seattle

Seattle was the city where the whole scene was put into motion. During World War I workers around the country won numerous concessions, especially in terms of wage increases. The government was willing to provide such benefits if workers would promise not to strike and to keep the wartime production machinery moving. After the war, many of the concessions began to disappear. Maintaining a higher wage scale, along with other benefits such as shorter hours, was no longer a wartime necessity; therefore, it was no longer a concern of employers or the federal government. Many members of American society believed workers were responsible for the rise in the cost of living during the war. Furthermore, organized labor maintained a reputation for being controlled by what were viewed as undesirable elements, namely the radical sector, many of whom were foreign born.

At issue here was the dissatisfaction of the shipyard workers. Seattle was known as a strong union town, and its shipyard workers numbered around 35,000. When pay raises came to a halt, the workers went out on strike in January 1919. In less than two weeks, more than 65,000 workers throughout the city had joined the strike, which crippled the city.

What gave many people pause about the strike was not the numbers involved; rather, it was how the city was run once the strike was in full swing. Parallels to the Bolshevik revolution were abundant. Since the Russian Bolsheviks were considered evil, and the workers of Seattle were supposedly behaving like their Russian counterparts, clearly some believed revolution was beginning in the United States. Mayor Ole Hanson had armed police and troops on hand, and he almost declared martial law. However, this was not a revolution. Rather, the strike was peaceful.

The General Strike Committee ran numerous services. In working out of community kitchens, the cooks' union was said to have served as many as 20,000 meals a day. Children were provided with milk. World War I veterans even served as patrolmen. But the experiment was not to last. Using pressure, major national labor leaders persuaded Seattle workers to end the strike before their demands were met. Although the strike ended, as did the workers' control of the city, what happened in Seattle inspired many others. To many radicals, what the General Strike Committee accomplished proved Marxist theory in that the workers could not only seize the economic and political system but could effectively control it as well.

Boston

Probably the most disturbing strike in 1919, in terms of public safety, came when the Boston police force went on strike after 19 officers who were trying to affiliate the police with the American Federation of Labor (AFL) were suspended. The strike was seen as a betrayal of public trust, especially because the strike prompted a crime wave. Massachusetts governor Calvin Coolidge stepped in and fired the entire police force, stating that none of the fired officers would ever be allowed to return. State troops were called in to maintain order, and Coolidge turned to war veterans to fill vacated spots. Such actions not only won Coolidge public favor but ultimately led the Republican Party to nominate him as vice president on Harding's ticket.

The Steel Industry

Another important strike of 1919 was the steel industry strike. U.S. Steel already had a reputation for vigorously fighting labor organization. The chairman of U.S. Steel, Elbert H. Gary, refused to meet with labor leaders

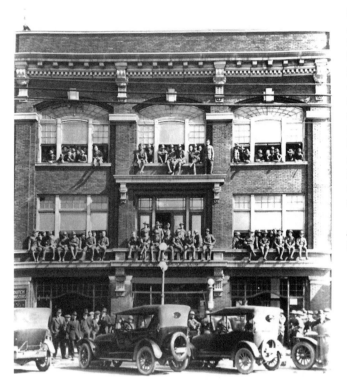

Elbert Gary was an American lawyer and industrialist involved in the steel industry. He improved the conditions of his workers on his own, but was opposed to unionization. His opposition led to a large-scale strike of steelworkers in 1919–1920. Here are the Troops in Gary during the strike. (*Calument Regional Archives, Indiana University N.W.*)

to try to avoid a strike, which then began on September 22. More than 350,000 workers in 10 states walked off the job, all but shutting down the steel industry. Taking center stage in the steelworkers' organization was the radical William Z. Foster. Joining in the fight alongside Foster was John Fitzpatrick, the longtime president of the Chicago Federation of Labor (CFL). Although the two would eventually have a falling out a few years later, their radical stance toward unionization frightened the more conservative elements of the AFL. For starters, the AFL was a craft union, meaning that only workers with a specific skill were eligible for unionization. Foster and Fitzpatrick believed in industrial unionism, meaning that anyone who worked and earned a wage was eligible for organization.

The steel companies were not going to sit by quietly. They fought back, often violently. Frequently supported by local governments, many companies had striking workers physically assaulted. Even though Wilson pleaded for the two sides to meet, the steel company owners refused to comply. And, as with any of the other strikes during 1919, the striking workers were characterized as radicals.

The steel strike eventually failed in January 1920, for reasons including apathy on the part of many workers, the strength of the government forces and steel companies, and the overall fear of revolution in the United States. Many believe the 1920s were a period of decline for labor, yet at the start of the New Deal labor still had the strength to win many concessions, some that would last for decades. The labor movement emerged from the 1920s with a sense of purpose and the will to continue to fight.

The Battle of Education and Americanization Programs

Beginnings

Not every issue during the Jazz Age had to do with labor strife. Education was one area in which people from both the Left and the Right were looking for reform. This was especially embodied in an annual event called *American Education Week* (AEW), which the Bureau of Education launched in 1920. Originally designed to promote improvements in the school system, it became instead a battleground where the Left and the Right stood toe to toe in what they saw as a battle over control of what would be taught in the educational system.

AEW can be considered part of the Americanization programs of the time, a reaffirmation of national principles. One must be careful, however, not to paint government education programs as merely an attempt to maintain the status quo. There were many sincere efforts to educate both the "ignorant" immigrant and the "unenlightened" citizen. AEW began innocently; its advocates had a genuine concern for the nation's schools. Within time, it became a program that was targeted for its seemingly ultra-conservative views.

The Bureau of Education was established as an independent agency in May 1867. Originally named the Department of Education, its independent status was stripped in 1868; it was renamed the Office of Education and placed under the Department of the Interior. In 1870, the agency was renamed the Bureau of Education, remaining as such until it was reestablished as the Office of Education in 1929. Its original function was to collect and analyze information about education. Within time, its duties were expanded to include providing vocational education, conducting conferences, and producing research surveys and publications. The bureau was involved in Americanization programs long before AEW. It sponsored conferences, printed posters and publications, and competed with other government agencies. One such competition took place in 1916 with the Bureau of Naturalization, which felt it had the better obligation to Americanize. As John McClymer writes, "neither bureau would consider working with the other save in terms of cooptation, and their brief attempt to coordinate fizzled in [the] argument over publicity" (McClymer 1978, 28).

American Education Week

The precursor to AEW came in 1920 with the announcement of *School Week*, which was to take place December 5–11. The goal was to improve the schools and "to take such actions as may be necessary to cause the people to use this week as will most effectively disseminate among the people accurate information in regard to the conditions and needs of the schools, enhance appreciation of the value of education, and create such

Boston police pose with literature and pamphlets seized from a raid at Communist Party head-quarters in Cambridge, Massachusetts, in November 1919. Anti-communist raids were held in most large cities across the nation, as "red scare," the irrational but rampant fear of communism, swept through the United States. A second wave of red scare occurred during the McCarthyism era in the 1940s and 1950s. (*Topical Press Agency/Getty Images*)

interest as will result in better opportunities for education" (National Archives, Records of the Office of Education 1920). The program was well received, and various government, civic, and religious groups were invited to participate.

In 1921, John Tigert was appointed commissioner of the Bureau of Education. Although he was relatively unknown, Tigert's appointment was a bit controversial. Opponents declared the move political, and some even claimed he was the nephew of Secretary of the Interior Albert Fall, who would later go to prison as a result of the infamous Teapot Dome Scandal. The Senate Committee of Education even held up Tigert's appointment for several weeks. To many, Tigert was a "red-baiter," and he even "declared his determination to eliminate 'communism, bolshevism, and socialism' from the schools" (Quoted in Iverson 1959, 13). But upon taking the oath of office, Tigert at once attempted to appease his critics by calling for more funds for education and making contact with his bitter opponents.

AEW got its official start when President Harding declared that the week of December 4–10, 1921, would be American Education Week. AEW would encompass many of the goals set forth by the original program: Care for public education, eradicating illiteracy, and the improvement of educational facilities. But Harding's proclamation also asserted that

". . . our future strength and security are much dependent on their education and commitment to American ideals" (National Archives, Records of the Office of Education 1921). One group volunteering to help with America's "future and strength" was the American Legion, a fiercely patriotic society.

In 1921, AEW passed without much fanfare. On October 13, 1922, Tigert issued a letter announcing the next event for the week of December 3–9. There would be days with designated purposes, each one addressing a particular concern. Tigert wrote that "Sunday shall be observed as God and Country Day; Monday, Citizenship Day; Tuesday, Patriotism Day; Wednesday, School and Teacher Day; Thursday, Illiteracy Day; Friday, Equality of Opportunity Day; and Saturday, Physical Education Day" (National Archives, Records of the Office of Education 1922).

To many, the week seemed to be becoming a forum for Tigert and the American Legion. However, Tigert did reach out to as many organizations as possible, offering literature and advice. Quite often, the American Legion distributed its own literature, presenting advice about how to act as a "proper" citizen. The 1922 AEW was not a headline-making venture either. It was the 1923 AEW where the true controversies would begin.

Although Tigert sincerely called for the usual focus on physical health, improving school conditions, and equal educational opportunities, ominous tones were growing. The program for 1923 was Sunday, For God and Country; Monday, Constitution Day; Tuesday, Patriotism Day; Wednesday, School Teacher and Community Day; Thursday, Illiteracy Day; Friday, Physical Education Day. Slogans were devised to correspond with each day. For God and Country Day, groups were to organize mass meetings and use speakers from the American Legion. For Constitution Day, Tigert and the American Legion pronounced "Revolutionists and Radicals a menace to [Constitutional] guarantees." For Illiteracy Day, the program announced "No immigration until illiteracy among native and foreign born is removed" (National Archives, Records of the Office of Education 1923).

During this period the immigration issue was indeed a hot topic; Secretary of Labor James John Davis, himself an immigrant from Wales, remarked that "I would admit to America only the alien who is able and willing to accept American customs, American ideals, American institutions, and who can contribute something to the advancement of our civilization" (Davis Papers 1923). The American Legion especially welcomed this kind of support. But when the Bureau of Education announced the 1924 version of AEW, a battle was in the works.

The 1924 Controversy

The press release, dated September 22, 1924, announced that AEW was scheduled for the week of November 17–23. Among the usual attention to overall school improvement, there were a few new twists:

Monday, Constitution Day

1. Life, liberty, justice, security, and opportunity
2. How our Constitution guarantees these rights.

3. Revolutionists, communists, and extreme pacifists are a menace to these guarantees.

Tuesday, Patriotism Day

1. The red flag means death, destruction, poverty, starvation, disease, anarchy, and dictatorship.

Even before President Calvin Coolidge could make the official proclamation, there were widespread protests across the nation. For example, the *New York World* printed articles reporting the program as "militaristic" and "marked by intolerant propaganda against progressive political and industrial thought under the guise of combating radicalism." Another article claimed "[It is] a deliberate attempt to stamp minority ideas as treasonable" (*New York World* November 4, 1924). Letters also came from all sectors of society, most of which argued that the 1924 AEW strayed from what was originally intended. L. E. Bowman, professor of political science at Columbia, stated "Surely true education speaks of truth, not inflammatory opinions against any set of people." Herbert A. Miller of Ohio State University wrote "I feel it to be a national disgrace. Its purpose is propaganda rather than enlightenment. The whole atmosphere . . . is very unhealthy." The Baltimore Department of Education protested because "the program proposed for Education Week this year departs from the purely educational purposes for which the week was established" (National Archives, Records of the Office of Education 1924). Many others used Christianity as their weapon when it came to denouncing "extreme pacifists." With so many antiradicals espousing American Protestant values, many pointed out that Jesus advocated peace.

This is not to say that Tigert was not without his supporters. Tigert was not a puppet of the American Legion; his views were merely identical. The *Washington Post* printed an unsigned editorial that complained about the protests, arguing that if "it were Soviet Education or Internationale Education Week, they would yell their throats hoarse in praise." Since AEW was devoted to American ideals, "they protest against it as the crime of all ages!" (*Washington Post* November 6–8, 1924).

Criticisms of AEW continued, though not as heavily, through the first half of 1925. On July 9, the program for that year was released. Once again held under the joint auspices of the National Education Association and the American Legion, the program, scheduled for November 16–22, promoted so-called American ideals, but in a more subtle context, and without condemning diverse points of view. The controversy was over. The following year the Bureau of Education announced it would no longer be part of AEW, turning such activities over to the states.

The Controversy over Evolution

In terms of radicals and reformers in the area of education, nothing exemplifies the battle between progress and preservation of traditional American

Portrait of John Scopes, tried for violating the Tennesse ban on teaching evolution. Scopes' defense team wanted a conviction in order to challenge the validity of the law in the state supreme court. (*Library of Congress*)

religious values more than the infamous Scopes "Monkey" Trial of 1925. Schoolteacher John Scopes was arrested and tried in Dayton, Tennessee, for teaching evolution in violation of state law. Both sides of this controversial issue would claim to be reforming the current system. It would also become the media event of the year.

The center of the storm here was the state of Tennessee's ban on the teaching of evolution in the schools. Kentucky considered such a law during 1921–1922, but Tennessee took a step further. In January 1925, John Washington Butler proposed an act to ban the teaching of evolution in the public schools. Although the bill passed the state house of representatives by an incredibly wide margin, the measure was debated with a lot more vigor in the state senate. The Butler bill was eventually passed, and signed into law, though Governor Austin Peay did not believe anyone would actually try to enforce the law.

At the heart of the matter, to supporters of the law, was the protection of the fundamentalist belief in the Bible, especially concerning the creation of the world in six days. Charles Darwin's theory of evolution, which held that all species of life developed and evolved over time through natural selection, seemed to contradict the teachings of the Bible. The Tennessee law banned the teaching of any theory holding that humans were descended from a lower form of animals.

Even within the scientific community Darwin's theory was hotly debated. To the fundamentalists who wished to preserve their way of life, Darwin's theory challenged their very beliefs; the Bible was to be taken literally. To those who believed in Darwin's theory, his scientific observations paved the way to further understanding how the world operated. Many supporters of evolution believed the theory of evolution and the Bible could be reconciled. After all, the Bible just related how the world came into being; it did not provide the step-by-step process or the ingredients.

The American Civil Liberties Union (ACLU) held that the law was unconstitutional and sought to challenge it in court, so they needed someone to stand up against it. The ACLU found their hero in John Scopes, who agreed to admit he taught evolution. Kentucky native Scopes was 24 years old at the time of the trial and had a good reputation as a teacher. It is not certain that Scopes actually ever taught evolution, but his admission was enough. On May 7, 1925, Scopes was arrested and charged for teaching aspects of evolution in an April 24, 1925 class.

The Trial Becomes a Media Circus

The trial became a national sensation. Both sides enlisted heavy hitters to forward their cause. The fundamentalist side secured the famous William Jennings Bryan to serve on the prosecution side. Bryan had a long life in politics. He had run for president unsuccessfully several times and had served as secretary of state under Wilson. During the 1890s, he had appeared to be quite liberal. Now he appeared to be a staunch conservative, upholding antiquated beliefs. Bryan supported the Butler bill but not the criminal penalties; now he was going to defend the law in court.

Opposing the law, and defending Scopes, was the infamous liberal Chicago lawyer Clarence Darrow. Darrow had a reputation for taking on difficult cases. Besides the Scopes trial Darrow's most famous case was defending the child murderers Leopold and Loeb and saving them from the death penalty. Darrow and Bryan were actually old friends; there are numerous photos of the two amicably conversing, even smiling at each other, during the trial. They had supported the same social causes in the past.

The trial began on July 10, 1925, and was a media circus. Presiding over the trial was Judge John T. Raulston, who had a minister open each day's proceedings with a prayer. On the streets of Dayton vendors sold food, toy monkeys, and Bibles. Newspapers across the country followed the trial intensely, and the proceedings were broadcast over the radio.

Darrow did his best to defend Darwinian theory by bringing in scientists to testify as expert witnesses. Judge Raulston refused to allow such

Clarence Darrow (leaning) during the Scopes trial. The trial of John T. Scopes, a high school teacher charged with illegally teaching the theory of evolution, took place in Dayton, Tennessee, in 1925 and was highly publicized as a battle between religion and science. (*Library of Congress*)

testimony. On the seventh day of the trial Darrow switched tactics. In a highly unorthodox move, he placed Bryan on the stand to testify as an expert witness on the Bible. At this point that trial was taking place outside the courthouse. Although Bryan testified that the Bible should be taken literally, he would later remark that portions of the Bible may use language consistent with the ancient times and not the present. But the big moment came when Bryan conceded that the story of the world's creation in six days might not have actually been a literal period of six days of 24 hours each. To the fundamentalists, this was a betrayal of all they held dear. The jury was not present for this testimony, there was no actual legal use for the cross-examination, and Judge Raulston would toss out Bryan's remarks.

Darrow never once claimed Scopes was innocent; on the contrary, even during his closing remarks he reiterated to the jury that Scopes was guilty. The reasoning was simple; Darrow wanted a conviction in order to appeal the case to the Tennessee Supreme Court, which might overturn the law. Scopes was found guilty and fined $100. Scopes did not testify at the trial, but before sentencing he did speak to the judge about opposing this ''unjust law.'' Upon appeal Scopes' conviction was tossed out. However, the antievolution law remained on the Tennessee books for another four decades. The trial would later receive further immortalization with the stage play, and later film, entitled *Inherit the Wind*.

The Move Toward a Third Political Party

Although many in the radical sector believed the times were difficult, for others there was a great deal of hope. In the realm of politics, the CFL attempted what had been tried many times before: creating a viable labor party that would appear beneficial for all of society, not just the working class. For the CFL, this would be a courageous, yet dangerous, step, for as intense anti-radicalism grew, the chances for success diminished. However noble an attempt, there were too many obstacles.

Longtime CFL president John Fitzpatrick, who was very much involved in the steel strike of 1919, had dreamed of a labor party for years. This dream became a reality on December 29, 1918, when the Labor Party of Cook County was created. Although this was a local political party for the Chicago area, Fitzpatrick established it with the hope that it would eventually develop into a national organization. But there were some concerns. The federal government was cracking down harshly on dissidents. People were still being prosecuted for opposing World War I under the controversial Espionage and Sedition Acts. Even within the labor movement itself, the AFL, under Samuel Gompers, opposed any sort of independent political action. Furthermore, opposition came from other segments of the radical community, namely the Socialist Party, who felt it best represented the needs of labor.

Echoing sentiments voiced many times over previous years, the Labor Party stated that the two existing main political parties did not represent the needs of the working class. Many of the party's platforms called for measures often considered socialistic. For instance, the democratic control of industry and public ownership of transportation and utilities were somewhat controversial ideas back in the 19th century. Other forward-looking measures included a reduced cost of living, equal gender rights in government and industry, the eight-hour workday, and, in an attack on the Espionage and Sedition Acts, complete freedom of speech. To keep these issues before the public, the CFL created a labor newspaper, the *New Majority*.

Any successes for the Labor Party were dismal at best, although it did place third overall in Chicago elections, outpacing the Socialist Party. However, with each new election came new disappointments. The CFL did not quit and moved swiftly to establish a national party. The first national convention of this new labor party met in Chicago in November 1919, with delegates from across the country. But while the CFL was creating a national party, the party saw a drop in attendance at conventions at the state and local levels. The national party met again in July 1920 and adopted the name Farmer-Labor Party. Although it was a creation of the CFL, the Farmer-Labor Party was a conglomeration of many groups. The Progressive politician Robert LaFollette was thought to be the favorite for the Farmer-Labor Party's presidential candidate, but they chose Parley Parker Christensen, with Max Hayes as vice president.

The presidential election of 1920 was a complete and utter disaster for the Farmer-Labor Party. The Republican candidate Warren G. Harding was swept into office. The Farmer-Labor Party could not even manage 1 percent of the vote. Eugene Debs, running for president from a prison cell (for violating the Espionage and Sedition Acts), garnered more votes. With each passing election and each passing year, the dreams of the CFL grew dimmer. In 1923, led by communist William Z. Foster, a former labor organizing partner of Fitzpatrick's, the communists would eventually take over the party. In 1924, the CFL officially abandoned the Farmer-Labor Party and returned to the AFL fold of nonpartisan political action. To further distance themselves from the communist-controlled party, the CFL changed the name of the *New Majority* to *Federation News*.

The Socialists

Another radical organization looking for survival during the Jazz Age, and having better luck than the Industrial Workers of the World (IWW), was the Socialist Party of America (SPA). The SPA was created in 1901, a combination of two previously existing groups, the Socialist Labor Party of America and the Social Democratic Party. Unlike many other radical organizations, the SPA did find some political successes across the country, sending numerous candidates to local offices and two candidates to Congress. The SPA's strongest supporters appeared to come from immigrant groups, especially from the German and Jewish segments.

The relationship between the SPA and other groups fluctuated between cooperation and outright disrespect. Many members of the SPA, such as Debs, were founding members of the IWW. As for the SPA's relationship with the AFL, there was not much love lost either way. The AFL was openly hostile to the SPA, even though some members of the SPA believed a merger was possible. Max Hayes, who was the CFL's 1920 candidate for vice president in their failed attempt at a labor party, held on to hope for such a merger.

As with many other radical groups, real or perceived, World War I proved to be a challenging time. Opposing the war meant bringing down the wrath of the government; supporting the war would be seen as a betrayal of their beliefs. Risking prison, many openly came out against the war, although some within the party supported the war. In 1918, Debs openly came out against the war and the draft. This action resulted in a prison sentence of 10 years. Despite a court challenge that made its way to the Supreme Court, his conviction was upheld. However, in 1921, in calmer times, Debs received a pardon from Harding. This did not prevent Debs from running for president from his prison cell; as mentioned earlier, he actually had a better showing than the Farmer-Labor Party. Debs earned fewer than a million votes, just over 3.4 percent of the total tally, whereas the Farmer-Labor Party as a whole could not garner even 1 percent. Debs was actually accustomed to such showings in the polls. In his 1912 presidential bid, he received just over 900,000 votes, or 6 percent of the total.

The SPA would not field a presidential candidate in 1924, preferring instead to support the Progressive Robert LaFollette. The SPA would eventually return to the political arena. As for their other political aspirations, in 1920, five of their members were expelled by the New York State Assembly for their political associations. Unlike the challenge Debs presented concerning his conviction, these five individuals also took their case to the Supreme Court and were allowed to return to office.

The Creation of the Communist Party

For the left-wing community, the debate over the communist takeover of Russia would be a dividing issue. The SPA would split over support for the Bolsheviks. As with the IWW, there was not necessarily ideological purity throughout the organization. Differences of opinion are only natural, especially with Lenin's January 1919 invitation for the left wing of the SPA to participate in the founding of the Communist Third International, also known as the Comintern. However, the SPA had expelled certain sections of the party, and those who were expelled and supported the Bolshevists met in June 1919 to make plans to return to the party. One group broke away, and, led by Louis Fraina and Charles Ruthenberg, formed the Communist Party of America on September 2, 1919.

The formation of an American Communist Party presented some competition. Writer John Reed, whose eyewitness account of the Bolshevik revolution, *Ten Days That Shook the World*, remains a classic work, and Benjamin Gitlow went forward with their plans to take over the SPA convention. However, word had gotten out, and the police were ready to escort Reed's group from the convention. On September 1, just one day before Fraina's move, the Communist Labor Party was created in Chicago, the same town as the subsequent group. Both groups sought recognition from Moscow; the Russian communists would not acknowledge either group, but, rather, urged them to become a single organization. In 1921, these two groups would in fact merge to create the Communist Party of the USA.

The Sacco and Vanzetti Case

Origins of the Case

The one case that probably exemplified the feelings toward radicals during the Jazz Age was the trial of Sacco and Vanzetti. What started out as a crime involving robbery and murder became a pronounced statement about the legal system, immigrants, and the freedom of political beliefs. As with the Scopes trial, even in contemporary times the case of Sacco and Vanzetti continues to elicit considerable discussion.

The story began in South Braintree, Massachusetts, on April 15, 1920. Frederick Parmenter, a paymaster, and Alessandro Berardelli, a guard, were transporting $16,000 in payroll money in two metal lockboxes for the Slater and Morrill shoe factory. Two criminals ambushed the men, shooting and robbing them. Nicola Sacco and Bartolomeo Vanzetti were arrested for the crime on May 5.

Bartolomeo Vanzetti (center left) and Nicola Sacco (center right), immigrant Italian anarchists con-victed of armed robbery and murder, enter the Dedham, Massachusetts courthouse in handcuffs. The two were executed in 1927 for the crimes they were convicted of committing in 1920. Their conviction and execution were debated throughout the world and called into question the fair-ness and objectivity of the American justice system. (*Library of Congress*)

Sacco and Vanzetti were Italian immigrants and anarchists. As noted, in 1920 there was enough fear of radicalism, not to mention that of immigrants, and Italian immigrants were looked at with little, if any, favor. People like Sacco and Vanzetti were hardly accepted into mainstream American society. When they were arrested, there was little chance of their being treated fairly, especially as both men were armed. Sacco was also carrying an anarchist meeting announcement, which had been written by Vanzetti.

The first questionings by the police and the district attorney did not work out well for the two men. They showed their distrust of the police and did not answer the questions truthfully. This would be brought up at their trial, although much of what the police asked them had nothing to do with the actual crime. Despite the lack of any real evidence linking Sacco and Vanzetti to the crime, the trial began on May 31, 1921, presided over by Judge Webster Thayer, who had asked for the case.

In addition to their ethnicity and political beliefs, the two defendants had another mark against them; in 1919, Vanzetti had been convicted of a different robbery in Bridgewater. That trial alone was a farce. Many of the witnesses for the prosecution had previously changed their stories several times—a fact not known to the defense—and some of the witnesses supporting Vanzetti's innocence testified in Italian, using an interpreter, which made their testimony suspect. Obviously, none of this was in Vanzetti's favor, and when his trial with Sacco began, the sentiments against the defendants—already highly negative in the first place—worsened.

The Trial

Prosecuting the case was Frederick Katzmann, who was also behind Vanzetti's earlier conviction. The defendants produced witnesses to show they were elsewhere at the moment that the crime was committed. As with Vanzetti's first conviction, the fact that these witnesses were Italian made their testimony suspect. In contrast, the testimony of the prosecution's witnesses was very much questionable; one witness actually testified under a false name. As with some of the witnesses in Vanzetti's solo trial, some of the testimony was revised from earlier statements. Other testimony did not ring true. For example, one woman had identified Sacco from a distance of approximately 80 feet, from in a moving car that was at its closest point 30 feet away. Attorneys on both sides were guilty of misconduct. Some prosecution witnesses were pressured into their testimonies; one of the defense attorneys used blackmail on one witness and got another one intoxicated to get him to sign a renunciation form (which was itself renounced). Regardless, the eyewitness testimonies against Sacco and Vanzetti were in doubt.

When examining the material evidence related to Sacco and Vanzetti the case turns even more controversial. The gun Vanzetti had on him at the time of the arrest proved problematic. It was difficult to place that particular gun at the crime scene, even though the prosecution said it was stolen from the guard. Other evidence, such as the stolen money and the car, could not be linked to either man. In the case of Sacco, the ballistic evidence would play a central role. One of the bullets matched the caliber of Sacco's gun, but whether the fatal shot was fired from Sacco's gun was a matter of mere speculation.

It has been noted time and again that the trial was really about the fact that Sacco and Vanzetti were Italian anarchists. Although many believe the defense attorneys failed to attack the flimsy and nonsensical evidence presented by the prosecution, there can be little doubt that an acquittal would never have happened. On July 14, 1921, the jury convicted both men, deliberating less than a single day. The appeals began at once and, as required under the current Massachusetts law, were heard by Judge Thayer, who not only refused each one (including four during a single day) but would brag about his actions to others. It is well known that Thayer referred to Sacco and Vanzetti as those "anarchist bastards." One man in prison, Celestino Madeiros, wrote a note confessing not only to the Braintree crime, but also exonerating Sacco and Vanzetti. This was ignored. Thayer sentenced the men to death on April 9, 1927. The defense attorneys won a series of stays of execution, but eventually Sacco and Vanzetti's luck ran out.

The Execution and the Legacy

By the time of their execution, Sacco and Vanzetti had become known around the world. Just before the execution, the current Massachusetts governor appointed a panel to review the case, although this was mostly the result of so much outside pressure. It was to no avail; the panel did not recommend a reversal of conviction. Shortly after midnight on August 23, 1927, Sacco and Vanzetti were put to death in the electric chair. The protests were worldwide.

Sacco and Vanzetti's story has been told countless times. In 1928, socialist author Upton Sinclair wrote *Boston*, a two-volume novel about the case. As with many of his novels, Sinclair combines historical fact with fictional narrative in telling the story of Cornelia Thornwell, a well-to-do grandmother who renounces the hypocrisy of Boston blueblood society to live among the working classes. In her adventures Thornwell meets, and befriends, Sacco and Vanzetti, sticking with them all the way to the bitter end. Sinclair makes it clear which portions of the novel are straight from the historical record and which are fiction. Regardless, *Boston* is an early, scathing indictment of the treatment suffered by the two men.

The Sacco and Vanzetti case would be reexamined over and over. The inappropriate handling of the court proceedings has been heavily criticized. Although Vanzetti's innocence is generally upheld, many have in fact questioned Sacco's innocence in the Braintree crime. Although the two men were hardly the first to be the victims of unfair justice, their story very much exemplifies the nation's fears during this period.

Conclusion

The Progressive Era was over. The Jazz Age was in full swing in so many ways. The radical sector presented a strong front. So did mainstream society. In the post–World War I years, the direction the country was to take was fiercely fought.

But was this necessarily a fight between radicals and mainstream society? Were the lines drawn that sharply? Of course not. Being a member of mainstream society did not mean one could not hold divergent viewpoints. At the end of World War I, the United States entered a long period of isolationism, whereby the country tried to keep itself away from foreign policy intrigues and to protect what were seen as traditional American values. Ideologies such as socialism, communism, and anarchism were not seen as traditional American values, and their infusion into American society was attributed to foreigners. Even the more conservative elements of the American labor movement, as embodied in Gompers, were often lumped in with that more radical sector. To maintain a peaceful society would be to understand that radicalism was poisonous.

For many radicals, the post–World War I era was a chance to truly start the world anew, for there were many lessons to be learned from the terrible conflict. Many believed correcting flaws within the political, social, and economic network would prevent future wars and would make society more beneficial for all. Society could not rely on traditional values, for many values change over time. What might have been acceptable in 1900 was antiquated in 1920. Although the fickleness of society was acknowledged, so was the notion that the world does not stand still; growth and development are inevitable, and with growth change must come.

The radicalism of the 1920s paints a vivid picture of how people viewed the purpose of values in society. What is especially interesting is that many of the ideas used to support the different sides of the issue came from earlier periods; what were embraced as traditional American values went back to the earliest years of the country. Yet radical ideologies also went back to another century. The *Communist Manifesto* was published in 1848, and vigorous activities on the part of anarchists, not to mention the formation of the Socialist Party, also took place during the 19th century. Both tradition and radicalism had their roots in times long ago. It is interesting to see each side pointing fingers at the other for being out of touch while reaching back into history for their justification to influence contemporary times.

References and Further Reading

Brecher, Jeremy. *Strike!* San Francisco: Straight Arrow, 1972.

Brody, David. *Labor in Crisis: The Steel Strike of 1919.* Philadelphia: Lippincott, 1965.

Davis, James John. Papers. Library of Congress. Manuscript Collections. Washington, D.C.

Dinnerstein, Leonard, and David M. Reimers. *Ethnic Americans: A History of Immigration and Assimilation.* New York: Harper and Row, 1975.

Eastman, Max. *Love and Revolution.* New York: Random House, 1964.

Iverson, Robert W. *The Communists and the Schools.* New York: Harcourt, Brace and Company, 1959.

Kellen, Stuart A. *The Roaring Twenties.* San Diego: Greenhaven Press, 2002.

McClymer, John. "The Federal Government and the Americanization Movement, 1915–1924." *Prologue* 10 (Spring 1978): 23–41.

McDonald, Forrest. *A Constitutional History of the United States.* Malabar, FL: Robert Krieger, 1986.

National Archives. Records of the Office of Education. Record Group 12. Entry 6, Historical File. Washington, D.C., 1920–1925.

New York Times, March 25, 1918.

New York World, November 4, 1924.

Olneck, Michael R., and Marvin Lazserson. "The School Achievement of Immigrant Children, 1900–1930." *History of Education Quarterly* (Fall 1969): 524–543.

Renshaw, Patrick. *The Wobblies: A Story of Syndicalism in the United States.* New York: Doubleday and Company, 1967.

Washington Post, November 6–8, 1924.

Writers | 9

Mitchell Newton-Matza

Writers draw inspiration from their own experiences and the times in which they live. Many writers, like the socialist Upton Sinclair, drew on historical events and personal political ideology to shape their works. A writer—F. Scott Fitzgerald—coined the term "the Jazz Age," to describe the period of 1918 to 1930. Although it is impossible to name one golden age of writing, the Jazz Age opened up many new ideas in expressive writing that influenced writers for decades to follow.

For many sectors of society, the post–World War I years held out a lot of hope. The era of World War I is often called the "end" or "loss" of innocence, whereby supposedly cherished Victorian era ideals of purity and proper behavior were lost forever. Although some considered this to be a negative, many others considered this change to be a liberation. No longer would antiquated norms of behavior and morality dictate society. For the most part, the Jazz Age writers embraced this view, and although they were hardly the first to challenge cherished society beliefs, this was a period in which freedom was expressed in ways not acceptable in previous times. One of the more interesting aspects of the Jazz Age writers is that so many of them were not even living in the United States at the time of their creative output. France could actually be considered one of the centers of American Jazz Age writing.

The End of the Victorian Era

What were the influences from which the writers drew their thoughts and inspiration? One of these was the rejection of the Victorian-era values. During the Victorian era, men and women were expected to conform to specific forms of behavior. Premarital sex was considered taboo. Sexual relations were reserved for married couples, and many believed even

The Soul of Jazz Age Writers

The characteristics of the Jazz Age writers can possibly be summed up in two words: exciting and energetic. To use such words as groundbreaking or trendsetters would be trite, for although the Jazz Age writers addressed topics not used as prominently in past times, each time period can lay claim to its own originality.

What makes the Jazz Age writers so exciting and energetic? Taking advantage of the post–World War I era, and the end of Victorian era protocols, topics previously thought taboo gained wider dissemination.

How these ideas were accepted is another topic.

One could argue that sales figures are a good indicator for mainstream acceptance. F. Scott Fitzgerald's successes not only made him a star but also helped glamorize a lifestyle of high living. John Dos Passos described a similar lifestyle that centered on certain pleasures, such as sex and alcohol, but his view was from a less lavish segment of society. Why anyone enjoys reading a certain work is a guess, but perhaps part of the appeal of these works was twofold: (1) Many

married couples should be intimate only for the purposes of procreation; sex was not meant to be enjoyed. For a woman to enjoy sex, especially admitting so openly in society, would be to tarnish her reputation, branding her a ''loose'' woman. Even during courtship, social functions where young men and women mingled were chaperoned.

With these Victorian values of mating and courtship, however, came a double standard that remained for years. Young men were still expected to sow their wild oats, although usually discreetly. Women were not allowed such discretions. Women were still expected to be virgins on their wedding night. Furthermore, it was considered acceptable for a married man of substance to have a lover on the side, but if a wife was caught being unfaithful, it not only meant divorce but also banishment from society. While this is not to imply that these behavioral patterns were accepted by all, it was exactly these ideals of sexual hypocrisy that the Jazz Age writers addressed.

Other Influences

Another impetus to the openness of Jazz Age writing was the road paved by the infamous muckrakers of late 19th and early 20th society, who helped set the standard for writers setting out to expose the inherent and deep problems in society. Upton Sinclair's infamous 1906 book, *The Jungle*, is known mostly for its exposé of the terrible conditions in Chicago's meatpacking plants, but Sinclair's main goals were to expose the evils of modern capitalist society and to convert readers to socialism. Other muckrakers, like Frank Norris, also sought to write about the underside of American life in hopes of changing minds. Although Jazz Age writers might not have agreed readers enjoy reading about a high-class life-style they have not experienced, and (2) many appreciated and could identify with the frankness and openness of the writing.

Although the energy and excitement of the Jazz Age writers can be partially attributed to the dramatic changes in society in the post–World War I years, it is also the very debate over their works that contributed. Sometimes what can drive an artist to creativity is a good controversy. Although it is impossible to say how much artists are going out of their way to be controversial,

all writers contemplate how a work will be perceived. Some do not intend to rock the boat, but others revel in it. Regardless, as some say, "There's no such thing as bad publicity."

From whatever inspiration an artist draws, be it his or her own personal experiences, the personal experiences of total strangers, or the events of the day, the Jazz Age writers drew on the excitement and energy of a new period in American history and a vibrant time in American literature.

with the muckrakers, they were certainly carrying on their tradition of being unafraid to voice their views, no matter how distasteful to so-called polite society.

The Postwar World

The disillusionment of postwar society was another influence in the Jazz Age. The so-called "war to make the world safe for democracy" proved to be anything but what it was supposed to be. The brutality of war was more real than ever before, and people wondered what exactly had been accomplished. The world appeared to be in no better condition than it was before the conflict began. Europe remained in turmoil. Before the war, many racial and ethnic groups fought to attain autonomous states, but achieving those ends was far more difficult than hoped. New countries were created, such as Czechoslovakia, although many of its inhabitants had no desire to live with each other. Even within the United States, many citizens, most notably African Americans, thought establishing their own identity would be part of the overall goal of the war; that is, by establishing worldwide democracy, their own status would be elevated.

Having the safety of oceans to separate it from the rest of the world, America turned inward. With this inward-looking view and the continued growth of mass production and culture, writers questioned what was actually being accomplished. Although some might have argued that the growth of mass culture meant more people could participate in society's pleasures, the Jazz Age writers did not see this as an advancement. Rather, they looked beyond the facade of mass culture, which covered an emptiness that lay underneath.

Finally, the writers of the Jazz Age were participating in what was happening across cultural and disciplinary lines. In keeping with the movement away from the Victorian-era values of sexuality and morality, both Hollywood and the academic community were exploring human relationships in ways once considered shocking. The field of psychology, especially the work of Sigmund Freud, examined human feelings and sexuality. The openness of Hollywood to depict its actors as objects of sexual desire was enjoyed by some but caused others to demand censorship of films. Writers during the Jazz Age found a better outlet for their expression of human relationships that went hand in hand with what others were doing elsewhere.

The Harlem Renaissance

In the Jazz Age, one movement that particularly embodied the idea of breaking free from convention was the Harlem Renaissance, a movement by African American artists across all disciplines. As with the Jazz Age itself, it is difficult to limit this cultural movement to specific years. Regardless, the Harlem Renaissance left a remarkable and lasting legacy during this time.

The popular image of the American black population was anything but flattering in this era. Besides the overall racism, blacks were often portrayed in films and other mediums of mass culture as simpletons, drunks, and ignorant of white cultured society. Black men were often stereotyped as dangerous and preying on virtuous white women. Films such as D.W. Griffith's infamous *Birth of a Nation* (1915) especially promoted these stereotypes, although Griffith later tried to atone for the images portrayed in the film. If not portrayed as drunken, predatory savages, blacks were the object of comic relief, showing stupid and childlike behavior.

The Great Migration

African Americans were certainly undergoing numerous changes along with the rest of American society. In the pre–World War I years the movement known as the Great Migration brought thousands of blacks in the South to northern cities such as New York and Chicago. The reasons for such moves were obvious, such as access to better jobs and education, a higher standard of living, and escape from the Jim Crow laws of the South. But racism was just as bad, if not worse, in the North. Blacks were still not welcome into the better, higher-paying jobs and usually had to take the lowliest jobs in northern industries. Although the South might have had codified segregation, in the North segregation was implied. Furthermore, northern blacks did not care much for southern "country bumpkin" blacks. Those African Americans who had managed to establish professional careers in fields such as law and medicine saw these southern blacks as a step backward; they believed the gains made in northern towns would be eradicated by the presence of the ignorant, transplanted southern blacks.

Rising Black Pride

Forms of black pride were emerging, however. Led by people such as the charismatic Marcus Garvey, founder of the Back to Africa movement, African Americans were examining their lives and culture in their own terms. Garvey himself was not necessarily promoting a mass migration; rather, he was trying to promote the notion of a strong black Africa as it was obvious the white-dominated American society would not protect the well-being of its black population. Garvey would eventually be convicted of mail fraud, based on thin evidence, but this did not stop the approximately 4 million members who joined his Universal Negro Improvement Association. President Calvin Coolidge pardoned Garvey in 1924, and he was eventually deported to Jamaica.

The Harlem Renaissance represented a flourishing of black culture. Centered in New York City, this movement, besides being a form of important self-expression, also strove to negate the terrible stereotypes of blacks perpetuated by other segments of American culture. The Baptist minister Adam Clayton Powell Sr., for instance, remarked that Harlem was "the symbol of liberty and the Promised Land to Negroes everywhere." The Harlem Renaissance involved writers—of both fiction and poetry—as well as artists and musicians. Although Harlem was the center of the movement, the participants lived across the country, and all were able to promote their works in ways never done before.

One social aspect of the Harlem Renaissance was the advent of the rent party. As a housing shortage fell upon Harlem, rents escalated and many black workers, who earned considerably less than whites, held rent parties to try to cover costs. The entry ticket ranged from 5¢ to 25¢, and additional money was raised through the sale of alcohol and soul food. By the end of the Jazz Age, approximately 300,000 blacks lived in New York, an incredible increase from the 1920 population of 50,000. And although Harlem would become known as a slum, it was also, as noted, the center of cultural expression.

Roots of the Renaissance

The writers of the Harlem Renaissance tended to draw from two sources: their African roots and new places they were visiting, such as France, most notably Paris, and black-centered cultures such as the Caribbean Islands. These writers were not necessarily finding their own voices, for those were already in place. What was being found more than anything was the outlet. One of the important outlets was Garvey's *Negro World*. In addition to promoting Garvey's agenda, the newspaper took a stand against racism by not accepting advertisements for items such as skin lighteners. *Negro World*'s influence was not limited to Harlem, for readers across the United States could access this paper. One of the writers who found access to readers through this paper was Claude McKay.

Claude McKay

Jamaican-born Claude McKay displayed enormous talent as a writer of fiction and poetry. And although his work was published in *Negro World*,

McKay actually disagreed with Garvey's ideas, and virtually nothing exists of his work for the publication. McKay published his first book of poetry, *Songs of Jamaica*, in 1912. He later moved to the United States where he was stunned by the Jim Crow–enforced segregation of the South. Although he did not care for communism under the Soviet Union, McKay did embrace socialism. McKay's personal life involved bisexual affairs. His own wife did not care for New York life and returned to Jamaica.

In 1928, McKay published his classic work *Home to Harlem*. The winner of the Harmon Gold Award for Literature, the book depicted a view of Harlem life in a manner that many did not appreciate. Its discussion of sexuality angered black leaders, such as W. E. B. DuBois. McKay's other works include the novel *Banjo* (1930) and two autobiographical pieces, *A Long Way from Home* (1937) and *Harlem: Negro Metropolis* (1940). He continued to write poetry, and *Selected Poems* was published posthumously in 1953. McKay eventually rejected his past dealings with communism and socialism and was baptized in the Catholic Church. He died in 1948.

Claude McKay was a Jamaican writer and part of the Harlem Renaissance. (*Library of Congress*)

Alain Locke and the New Negro

Another key figure in the Harlem Renaissance was Alain Locke, who was often referred to as the "Father of the Harlem Renaissance." Born in 1886, Locke was the first African American Rhodes scholar. In keeping with many others in the Harlem Renaissance, Locke believed black Americans should look to their African roots and move away from tradition and convention. Well trained in philosophy, a field he taught at such schools as Howard University, Locke became best known for editing *The New Negro*, an anthology of African American writings. According to Locke, "Negro life is seizing upon its first chances for group expression and self-determination."

The New Negro was a collection of black writings that served several purposes. It was not only a form of self-expression, but it also helped others to understand the world of African Americans. Black people were to examine themselves in their own way, not by the standards of white Americans. DuBois himself addressed this situation when he said it was a way "to be both a Negro and an American." Before *The New Negro*, Locke edited the March 1925 issue of *Survey Graphic*, which centered on the Harlem Renaissance. Locke especially wanted white America to have a notion of what it meant to be a black American.

Zora Neale Hurston

Trained anthropologist Zora Neale Hurston was another unique voice of the Harlem Renaissance. Hurston's life was one of struggle, but she persevered in the face of obstacles like losing her mother at the age of 13. In 1926, along with other noted Harlem Renaissance figures such as Langston Hughes, Hurston helped to publish the journal *Fire!* As with *The New Negro*, this magazine was aimed at African American readers. Hurston's best-known novel was *Their Eyes Were Watching God* (1937). The book follows the life of Janie Crawford, an African American woman whose three marriages make a profound impact on her life. The dialogue is presented in the southern dialect of the time, which some considered to be degrading to black Americans. Despite this criticism, the book had a wide audience. Although Hurston struggled as a writer later on in life, her works remain significant contributions to American literature.

The Lost Generation

Outside the Harlem Renaissance other writers were also exploring their interests and openly expressing their opinions of modern society. As with their African American comrades, these writers often expressed their views in ways many felt offensive or obscene. Openly frank discussions of sex and substance abuse might have shocked some, but to others the times were right. The Victorian ideals were quickly disappearing, and writers were now openly expressing what many felt inside. Many such writers were lumped in a group of their own known as the "Lost Generation."

Portrait of Zora Neale Hurston, an influential artist of the Jazz Age. (*Library of Congress*)

The coining of the phrase "Lost Generation" is attributed to the American writer and artist Gertrude Stein. Although the story surrounding how the phrase came to be is unclear, the impact has been lasting and the term was picked up by other writers, in particular Ernest Hemingway. Stein (1874–1946) was born into a comfortable lifestyle, which provided her with a college education and the opportunity to travel. She spent most of her life in France. She did not share the middle-class lifestyle of most of her Jazz Age colleagues, but she was anything but an outsider and cultivated friendships with many Jazz Age artists, such as Ernest Hemingway.

Many Jazz Age writers demonstrated their disaffection toward American life. Many of these feelings were prompted by the war, but these emotions did not arise overnight. Some of these writers had come of age

John Dos Passos (1896–1970) is just one of the Lost Generation writers. (*National Archives*)

before the war, others during the conflict. What they had in common was the belief that America was not living up to the ideals it projected. In moving from trying to adhere to outmoded Victorian-era morals to experiencing the horrors of World War I, American culture was not what it should have been. Many of these writers therefore decided to seek artistic freedom abroad, especially in places like Paris. Although each writer had his or her own ways of criticizing American culture and life, they all shared a common bond and sentiment.

John Dos Passos

John Dos Passos (1896–1970) was one of the Lost Generation writers. Born in Chicago, Dos Passos wrote several novels that explored the disaffection and liberation so many felt and lived, but could not express previously. A Harvard graduate, Dos Passos first sought to pursue his artistic career by studying architecture. He served with the U.S. Army Medical Corps in World War I, and after the war he studied anthropology at the Sorbonne. Two of his novels, *One Man's Initiation* (1920) and *Three Soldiers*

(1921), drew on his wartime experiences. A prolific writer, Dos Passos produced 42 novels. He also wrote plays, poems, and essays, as well as created hundreds of works of art.

Dos Passos embraced leftist ideology and promoted such views through his protests concerning the infamous Sacco-Vanzetti case and his glowing endorsement for the Industrial Workers of the World (IWW), also known as the Wobblies (see chapter on *Reformers, Radical and Socialists* for more details). For a brief period in 1928 he spent time in the Soviet Union, observing their socialist system, but he eventually turned away from leftist ideals, something that earned him scorn from colleagues.

Dos Passos made his mark on the literary world with his 1925 novel, *Manhattan Transfer*, in which his fascination with city life was also a backdrop for his views on modern-day living. The techniques he used, especially narrative collages and stream of consciousness, revealed a complex society characterized by apathy, sorrow for the past, and yet energy for life. As Ethan Mordden writes, Dos Passos "abstracted the disorientation of city life, its loss of man-to-man contact, in the tempos, colors, and smells of characterful anonymity" (Mordden 1978, 85).

Toward the end of the Jazz Age, Dos Passos began to publish the three separate, yet interconnected, novels that would make up the *U.S.A. Trilogy*. In *The 42nd Parallel* (1930), *1919* (1932), and *The Big Money* (1936), he presented an image of America from the Spanish-American War to the economic collapse of 1929 that led to the Great Depression. He does not use a typical linear narrative; rather, his pessimistic views of American political and economic culture are shown through interweaving narratives, newspaper clippings, song lyrics, and actual political speeches and slogans. Through his innovative "camera eye" technique of autobiographical stream of consciousness narratives, Dos Passos interjected his own experiences into the fictional portions of the book, allowing readers to see the situation as the author saw and lived it. Dos Passos's style influenced numerous future writers and helped project the image of America as seen by many of his other Lost Generation colleagues.

Ezra Pound

Ezra Pound (1885–1972) was an artist before, during, and after the Jazz Age who had an enormous impact on the break from traditionalism in all forms of art. Before the Jazz Age, Pound already had a reputation as a poet, but in the 1920s he continued to experiment with many different forms of expression. His reputation in modern times is somewhat controversial because of his support for Italian dictator Benito Mussolini, but he is known as a trailblazer.

In the pre–World War I era, imagism in poetry gained notoriety, especially due to the efforts of Pound. In a movement away from previous forms of poetry, the idea of images, rather than romantic stanzas, took center stage. Imagism rejected sentiment in favor of more direct, descriptive language in order to invoke mental images. In one of his innovative works, *Cathay* (1915), he used free-verse translations of Chinese poetry in his

Regarded by some as the "poet's poet," Ezra Pound wrote verse whose vivid imagery and spare language strongly influenced poetic technique in Britain and the United States during the first half of the 20th century. An iconoclast in literature, art, and music, he produced a body of poetry and criticism that remain controversial. (*National Archives*)

writings. Although criticized for not using literal translations, Pound was not trying to be precise; rather, the point was to invoke images and ideas.

Pound continued to turn away from traditionalism. Like so many others, the horrors and disillusionment of World War I weighed on him. This led him to move to Paris in 1920, where he associated with other artistic free thinkers, with whom he shared a common bond. The result was a new form of artistic expression, surrealism.

While in Paris, Pound also became involved in music. He promoted many concerts and concepts and dabbled in music composition. Working with other notable musical artists, such as Olga Rudge and George Antheil, he experimented with dissonance, irregular rhythms, and other new and challenging forms of musical expression. As with Pound's poetry, the music was meant to invoke images as opposed to basic emotions.

Pound left France for Italy in 1924. In Italy he continued to promote new forms of expression, which he believed could not be achieved in America. Soon, however, Pound found himself in trouble with the U.S. government for supporting Mussolini's regime, and he was brought back

If there is any single writer of the Jazz Age and Lost Generation who came to embody the sentiment, spirit, and even frustration of the period, it was F. Scott Fitzgerald. (*Library of Congress*)

to the United States under the charge of treason. Pound escaped a prison term, but he was sent to St. Elizabeth's Hospital in Washington, D.C., for 12 years. Upon his release in 1958, Pound returned to Italy where he remained the rest of his life, a constant critic of the American system. Pound is still highly regarded as a pioneer of modernism. More importantly, although Pound was certainly an artist in his own right, he was also highly active in promoting the achievements of others.

F. Scott Fitzgerald

If there is a single writer who has come to embody the sentiment, spirit, and even frustration of the the Jazz Age and the Lost Generation, it is F. Scott Fitzgerald (1896–1940), who actually coined the term "Jazz Age." Still considered a major literary figure, Fitzgerald helped to elucidate the disillusionment of the age, a disillusionment that existed no matter what one's social status might be.

Born in St. Paul, Minnesota, Francis Scott Key Fitzgerald (he was a distant relation to the composer of the national anthem) published his first piece was when he was 13—a detective story in his school's newspaper. He enrolled in Princeton in 1913 and became very involved with the Princeton Triangle Club. To the detriment of his studies, he wrote numerous pieces for the club's musicals, as well as providing material for a collegiate humor magazine.

In 1917, Fitzgerald left Princeton to join the army, just as the United States was becoming involved in World War I. He met Zelda Sayre while he was in the military and the two became engaged, although she broke it off because of Fitzgerald's financial struggles. Unlike other writers of the

Lost Generation, Fitzgerald did not see military action overseas; World War I ended just before his deployment. His first novel, *The Romantic Egotist*, drew on his feelings about his military service, but was eventually rejected. Some of this book was later reworked into *This Side of Paradise*, which was published in 1920.

Like other works of the Lost Generation, *This Side of Paradise* examines post-World War I life among the youth through the life of the central character, Amory Blaine, a young Princeton student, some of whose experiences are similar to those of Fitzgerald himself. Blaine, like so many others, becomes disillusioned and cynical about American life. The openness of romantic relationships between men and women is also explored—one girl for example extols the number of men she has kissed and will kiss in the future—along with Freudian notions of sexuality. According to Fitzgerald, his younger generation is not necessarily doing anything new, they are just expressing it in ways never before seen. In one interview, he said *Paradise* was "a novel about Flappers written for Philosophers" (Jenkins 1974, 156). *Paradise* was a success and made a star of Fitzgerald. With this success, Zelda returned and the two were married.

Fitzgerald was also known for writing stories for magazines, something that would become the staple of his income, especially in later years. He wrote for smaller and lesser-known publications, as well as national magazines, including the *Saturday Evening Post*. In such stories as "Bernice Bobs Her Hair," he described the lives of women who were breaking with convention. But although Fitzgerald hoped for respect as a writer, his personal life of extravagance and drinking tended to grab attention from his literary works.

Fitzgerald's second novel, *The Beautiful and the Damned* (1922), also draws on his own life. Another tale of American morality, the story of Anthony and Gloria Patch, members of the East Coast upper class, deals with marital life and alcoholism. Fitzgerald was writing about a social class that was far from content. Although they might have money and very few material wants, life was far from perfect. Having struggled with financial uncertainly himself, both as a child and an adult, he portrayed life as being empty and, at times, without much meaning.

What solidified Fitzgerald's mark on American literature was his 1925 novel *The Great Gatsby*. Although it was not a financial success upon its initial publication, *Gatsby* remains his most famous work. The story of Jay Gatsby is told through the eyes of Nick Carraway as he remembers past events. This is a story of the excessive lifestyle of the rich on New York's coast. It tells of lavish parties, adultery, accidental death, and murderous revenge, all centering on a mysterious character named Jay Gatsby. *Gatsby* is a prime example of how Fitzgerald, and others, viewed the excesses and over-the-top behavior of those who were now openly defying what was once considered proper social behavior. Though *Gatsby* was forgotten for a time, it enjoyed a future renaissance and remains an example of classic American writing. Productions of *Gatsby* include stage, film, and even an operatic version.

Fitzgerald was in Europe when *Gatsby* was published, but he and Zelda returned to America in 1926. Zelda's mental health deteriorated, and

Fitzgerald's alcoholism continued. He continued to write short stories, which brought in a decent income, but he was unable to control his spending. His third novel, *Tender is the Night*, was not published until 1934, and his final novel, *The Last Tycoon*, was published posthumously in 1941.

Fitzgerald continued to spiral downward while attempting to bring in money as a Hollywood screenwriter. He died of a heart attack in 1940. (Zelda passed away two years later in a fire.) Fitzgerald considered himself to be a failure. Despite his shortcomings, however, Fitzgerald projected an image of Jazz Age America that has lasted into contemporary times.

Ernest Hemingway

Although not necessarily thought of as a Jazz Age writer per se in terms of his subject matters, Ernest Hemingway (1899–1961) was definitely part of the Lost Generation who helped to describe disaffection with American life. One of the best-known writers of all time, Hemingway produced novels and short stories and worked as a reporter.

Hemingway was born in Oak Park, Illinois, just outside Chicago. His father was a country doctor, and his mother was a music teacher who once had opera aspirations. His mother often dressed Hemingway in feminine clothes alongside his older sister, the reason being that she originally wanted twins. Gender ideas often surfaced in his works. Although his mother stressed more domestic ideals, Hemingway developed a taste for the outdoors, cultivated by his father.

Hemingway excelled in high school academics and sports and was editor of the school newspaper. Despite his parents' insistence on his attending college, Hemingway became a reporter for the *Kansas City Star*. When the United States entered World War I, Hemingway attempted to join the army, but was rejected for failing the vision test. He then joined the Red Cross Ambulance Corps. In France and Italy he witnessed the horrors of war firsthand, something that never left him, especially after he was wounded in 1918. His failed romantic relationship with a nurse provided material for his works. After the war he lived in Oak Park and Chicago, but in 1921, he and his wife headed for Paris, where he met other writers and artists.

Although Hemingway was known as a short story writer during the Jazz Age, his two novels of that time, *The Sun Also Rises* (1926) and *A Farewell to Arms* (1929), helped describe the mood of American expatriates. As with Fitzgerald and others, Hemingway drew on personal experiences. While writing about war, he refused the idea of the hero. He knew all too well what combat meant, and from his background in boxing he knew that winning could be just as devastating as losing.

Hemingway's first novel, *The Sun Also Rises*, was a success. Semiautobiographical, the book centers on Jake Barnes and his friends as they are on their way to Pamplona, Spain. A war injury has made Barnes impotent, though he wishes for a sexual relationship with Brett Ashley, who enjoys sexual escapades outside her relationship with her fiancée. Alcohol plays an important part of the story, and the characters all need more in terms of emotional fulfillment. The characters are looking for a new path after society's destruction in the war. Although freedom is desired, the postwar world has created a situation as much fearful as it was liberating.

A Farewell to Arms is another semiautobiographical work that deals with the war. The protagonist is Frederic Henry, who, like Hemingway, drove an ambulance in Italy. Henry is also wounded, and begins a tragic affair with a nurse. Many consider *Farewell* to be one of the greatest war novels.

Hemingway continued to write novels and short stories and was critical when Dos Passos turned away from communism. Hemingway also shared a common bond with many of his colleagues—the heavy use of alcohol. His heroes were stoic and not flashy, yet had their own place in the Jazz Age. Considered one the greatest writers of all time, Hemingway tragically committed suicide in 1961.

Sinclair Lewis

Next to F. Scott Fitzgerald, the other author most closely associated with the Jazz Age is Sinclair Lewis (1885–1951). Like Fitzgerald, Lewis's works remain a staple of American literature, although Lewis was by far the more successful writer of the two. In 1930, Lewis had the distinction of being the first American to win the Nobel Prize for Literature. His presentations of life during the Jazz Age had just as much impact as those of the Lost Generation. Known as a prolific writer, Lewis wrote novels, plays, short stories, and various commentaries throughout his career.

Born in Sauk Centre, Minnesota—a locale that would serve as the inspiration for many of his works—Harry Sinclair Lewis developed a love for books. A bit gawky when growing up, during the Spanish-American War Lewis tried to run away and join the war effort as a drummer boy. He completed his college studies in 1908 at Yale. Lewis embarked on a writing career after Yale, producing short stories for magazines and following other pursuits. His first book was published in 1912, but it was not until the Jazz Age that he truly made his mark.

In 1920, Lewis published his first major success, *Main Street*. A commentary on small-town life, *Main Street* is the story of Carol Kennicott, the wife of the local doctor in the town of Gopher Prairie. Her husband loves the locale while Carol thinks the town is backward and stifling. Her attempts to infuse culture into the town are met with scorn. Although Carol experiences big-city life away from her husband, she eventually returns to Gopher Prairie.

Babbitt, published in 1922, was not only met with huge success but is also considered by many to be Lewis's finest work. The novel probably makes the best statement about conspicuous consumption during the Jazz Age. Centered on the life of its main character, George Babbitt, in the imaginary town of Zenith, the book, like *Main Street*, also examines the issue of conformity. Babbitt is a shallow man who is more concerned with his personal social status than with any other living being. The depiction of a middle-class businessman making himself out to be more than he really was had a huge impact across the nation. Many cities claimed to be the inspiration for Zenith. As Geoffrey Perrett points out, "far from being insulted by Lewis's mockery, cities all over the Midwest competed for recognition as the original Zenith" (Perrett 1982, 269).

Arrowsmith (1925) turned away from themes of middle-class conformity to the world of science and medicine. The book is about Dr. Martin Arrowsmith, a man who could make extreme fame and fortune but instead fights the bubonic plague in the Caribbean. Although the central character loses his sense of himself, what is interesting is that Arrowsmith abandons a high-profile life to work in a remote rural setting.

Lewis addressed the sensitive issue of religion in *Elmer Gantry* (1927). Gantry is a self-centered hedonist who realizes how much more power and attention he can achieve by becoming a Pentecostal minister. Through numerous scandals, Gantry manages to survive and continue, despite being a fraud. The book was controversial, and banned in many areas, especially because it may have been based on actual people. Congregations refused to believe such hypocrisy and fraud could exist in the Christian religion. Just a few years after the infamous Scopes "Monkey" Trial— whereby both science and religion were called into question—a novel addressing the idea of a man manipulating religion for the sake of personal gain was considered to be a gross insult. There was enough of a battle during the Jazz Age between the religious Right and the increasingly open liberal attitudes toward personal lifestyles. For those who opposed the book, *Elmer Gantry* was an unfair indictment; to the book's supporters it was a story that desperately needed to be told.

Dodsworth (1929), Lewis' last novel during the Jazz Age, tells the story of an automobile designer and his wife, a married couple who have differing views of how to live life. What is interesting about the novel is Lewis' discussion of the expatriate sentiment, something generally not associated with his works. Lewis's work remains as an important indictment of Jazz Age life.

Algonquin Round Table

For many Jazz Age writers and intellectuals, postwar life was not all gloomy. While still sharing the disillusionment of the Lost Generation, some took a more lighthearted approach, and humor and games tended to take the place of the sadness others described. The group known as the Algonquin Round Table was certainly a lively group, one that garnered national attention, although that attention was not always favorable.

Not all members of the Algonquin Round Table were writers, but their daily luncheons at the Algonquin Hotel, in New York City, made considerable press during the Jazz Age. Many of the group used the gatherings for collaboration, but much meeting time was used for an exchange of wit and criticism of society. Algonquin Round Table members included Dorothy Parker (poet and writer), George S. Kaufman (playwright and director), as well as various newspaper columnists and artists. Many famous people, including the film comic Harpo Marx, floated in and out of the group. Their antics, which often included practical jokes, made for nationwide reading. In 1922, the group produced *No Siree*, a one-night-only revue. However, despite the strong reception this sole performance received, their attempt to offer the show to the general public proved to be a disaster.

Although these various artists and writers were impressed with each other, others were not. Many, including H. L. Mencken, considered the group to be self-serving and self-promoting, a group who disparaged society to make themselves appear superior in intellect and lifestyle. Even Parker herself would later dismiss the Algonquin Round Table as a bunch of show-offs.

Reader's Digest

In contrast to the literary elite and the wits of the Algonquin Round Table, *Reader's Digest* was the reading choice of the common folk. A magazine founded in 1922 by Lila Bell Wallace and DeWitt Wallace, the family-oriented magazine appealed primarily to middle-class readers, although its appeal went beyond class lines. Noted for its condensed versions of writings from other sources, as well as shorter pieces of humor and human interest, *Reader's Digest* gave many readers access to topics they might not have previously considered.

Conclusion

When the Great Depression began, literature changed to reflect the times. Books such as *Vein of Iron* and *Grapes of Wrath* reflected the hardships of the times rather than the flash and conspicuous consumption of the Jazz Age, although many Hollywood films still showed the joys of high living. Many Jazz Age writers, such as Hemingway and Lewis, continued to produce works and remained successful well after the period. Others, such as Fitzgerald, struggled to maintain the expectations placed upon them.

Whether living in the United States or abroad as an expatriate, the writers of the Jazz Age helped to create not just a whole unique body of work but a body of work that also became infused with American culture. From the incorporation of terms like "Babbittry" or the "Harlem Renaissance" to the staging of an opera version of *The Great Gatsby*, Jazz Age writing remains a treasured part of American cultural achievements. As any body of literature reflects the tone of its time, whether through conformity or counterculture, the Jazz Age writers present a fascinating view of America at a time of tremendous change.

References and Further Reading

Arnesen, Eric. *Black Protest and the Great Migration*. Boston: Bedford/St. Martin's, 2003.

Bainbridge, John. *Little Wonder: Or, the Reader's Digest and How it Grew*. New York: Reynal & Hitchcock, 1945.

Baker, Carlos. *Hemingway: The Writer as Artist*. Princeton, NJ: Princeton University Press, 1972.

Bogart, Max. *The Jazz Age*. New York: Charles Scribner's Sons, 1969.

Canterbury, Ray E., and Thomas Birch. *F. Scott Fitzgerald: Under the Influence*. St. Paul, MN: Paragon House, 2006.

Carpenter, Humphrey. *A Serious Character: The Life of Ezra Pound*. Boston: Houghton Mifflin, 1988.

Cowley, Malcolm, and Robert Cowley. *Fitzgerald and the Jazz Age*. New York: Charles Scribner's Sons, 1966.

Drowne, Kathleen, and Patrick Huber. *The 1920s*. Westport, CT: Greenwood Press, 2004.

Heidenry, John. *Theirs Was the Kingdom: Lila and DeWitt Wallace and the Story of Reader's Digest*. New York: W.W. Norton, 1993.

Hermann, Dorothy. *With Malice Toward All: The Quips, Lives and Loves of Some Celebrated Twentieth Century American Wits*. New York: G. P. Putnam's Sons, 1982.

Jenkins, Alan. *The Twenties*. New York: Universe Books, 1974.

Kenner, Hugh. *The Pound Era*. Berkeley: University of California Press, 1973.

Kyvig, David. *Daily Life in the United States, 1920–1940*. Chicago: Ivan R. Dee, 2002.

Lingeman, Richard. *Sinclair Lewis: Rebel from Main Street*. New York: Random House, 2002.

Lynn, Kenneth. *Hemingway*. New York: Simon and Schuster, 1987.

Meade, Marion. *Dorothy Parker: What Fresh Hell Is This?* New York: Penguin Books, 1987.

Mordden, Ethan. *That Jazz! An Idiosyncratic Social History of the American Twenties*. New York: G. P. Putnam's Sons, 1978.

Perrett, Geoffrey. *America in the Twenties*. New York: Simon and Schuster, 1982.

Redman, Tim. *Ezra Pound and Italian Fascism*. Cambridge, MA: Cambridge University Press, 1991.

Schorer, Mark. *Sinclair Lewis: An American Life*. New York: McGraw-Hill, 1961.

Stock, Noel. *Life of Ezra Pound*. London: Routledge and Kegan Paul, 1970.

Wood, James Playsted. *Of Lasting Interest: The Story of the Reader's Digest*. Westport, CT: Greenwood Press, 1958.

Businesspersons | 10

Sean O'Connor

The second decade of the 20th century was a time of great turmoil for virtually the entire human race. The Mexican Revolution (1910) and subsequent Mexican Civil War (1910–1920), the Chinese Revolution (1911), World War I (1914–1918), the Russian Revolutions (1917) and subsequent Russian Civil War (1917–1923), and the global flu pandemic (1918–1920) killed millions of people, devastating the lives of wounded war veterans and people who lost friends and relatives to war and plague. These events also disrupted trade, causing additional economic suffering.

The interwar years are often thought of as being divided cleanly between a decade of prosperity—the Roaring Twenties—and the Great Depression of the 1930s, which began with the stock market crash of October 1929. Many forget that there were two recessions in the 1920s (1920–1924 and 1926–1927), and although urban-dwellers saw their incomes rise in the 1920s, farmers saw their incomes fall. For the working classes, disposable income rose at a rate of approximately 1 percent per year, but for the richest 1 percent of the population disposable income rose eight times as fast. By contrast, farmers saw the price of wheat decline from $2 a bushel during the war to 67¢ a bushel. During the war, the federal government had nationalized railroad and shipping lines. After brief debate about the desirability of continued government ownership or control of these companies, government control was relinquished by passage of the Esch-Cummins Transportation Act on February 28, 1920 and the Jones Merchant Marine Act on June 5, 1920.

During the postwar period of 1920–1921, the Dow Jones Industrial Average declined 47 percent from its peak in 1919 in the immediate aftermath of the war, and unemployment rose to 15 percent of the workforce as the U.S. government cancelled contracts for war material, leading defense contractors to lay off workers. Soldiers were mustered out of the service, returning home to compete for civilian jobs. Business profits had amounted to $8 billion in 1919 and fell to $1 billion a year later. In 1920, the unemployment rate hit 20 percent.

Today, commentators like Noam Chomsky often use the phrase "welfare capitalism" to describe government programs that directly or indirectly allow private enterprise to profit at public expense (such as when Congress purchases more weapons or vehicles of a particular kind that the Defense Department requests). However, when historians use the phrase in reference to the 1920s, they are talking about programs, similar to, or better than, modern benefits packages, that were created by employers to win greater loyalty from employees than could be had by paying salaries or hourly wages alone. Employers offered perks such as pensions and vacation time out of a sense of paternalistic care for employees, to reduce the attraction of labor unionization, or both. Other influences on the creation of such programs would have been the Progressive political reform movement of the late 19th and early 20th centuries and Frederick Winslow Taylor's scientific management industrial efficiency movement.

Other medium- and large-scale employers held an antithetical position and refused to negotiate with labor organizers and neglected to treat employees humanely to make unionization seem unnecessary. For example, once wartime government controls on the economy were removed, the steel industry planned to reinstate the seven-day workweek and the 12-hour workday and pay weekly wages of $20. During World War I (and later during World War II), the federal government mandated collective bargaining between workers and their employers, a logical way to ensure war material was produced on a predictable timetable. American Federation of Labor (AFL) president Samuel Gompers assumed that since this had been the case when he had backed the war effort he would continue to enjoy the support of the federal government when he sought unionization of the steel industry after the war, but he was to be disappointed.

When the economy recovered in the mid-1920s, and the unemployment rate fell, wages rose for many, but not all, employed workers. Few of those workers who shared in the new wealth saw their earnings increase as dramatically as investors and other business owners in that same period. Between 1922 and 1929, industrial productivity increased 32 percent, but average wages increased only 8 percent. In 1923, the United States Supreme Court struck down the minimum wage law.

Skyscrapers

During the 1920s, various business enterprises in New York City and Chicago vied to build the tallest skyscrapers in the world. In 1922—the year the *Chicago Tribune* celebrated its 75th anniversary—publisher Col. Robert R. McCormick announced a contest with $100,000 in prize money to design what would become the Tribune Tower to be built at the north end of the new Michigan Avenue Bridge. Winners Raymond M. Hood and John Mead Howells submitted a design that merged elements of New York City's neo-Gothic Woolworth Building (1913)—then America's tallest building—with

Woolworth building, New York. (*Library of Congress*)

France's Gothic Rouen Cathedral. The limestone-clad steel-frame building, erected in 1925, was innovative in that it had windows in its rounded corners and rose straight up instead of becoming progressively smaller with gradually recessed walls known as setbacks. The building is also notable because it contains small fragments of other famous buildings, including the Colosseum of Rome, the Alamo in Texas, and the Great Wall of China. A traveling exhibition allowed for widespread exposure to multiple designs submitted for the competition, which is why not only was Hood able to go on to contribute to the designs of New York City's McGraw-Hill building and Rockefeller Center, but the competition's second prize winner, Finnish architect Eliel Saarinen, was able to emigrate to the United States and establish a thriving business. Hood and Howells later provided the Art Deco design for the News Building at 220 East 42nd Street in New York City, headquarters of the *New York Daily News*, which was completed in 1930. The rotating globe in the building's lobby was later copied for the fictional

The Florida Land Boom

The real estate market saw a flurry of activity during the Jazz Age. In the state of Florida, both buyers and sellers were roaring with action. Florida had many appeals, especially for those who could afford to go there. For people from the North, it was a place to vacation in a warm climate. For investors, there was a large amount of property that could be acquired and resold at a profit.

Florida gained enormous popularity in a very short time. As with the stock market during the Jazz Age, it took little money to invest in property. People would acquire lots—both improved and unimproved—in the morning for one price and sell them for as much as double or triple the price by the end of the day. Naturally, property located along the oceanfront was the most desirable and expensive. Homes, mansions, golf courses, and even retirement communities sprang up almost overnight. It was noted that the weight of the *Miami Herald* was the heaviest in the nation because of the many

Metropolis *Daily Planet* in the syndicated TV series *The Adventures of Superman* (1952–1958) starring George Reeves.

Much as McCormick built the Tribune Tower (as well as his house) to advertise his newspaper organization, Walter Chrysler, founder of Chrysler Motors Corporation, commissioned architect William Van Alen to design New York's Chrysler Building at 42nd Street and Lexington Avenue. Van Alen had been given a mandate to erect the tallest structure in the world, and received unanticipated competition from his former partner, H. Craig Severance, who was designing a bank tower at 40 Wall Street. Both men altered their designs halfway through construction to outdo each other, but while Severance's building topped out at 927 feet, Chrysler secretly built a stainless steel spire inside the Chrysler Building and then had it raised up through the roof and bolted on top. Van Alen's Art Deco, white, brick-clad, steel-frame building sports multiple references to automobiles. It features a frieze of hubcaps, a band of abstract automobiles, and, in place of gargoyles, winged radiator caps and streamlined eagles modeled on Chrysler hood ornaments. The gleaming stainless steel crown combines arcs and chevrons that narrow in a series as it rises in a series of setbacks toward the spire. At 1,046 feet, the Chrysler Building surpassed not only Severance's Manhattan Company Building skyscraper at 40 Wall Street but also the 984-foot Eiffel Tower. However, it held the record as the world's tallest manufactured structure for only a year before the Empire State Building set a new record at 1,250 feet.

Unable to live with the idea that Chrysler Motors Corporation had the world's tallest skyscraper, former General Motors executive John Jakob Raskob, KCSG (1875–1950), commissioned architect William Lamb to real estate ads. The Florida market boom seemed to be a place for anyone to get in on the real estate business. One did not need to be a Wall Street mogul. With a small amount of money, coupled with readily available credit, one could net a profit in no time.

But there was a roar no investor and no amount of money could counter. In September, 1926, a Category Five hurricane struck the Miami area, state of Alabama, and the Bahamas. Known as the Great Miami Hurricane, this violent storm brought a roaring end to the Florida land boom. Hundreds were killed, as many as 50,000 were homeless, and there was approximately $100 million in damage. Not only were investors scared away, but the state of Florida had to raise taxes to high levels to help pay for public works. South Florida began to show a slight recovery toward the end of the 1920s, but with the start of the Great Depression, recovery was put on hold.

design a skyscraper to surpass the Chrysler Building in height. He then organized a consortium that demolished the Waldorf Astoria hotel at Fifth Avenue and 34th Street to make way for the skyscraper. The land cost $16 million and erecting the building cost $29 million. It was to be called the Empire State Building in honor of George Washington's observation while sailing up the Hudson River that New York was "key to the new empire." Built at a cost of $41 million, the 102-story Art Deco tower rests on a two-story deep foundation composed of 210 steel and concrete columns that were sunk into Manhattan's granite bedrock.

Despite 16 changes to its design and construction while under way, the building was erected in 14 months over 1930–1931, coming in 45 days and $5 million under budget. To accomplish this, a veritable army of craftspeople and laborers had to be employed, about 3,000 of whom were working at any one time. Working 13-hour shifts at $1.92 per hour, seemingly fearless steelworkers—many of them members of the Mohawks or other nations in the Iroquois Confederacy—riveted more than 50,000 one-ton steel beams to tolerances of less than one-eighth of an inch. The steel arrived at the site eight hours after leaving the mill in Pittsburgh. A total of 14 men were killed in the construction process. Once the building opened, the 73 elevators were run by a staff of 125 operators, one of whom, Harold Mauer, was still an elevator operator as late as 1981. He recalled being paid $300 a week when he started on opening day for what he thought would be a temporary job.

Opening day was May 1, 1931 (a propitious day for laborers), when former governor and Democrat presidential candidate Al Smith's grandchildren cut a ribbon, and President Herbert Hoover pressed a button in Washington, D.C., turning on the lights. The ceremony was also attended by Governor (and future president of the United States) Franklin Delano Roosevelt and Mayor Jimmy Walker. As this was the beginning of the Great Depression, it was initially difficult to find tenants to fill the 2 million square feet of office space, and detractors dubbed it the "Empty State Building," which is why a former governor of New York was hired as president of Empire State Building, Inc. to attract tenants.

The building was sturdy enough to withstand the impact of an airplane that crashed into the 34th Street side on Saturday, July 28, 1945, when a pilot got lost in thick fog on his way to Newark Airport. The three men aboard the plane and 11 people inside the building were killed, but the tragedy could have been worse.

The Clock- and Watch-Manufacturing Industry

During the war, the American clock- and watch-manufacturing industry benefited from having little or no competition from European manufacturers, but the Swiss timepiece manufacturers in particular rebounded in the postwar years. Annual imports of Swiss watch movements climbed from 2,019,000 to 4,375,000 in the 1920s. During this period, the Elgin National Watch Company emerged as the leading American firm in the industry.

Although the Elgin National Watch Company's corporate headquarters had always been in Chicago, most of its manufacturing facilities were located in Elgin, Illinois, from which the company's name was derived. The Elgin National Watch Company only started casing watch movements in the 1920s; before that, many customers had their Elgin watches cased by jewelers in Illinois Watch Case Company cases marketed with such names as the "Giant Elgin," "Elgin Tiger," "Elgin Commander." After a 1901 U.S. Supreme Court decision that a geographic name could not become an exclusive trademark, a number of companies traded on the goodwill the Elgin National Watch Company had earned by selling products with the Elgin name, including the Elgin automobile manufactured in Argo, Illinois, between 1916 and 1924, which was advertised as being "built like a watch."

Between 1915 and 1924, Elgin leased space to the Van Slicken Speedometer Company and Stewart-Warner Corporation, which acquired Van Slicken in 1917 based on Van Slicken's contracts with automakers like Cadillac and Oldsmobile. The Elgin Clock Company, chartered in 1922, was a direct outgrowth of the Elgin National Watch Company's development of a car dashboard clock for Van Slicken and Stewart-Warner. When Elgin established a trade school, the Elgin Watchmakers College, it at first shared a building with the Elgin Clock Company.

In the late 1920s, the top executives moved into offices in the Jeweler's Building, at the intersection of Hubbard and Upper Wacker in downtown Chicago just south of the North Branch of the Chicago River. In 1928, Elgin donated an eight-ton steel-and-bronze ornamental clock to the 41-story Jeweler's Building (then the tallest skyscraper outside New York

Drilling holes in watch
plates, Elgin National
Watch Co., Elgin, IL.
(*Library of Congress*)

City). Now known by its address—35 East Wacker—the building, which
was erected in 1925–1926, housed the businesses of various jewelers, as
well as the corporate offices of Elgin. Surmounted by the company's Father Time symbol, it was originally a slave clock, meaning it received electric impulses from a master clock in the Elgin National Watch Company
Observatory at 123 Watch Street in Elgin, Illinois, that slowed or sped up
the slave clock's pendulums so it was accurate to one-hundredth of a second. The clock proved to be one of the company's most enduring legacies,
because, unlike the company's largest factory in Elgin, Illinois, with its
great clock tower, which was torn down in 1966, the clock on the old Jeweler's Building can still be seen.

In the very early 20th century, wristwatches had been considered jew-
elry for women (like early 19th-century French bracelet watches); consequently, the clock- and watch-manufacturing industry did not give
wristwatches the same respect given men's pocket watches, or they were
considered specialized timepieces for pilots (virtually all of whom were
men), but this changed during World War I. The U.S. government purchased large numbers of wristwatches for soldiers in General John "Black
Jack" Pershing's Allied Expeditionary Force. The trend was toward
smaller watches in general, and in 1920 Elgin found that size 12 pocket

watches were outselling bulkier size 16 and 18 models. Elgin was faster than its competitors in retooling to focus on the manufacture of wristwatches.

In 1920, Elgin workers were receiving a 10 percent wage increase and participating in a new profit-sharing plan that allowed them to purchase stock at below-market prices. The sense of being part of a tight-knit group that insiders called "Father Time's Family" was increased by a magazine called *The Watch Word*, published by the Employees Advisory Council beginning in 1921, which kept employees abreast of changes in each others' personal and professional lives (such as births and promotions). The number of employees peaked at 4,379 in 1927, but the numbers were already declining before the stock market crash of 1929, which caused watch sales to plummet and thus thousands of people to be laid off. In the 1920s, Elgin's daily output climbed to a peak of 4,000 watch movements before slipping to 3,500 in 1929.

Meanwhile, the American Waltham Watch Company of Waltham, Massachusetts, the company from which the first Elgin watchmakers had been recruited in 1864, started losing money in 1920–1921; employees were facing wage cuts of 10 percent and curtailed fringe benefits. In 1924, another wage cut at Waltham led to a strike, which at times became violent, that began on August 11 and did not end until January 7, 1925. The settlement recognized the unionization of workers but also confirmed the second wage cut. Only then could Waltham finish retooling to concentrate on the manufacture of wristwatches, yet another reason Elgin surpassed Waltham as America's largest watch manufacturer. By 1927, some jewelers were reporting that up to 90 percent of all watch sales were for wristwatches.

In addition to facing increasing competition from Swiss imports and the challenge of retooling to produce wristwatches instead of pocket watches, another gruesome problem beset American clock and watch manufacturers in the 1920s: the discovery that the teenage girls and young women employed as dial painters—who had been taught to place their paintbrushes between their lips when applying luminous paint to watch faces—were at risk of dying of radium poisoning. Watches with luminous dials were particularly popular with infantrymen fighting trench warfare. When the war ended, veterans spread the popularity of such watches at home (during this period, the government also purchased luminous instruments for ships, airplanes, and other military vehicles). Approximately 8,500 luminous watches were manufactured in 1913, but demand had grown to 2.2 million luminous watches by 1919.

Between 1917 and 1927, about 2,000 young women and teenage girls were employed as dial painters, of whom about 1,600 have been identified by researchers. At least 441 dial painters were employed between 1927 and 1940, and there was a minimum of 1,350 dial painters in the 1940s, when World War II once again drove up demand for luminous dials. Only the workers in the period between 1917 and 1927 developed cancers and other illnesses that were definitely attributable to radium poisoning. Of the 1,600 identified dial painters in that period, 63 suffered bone cancer and

23 suffered cancer of the nasal cavities or mastoid cavities. However, the first dial painters to die of radium poisoning were killed not by cancer but by anemia or necrosis of the jaw (death of jaw bone and tissue). In 1929, the U.S. Department of Labor listed 23 such fatalities. The first cancer victims started to die in 1929. In New Jersey, 18 women had died as a result of radium poisoning, 13 of whom had been stricken with fatal conditions other than cancer, and five had died of cancer by 1931. In Connecticut, 15 women had died of radium poisoning by 1940, nine from cancer and six from other causes.

Elgin, which began applying luminous paint to watch dials on-site in 1914, claimed that none of its workers suffered ill health due to exposure to radium, as a result of various precautions. First, the workroom where dial painters worked was equipped with suction vents to carry away radium in the air. Second, cabinets in the room had a glazed finish. Third, employees were supplied with lead workbenches. Fourth, employees were given periodic physical examinations to monitor their health, and they were observed under argon lamps for signs of radium on the skin. Other companies had evidently been less cautious than the highly paternalistic Elgin.

In 1919, U.S. Radium Corporation began to arrange for customers like the Waterbury Clock Company (now Timex) of Waterbury, Connecticut, to paint dials themselves. Lip-pointing was one of the techniques U.S. Radium instructors taught Waterbury's new dial painters. Waterbury was not the only timepiece manufacturer in Connecticut to begin painting its own luminous dials on-site. New Haven Clock Company of New Haven, the E. Ingraham Company of Bristol, and the Seth Thomas Clock Company of Thomaston did so as well. In February 1925, a 21-year-old Waterbury employee, Frances Splettstocher, who had worked for the company for four years, died after developing necrosis of the jaw and anemia a month earlier. Without admitting she had died of radium poisoning, in March the company forbade lip-pointing and later hired Dr. Frederick Flinn to inspect all 26 dial painters employed in August 1925. He found no ill health or radioactivity among them, but in 1926 he revealed that he knew of two other victims of radium poisoning at the Waterbury plant.

Hearst Corporation newspapers took up the cause, bringing the plight of poisoned dial painters to public attention. In 1924, underfunded New Jersey government officials prodded a private organization, the Consumers' League of New Jersey, a middle-class women's group dedicated to improving workplace conditions for women and children, into pressing the government and corporations for reforms that would compensate victims and introduce regulation to prevent further victims. The Consumers' League consequently provided Harrison Martland, the scientist credited with discovering radium poisoning, with data and helped win compensation for former radium-poisoned dial painters in New Jersey. The group also pressured the New Jersey state labor commissioner to ban radium dial painting within the state. Sickened dial painters also found a powerful advocate in Dr. Alice Hamilton, a professor at Harvard University and government inspector at the federal and state level. Martland estimated that dial painters ingested 15 to 215 micrograms of radium a week, of which a small amount was permanently deposited in the body, but a mere half microgram ultimately proved to be dangerous. Once employers forbade lip pointing instead of encouraging it, the risk of contracting cancer was greatly reduced but not altogether eliminated.

Flinn privately confided to Harvard University's Dr. Cecil Drinker that radioactive material was to blame for worker illnesses at the U.S. Radium Corporation's plant in Orange, New Jersey, but in his article "Radioactive Material: An Industrial Hazard?" Flinn denied that any cases of jaw necrosis had been found in dial painters outside Orange and blamed cases of jaw ne-crosis there on syphilis, trench mouth, or bacteriologic infection, insinuating that the victims might be to blame for their illnesses by sexual promiscuity.

Executives of the Radium Chemical Company and the Radium Dial Company, both subsidiaries of the Standard Chemical Company, hid knowledge of illnesses among executives and dial painters in Pennsylvania and Illinois from the federal government until 1928. As Claudia Clark points out in *Radium Girls: Women and Industrial Health Reform, 1910–1935*, executives of the Standard Chemical Company, U.S. Radium, and other companies resisted governmental regulation for a number of reasons. They stood to lose money to liability suits if workers' claims were proven accu-rate; to lose money if more precautions were taken in dial painting, driving up the cost of production (and thus the price) of luminous watches; and to lose money selling radium for internal medicine if radium became widely considered dangerous. Further, a number of executives in the industry were research scientists who may have been in denial about how much danger they had placed themselves in by handling radium.

There were unexpected benefits of research into radium poisoning, however. The study of the effects of radiation on living tissue led to human radiobiology. At Harvard University, Cecil Drinker, who stressed the dangers of inhaling radium, researched the effects of inhaling other dusts with his engineer brother Philip, which led to the development of the iron lung that prolonged the lives of many polio sufferers. Philip Drinker became increasingly adept at designing ventilation systems that removed dusts and fumes from the air in factories. By 1932, his new Public Health Engineering Department had absorbed his brother's Industrial Hygiene Department, and upon Dr. Alice Hamilton's retire-ment in 1936, her Industrial Medicine Department. The emphasis had shifted from studying the health of workers to making the workplace healthy.

Charles Walgreen and the Rise of Chain Pharmacies

The world's first drugstore chains evolved in England and Scotland at the end of the 19th century. In the United States, the first chains were Hegeman & Company of New York City; Charles B. Jaynes of Boston; the Hall & Lyon Company of Providence, Rhode Island; and Cora Dow of Cincinnati, Ohio. After working for several successful Chicago pharmacists, Charles R. Walgreen Sr. (1873–1939) opened his first pharmacy in 1901. Louis

K. Liggett founded the United Drug Company in 1907. In the short term, Liggett would be more successful, but Walgreen would have the longer-lasting legacy. The former had 45 drugstores by 1916, and added 107 more by acquiring the amalgamated Riker-Hegman-Jaynes stores, reaching a peak of 672 drugstores by 1930. And that was just in the United States. Combining with pharmaceutical companies to form Drug, Inc., Liggett gained control of a chain of English chemist (druggist) stores, Boots, Ltd. At the height of the Roaring Twenties, Drug, Inc. operated 1,000 pharmacies in the United States and United Kingdom, but the consortium dissolved in 1933.

By contrast, Walgreen slowly and steadily expanded his enterprise from a single shop located in Barrett's Hotel at Cottage Grove and Bowen Avenue on Chicago's South Side. He had acquired 16 stores by 1916 and 29 stores by 1922, growing fourfold by 1927—the year the privately held company became a publicly traded corporation. The one hundredth store opened in Chicago in 1926. The company had grown fourfold again by 1961. The company attributed no small measure of its growth to the popularity of chocolate malted milkshakes developed by Ivar "Pop" Coulson at a Walgreens soda fountain in 1922, by adding vanilla ice cream (produced in-house at a plant the company owned on 44th Street on the South Side of Chicago) to the traditional recipe of milk, chocolate syrup, and malt powder.

Expansion and Collapse of Samuel Insull's Utilities and Transportation Empire

Samuel Insull Sr. (1859–1938) did more than anyone else, including his mentor, Thomas Alva Edison, to create the modern electric utility infrastructure of the United States. In a few short years he went from being Edison's secretary to becoming one of the founders of General Electric, now one of the largest conglomerates on Earth, synthesizing technological innovations to provide cheap electricity to millions and providing a business model that is still used to this day. The latter, though it would make him extremely rich, would ultimately lead to his ruin because his investment schemes would be viewed as the sort of stock market speculation that had led to the stock market crash of 1929 and subsequent onset of the Great Depression. With time, his notoriety has become ingrained on a national level, but he is well remembered in Chicago not only for establishing or expanding Commonwealth Edison, People's Gas, and the Northern Indiana Public Service Company but also for the parts he played in the foundation of Chicago's Lyric Opera House, Chicago's mass transit grid, and the Museum of Science and Industry. His son, Samuel Insull Jr., would follow his example in becoming a member of the museum's board of trustees. Both Insulls were also trustees of Chicago's A Century of Progress World's Fair of 1933–1934.

With General Electric and Westinghouse following Insull's lead at Commonwealth Edison, the number of electrified homes rose from 14 to 70 percent from 1910 to 1930. Despite the efforts of these companies and

An immigrant who came to America with little money, Samuel Insull amassed a fortune only to lose it in the Great Depression, undergo trial for fraud, and find his name vilified throughout the nation. (*Library of Congress*)

their promises of electric appliances leading to greater leisure, however, most people found iceboxes to be cheaper and easier to use than refrigerators well into the 1930s, and a number of studies have shown that housewives spend about as much time cleaning their homes with electric appliances as their foremothers did without them.

Insull was born in London in 1858, and in 1879 he became a secretary to George A. Gouraud, a representative in England of one of his idols, Thomas Alva Edison. In 1881, at the age of 22, Insull immigrated to the United States and became secretary to Edison himself. Just eight years later, in 1889, he had risen to become vice president of Edison General Electric Company in Schenectady, New York. After banker J. P. Morgan assumed control of Edison's electric companies in 1892, he dispatched Insull to Chicago to head Chicago Edison. During the Panic of 1893, Insull used funds from Morgan to purchase all of the other electric companies competing with him in the area.

Next, he established the industry principle of achieving economies of scale with large electric generating plants that could generate more energy for less money by constructing a large steam-powered turbine plant where Harrison Street met the Chicago River. Insull achieved economies of scale by constructing larger dynamos that used steam turbines that could generate more electricity for less money, especially if they generated DC rather than AC power. In switching his support from Edison's direct current (DC) format to the alternating current (AC) format championed by Edison's rivals Nikola Tesla and George Westinghouse, Insull was not merely riding the tide but ensuring a Tesla-Westinghouse victory in the so-called "war of currents." Insull was an innovator in other ways as well, foreseeing the value in selling electric generator sets to individual companies that wanted to generate their own electricity instead of restricting himself to generating electricity at Edison-owned plants and selling it to the public. To decrease the cost of generating electricity and increase demand for it, he convinced business to buy electricity at a reduced rate during off-peak hours.

By 1907, Insull had consolidated 20 utility providers under the name Commonwealth Edison. Beyond his control of Commonwealth Edison, he gained controlling interest in utilities in northwest Indiana, through a holding company called the Middle West Utilities Co., changing its name in 1924 to Midland Utilities Co., and changing its name again in 1929 to Midland United Co. In addition to owning these utilities and selling electrification (as a concept as well as a product) to railroads, he came to own all or part of several railroads. In November 1910, he had been named receiver of his company's largest customer, the Chicago & Oak Park Elevated Railroad Company. This placed him in a good position to facilitate the consolidation of Chicago's four elevated railroads, and he pledged $6 million of Commonwealth Edison money to a syndicate trying to do just that by purchasing outstanding shares of the South Side, Metropolitan, and Northwestern Elevated Railroads. The syndicate, which was led by the investment firm of Blair & Company, named Insull chairman of the new Chicago Elevated Railways Collateral Trust, which was described as a "voluntary association" rather than a holding company. Insull made Metropolitan Elevated Railroad president Britton I. Budd (1871–1965) president of the new voluntary association as well as president of each of the other three component elevated railroads. Riders complained that under the new system they should be getting free transfers and there should be through-routing but they were not enjoying any such advantages, and the Insull-Budd response was to inform the City of Chicago that these things could be had in return for permission to lengthen the Loop's train platforms.

In 1916, Insull gained control of the bankrupt Chicago North Shore & Milwaukee interurban railroad, which ran from Milwaukee to Evanston, an inner-ring suburb immediately north of Chicago. He made Budd president of this railroad, too, and Budd arranged for the Chicago North Shore & Milwaukee to serve Chicago proper by using the Northwestern Elevated Railroad's tracks, which were leased from the Chicago Milwaukee & St. Paul Railroad, starting in 1919. He purchased two other interurban lines as well, the South Shore Line and the Chicago, Elgin, and Aurora Railroad, as well as three streetcar lines he consolidated under the name Chicago Rapid Transit Line. In 1922, despite all their achievements, the elevated railroads were still only breaking even, and Insull told Chicago's City Council that the Chicago Elevated Railways Collateral Trust would accept any reasonable offer from the city, but none was forthcoming, so Insull and company reorganized the elevated companies into a single entity, the Chicago Rapid Transit Company, in 1924. The Chicago Rapid Transit Company purchased the Chicago & Oak Park Railroad at a court-ordered auction.

Beyond providing utilities and mass transportation for the area, Insull also left a mark on Chicago by founding the Lyric Opera House (as a showplace for his young bride, an opera singer). By the mid-1920s, Insull had long been admired for his shrewd business strategies and reviled not only for the monopolies he had created himself but also for monopolies others had modeled off of his.

On October 14, 1926, President Calvin Coolidge threw a switch in the White House to activate a mile's worth of 2,100-watt street lamps along State Street in the Chicago Loop, creating the "brightest outdoor mile ever made" (Platt 1991, 260). Presumably, the investment the merchants of State Street had made in upgrading the street lamps was quickly realized, because more than 200,000 people witnessed the event, and merchants on Randolph Street soon followed suit.

In 1928, the Federal Trade Commission launched what would become a six-year investigation of Insull's economic empire. Franklin D. Roosevelt vilified him when running for the presidency in 1932, speaking of the "the Insulls whose hand is against everyman's." If government officials meant to strip Insull of what they considered ill-gotten gains, they were acting too late. After the stock market crash in 1929, and over the course of 1930, elevated train ridership fell by 13.8 million people, and plummeted by an additional 30.5 million people in 1931 as a worsening Great Depression caused mass layoffs.

Philanthropy

A number of super-rich individuals of this age founded museums. With the notable exception of New York City's Museum of Modern Art (MOMA), these were museums devoted to science rather than art. Three museums were modeled on the Deutsches Museum in Munich, Bavaria, the world's first interactive museum of science and industry. Three of Chicago's four great science museums were founded in this era, and all four were founded by wealthy men whose fortunes could be traced to just two companies: the department store Marshall Field & Company and the catalog retailer Sears, Roebuck & Company.

MOMA was founded in 1929 at a luncheon in John D. Rockefeller Jr.'s house. The founders were his wife, Abby Aldrich Rockefeller (1874–1948); Mary Quinn Sullivan (1877–1939), an art teacher who was married to the rich lawyer Cornelius J. Sullivan; Lizzie Plummer Bliss (1864–1931), patroness of the arts and daughter of the wealthy textile merchant and Republican Party leader Cornelius Newton Bliss (1833–1911); and A. Conger Goodyear, a former president of the Buffalo Fine Art Academy's Albright Art Gallery (now the Albright-Knox Art Gallery) in Buffalo, New York, who became chairman of the board of trustees for the new enterprise. Goodyear recruited two very important men from the American art world to become trustees of the new museum. One was the Paris-born Boston Brahmin art critic and *Vanity Fair* editor Francis Crownin-shield (1872–1947). The other was Paul J. Sachs, who was a partner in the investment bank founded by his father and maternal grandfather, Gold-man, Sachs. Sachs's love of art had led him to become an art history pro-fessor at Harvard University and an associate director of Harvard's Fogg Art Museum. The museum founders rented space on the 12th floor of Man-hattan's Heckscher Building (now the Crown Building) and MOMA opened its doors on November 7, 1929, a few days after the stock market crash that started the Great Depression. MOMA survived the Great Depres-sion, moving into the Time-Life Building in Rockefeller Center in 1937, before opening on May 10, 1939, in its permanent home on 53rd Street, a building designed in the International Style (known as Bauhaus in Ger-many and Art Modern in France) by Philip Goodwin and Edward Durell Stone (1902–1978).

Chicago's John G. Shedd Aquarium, more popularly known simply as the Shedd Aquarium, was endowed with a gift of $3.25 million by Mar-shall Field's protégé John Graves Shedd (1850–1926), who had succeeded Marshall Field I (1834–1906) as president and chairman of the board of directors of Marshall Field & Company upon Field's death in 1906. The ar-chitectural firm of Graham, Anderson, Probst, and White designed the Shedd Aquarium, just as they had designed the White City's Palace of Fine Arts, the Wrigley Building, Marshall Field & Company's flagship store on State Street in the Chicago Loop, and the Field Museum of Natural His-tory. They would later design the reconstruction of the Palace of Fine Arts to house the Museum of Science and Industry.

In 1924, a group of businessmen rallied behind Shedd's project to form the Shedd Aquarium Society, asking the South Park commissioners to use the space adjacent to Grant Park created with landfill where what is now Roosevelt Road met Lake Michigan. This was in keeping with the *Plan of Chicago*, written by Daniel Burnham (1846–1912) and assistant Edward H. Bennet with the sponsorship of the Commercial Club of Chicago. The Burnham plan had called for museums to be built in parklands overlook-ing the lakeshore.

The groundbreaking took place on November 2, 1927. On December 19, 1929—just after a blizzard had blanketed the city and two months after the stock market crash—the Shedd Aquarium had a preview for the public. Thousands of people turned out to see the sole exhibit at the moment: a freshwater pool with fish, lizards, and amphibians. To fill Shedd Aquarium's tanks with 1 million gallons of seawater, 20 railroad tank cars had to make eight round trips between Key West, Florida, and Chicago in 1930. As John Shedd had only lived long enough to see the architect's first set of plans of the proposed aquarium, it was his widow, Mary R. Shedd, who cut the rib-bon at the opening ceremony on May 8, 1930.

In 1926, Julius Rosenwald founded the Museum of Science and Indus-try (MSI) in Jackson Park in the Hyde Park neighborhood on the South Side of Chicago. It opened in three stages between 1933 and 1940, as

Julius Rosenwald took the mail order business founded by Richard Sears, modernized it, and with the fortune he made, engaged in extensive philanthropy during the early 20th century. One of his greatest successes was being behind the creation of the world famous Museum of Science and Industry in Chicago. (*Library of Congress*)

construction work was completed and exhibits were installed. Rosenwald acted through the Commercial Club of Chicago, which had earlier commissioned Burnham's plan of Chicago.

In November 1921, Rosenwald had revealed to Samuel Insull, who was then president of the Commercial Club, that he wanted to found an interactive science museum modeled on the Deutsches Museum in Munich, Bavaria. Rosenwald received support in this venture from several Commercial Club members, including U.S. Gypsum president Sewell Avery, Illinois Bell chairman William Rufus Abbott, and banker and utilities executive Rufus Dawes, who served, respectively as first, second, and third presidents of MSI.

In 1925, the Commercial Club elected to transform the Palace of Fine Arts into an industrial museum, and received the private endorsement of Dr. Charles R. Richards, director of the American Association of Museums. This building, designed by Charles Atwood (1849–1895), was the last remaining palace from the White City fairgrounds of Chicago's first world's fair, the World's Columbian Exposition (1893), that was still standing in situ in Jackson Park. It had housed the Field Columbian Museum (which evolved into the Field Museum of Natural History) from 1894 to 1920, when that organization vacated the building to occupy a new home in Burnham Park closer to the commercial heart of the city. The South Park Commission (SPC) had initially wanted to raze the building after the Field Museum organization left, because it had fallen into such unseemly disrepair, but the sculptor Lorado Taft (1860–1936) rallied architects and civic groups around the idea of restoring the building to its neoclassical architectural glory. In 1924, the SPC gained permission from voters to raise money to restore the building by selling $5 million in bonds.

The reconstruction and restoration project was twice delayed by lawsuits brought in 1926 and 1929 by William E. Furlong, a lawyer who wanted the Palace of Fine Arts to house a convention center instead of or in addition to Rosenwald's museum. Because of these delays, Rosenwald did not live to see the museum open. He died at 2:55 P.M. on January 6, 1932, about 18 months before the museum's first opening ceremony on June 19, 1933. Ultimately, reconstructing the Beaux-Arts staff facade in limestone, restoring the brick substructure, constructing the Art Moderne interior, installing exhibits, and landscaping cost the South Park District, the Rosenwalds, and the Museum Corporation just over $8 million.

The Adler Planetarium & Astronomy Museum was founded by Sears, Roebuck & Company executive Max Adler and famed Northwestern University astronomer Philip Fox, two men intimately connected with the MSI. Fox, who had risen to the rank of major during World War I and remained active in the U.S. Army Reserves, eventually achieving the rank of full colonel and earning the nickname "The Fighting Star Gazer," was a professor of astronomy and director of Northwestern University's Dearborn Observatory when he was tapped to serve as first director of the Adler Planetarium.

Fox went from being the founding director of the Adler Planetarium & Astronomy Museum to being the third director of the MSI. Max Adler, the brother-in-law of Sears, Roebuck & Company president and MSI founder Julius Rosenwald, initially wanted the Adler Planetarium to be firmly associated with MSI. Instead, the first planetarium in the Western Hemisphere was built as a 160-foot diameter dodecagon at what is now known as the Museum Campus, which is also home to the Field Museum and Shedd Aquarium, north of Soldier Field at the northwest corner of Burnham Park, adjacent to Grant Park. In his 1935 book *Adler Planetarium and Astronomy Museum Operated and Maintained by Chicago Park District: An Account of the Optical Planetarium and a Brief Guide to the Museum*, Fox says of the three museums in Burnham Park, "The three are fittingly closely associated and form a trinity dedicated to the study of 'The Heavens above, the Earth beneath, and the waters under the Earth'" (Fox 1935, 6).

Max Adler (1866–1952) was the Elgin, Illinois–born son of Ashkenazi (German Jewish) immigrants who came to the Unites States in or about 1850. He was a violinist until he married MSI founder Julius Rosenwald's sister Sophie, at which time Rosenwald employed him as a vice president of Sears, Roebuck, & Company. In 1928, the year Robert E. Wood became president of Sears, Roebuck & Company, Adler retired from Sears to pursue philanthropic interests, much as Rosenwald had scaled back his direct involvement in Sears management to find more time for philanthropy by going from president of the company to chairman of its board of directors. That year, Max and Sophie Adler traveled with Adler's cousin, the architect Ernest Grunsfeld, to Germany, including stops at the Deutsches Museum and Jena, Germany, where five years earlier Dr. Walther Bauersfeld had invented the Zeiss Projector. Fox wrote that "the cost of the building was somewhere in the neighborhood of $550,000" (Remarks made at the American Association of Museums Annual Meeting and Museum Expo, Knappenberger 2007).

The Adler Planetarium was presented to the South Park District on May 10, 1930. Fox quoted Adler as saying, "Chicago has been striving to create, and in large measure has succeeded in creating, facilities for its citizens of today to live a life richer and more full of meaning than was available for citizens of yesterday. Toward the creation of such opportunities I have desired to contribute" (Fox 1935, 6–7). The popular conception of the universe is too meager; the planets and the stars are too far removed from general knowledge. In our reflections, we dwell too little upon the concept that the world and all human endeavor within it are governed by established order and too infrequently upon the truth that under the heavens everything is interrelated, even as each of us to the other. The Adler Planetarium & Astronomy Museum opened its doors to the public on May 12, 1930.

Conclusion

A few inventions of the Jazz Age that initially seemed beneficial to humankind subsequently proved to be toxic to humans or destructive to the global environment. As in other eras of human history, in the Jazz Age research scientists, inventers, and other innovators who discovered new technologies or ways of doing things garnered fortunes for the business enterprises they led or worked for and were enriched by their discoveries. Others were cheated or otherwise deprived of the money and prestige rightfully due them by their financial backers, though in the case of Billy Durant, he arguably undermined himself with reckless investments. Workers were sometimes killed or otherwise harmed by the technologies they developed.

The Jazz Age featured a wide variety of activities in the economic sphere. From the benevolent to the overtly greedy, business activities during this time display a dynamic approach to participation in the economic sphere. Whether this period is viewed as merely a precursor to the Great Depression or judged on its own, business activities in the Jazz Age, and those who participated in such activities, demonstrate the ability to take advantage of the opportunities available.

References and Further Reading

Alft, E. C., and William H. Briska. *Elgin Time: A History of the Elgin National Watch Company, 1864–1968*. Elgin, IL: Elgin Historical Society, 2003.

Barck, Oscar Theodore, ed. *America in the World: Twentieth-Century History in Documents*. New York: Meridian Books, 1961.

Bellis, Mary. "Freon." Available at http://www.inventors.about.com.

Bellis, Mary. "The Father of Cool." Available at http://www.inventors.about.com.

Boyd, Tomas Alvin. *Charles F. Kettering: A Biography*. Frederick, MD: Beard Books, 2002.

Clark, Claudia. *Radium Girls: Women and Industrial Health Reform, 1910–1935*. Chapel Hill: University of North Carolina Press, 1997.

Cox, James A. *A Century of Light*. New York: Benjamin Company, 1979.

Edsforth, Ronald. "Sloan, Alfred Pritchard Jr." *American National Biography* 20, 1999.

Fox, Philip. *Adler Planetarium and Astronomy Museum Operated and Maintained by Chicago Park District: An Account of the Optical Planetarium and a Brief Guide to the Museum*. Chicago, IL: Lakeside Press, R. R. Donnelley & Sons & Company, 1935.

Goldman, Jonathan. *The Empire State Building Book*. New York: St. Martin's Press, 1980.

Howells, Trevor, ed. *A Guide to the World's Greatest Buildings: Masterpieces of Architecture and Engineering*. San Francisco: Fog City Press, 1996.

Knappenberger, Paul. "Adler 75: Reshaping America's First Planetarium." American Association of Museums (AAM) Annual Meeting & Museum Expo, Chicago, IL, May 16, 2007.

Landes, David S. *Dynasties: Fortunes and Misfortunes of the World's Great Family Businesses*. New York: Penguin Books, 1996.

Minutes of the Executive Committee Meeting. Museum of Science and Industry, 1930.

Nelson, William T. *Fresh Water Submarines: The Manitowoc Story*. Manitowoc, WI: Hoeffner Printing, 1986.

Parrish, Thomas. *The Submarine: A History*. New York: Penguin Group, 2004.

Platt, Harold L. *The Electric City: Energy and the Growth of the Chicago Era, 1880–1930*. Chicago: University of Chicago Press, 1991.

Sklar, Robert. *Movie-Made America: A Cultural History of American Movies*. New York: Vintage Books, 1975.

Sonnedecker, Glenn, ed. *Kremer and Urdang's History of Pharmacy*. Philadelphia: J. B. Lippincott, 1976.

Walgreen.com. "Our Past." *Our History*. Available at http://www.walgreens.com/about/history.

Primary Documents

Mitchell Newton-Matza

The National Origins Act (1924)

The issue of immigration has been a national concern since the early years of the new Republic. During the first half of the 19th century, much of the anti-immigration bias was directed at the Irish, who were not only considered inferior but also faced a strong anti-Catholic bias. In the later decades of the 19th century and into the 20th, newer groups from Central and Eastern Europe entered the country in increasing numbers. Many of these groups were of Slavic descent, so besides the long-standing anti-Catholic bias, a strong anti-Semitic bias also emerge. The National Origins Act, also known as the Johnson-Reed Act, severely limited immigration to 2 percent of any particular group's U.S. population according to the 1890 census. A cap was placed at 150,000 for any group. To some critics of the law, it was closing the barn door after the horses had escaped as the presence of these newer groups was already numerous and strong.

SIXTY EIGHTH CONGRESS. SESS.I. Ch. 185, 190. 1924. Be it enacted by the Senate and House of Representatives of the United States of America in Congress assembled, That this Act may be cited as the "Immigration Act of 1924" Sec. 2. (a) A consular officer upon the application of any immigrant (as defined in section 3) may (under the conditions hereinafter prescribed and subject to the limitations prescribed in this Act or regulations made there under as to the number of immigration visas which may be issued by such officer) issue to such immigrant an immigration visa which shall consist of one copy of the application provided for in section 7, visaed by such consular officer. Such visa shall specify (1) the nationality of the immigrant; (2) whether he is a quota immigrant (as defined in section 5) or a non-quota immigrant (as defined in section 4); (3) the date on which the validity of the immigration visa shall expire; and such additional information necessary to the proper enforcement of the immigration laws and the naturalization laws as may be by regulations prescribed. b. The immigrant shall furnish two copies of his photograph to the consular officer.

One copy shall be permanently attached by the consular officer to the immigration visa and the other copy shall be disposed of as may be by regulations prescribed. c. The validity of an immigration visa shall expire at the end of such period, specified in the immigration visa, not exceeding four months, as shall be by regulations prescribed. In the case of an immigrant arriving in the United States by water, or arriving by water in foreign contiguous territory on a continuous voyage to the United States, if the vessel, before the expiration of the validity of his immigration visa, departed from the last port outside the United States and outside foreign contiguous territory at which the immigrant embarked, and if the immigrant proceeds on a continuous voyage to the United States, then, regardless of the time of his arrival in the United States, the validity of his immigration visa shall not be considered to have expired. (d) If an immigrant is required by any law, or regulations or orders made pursuant to law, to secure the visa of his passport by a consular officer before being permitted to enter the United States, such immigrant shall not be required to secure any other visa of his passport than the immigration visa issued under this Act, but a record of the number and date of his immigration visa shall be noted on his passport without charge therefore. This subdivision shall not apply to an immigrant who is relieved, under subdivision (b) of section 13, from obtaining an immigration visa. (e) The manifest or list of passengers required by the immigration laws shall contain a place for entering thereon the date, place of issuance, and number of the immigration visa of each immigrant. The immigrant shall surrender his immigration visa to the immigration officer at the port of inspection, who shall at the time of inspection endorse on the immigration visa the date, the port of entry, and the name of the vessel, if any, on which the immigrant arrived. The immigration visa shall be transmitted forthwith by the immigration officer in charge at the port of inspection to the Department of Labor under regulations prescribed by the Secretary of Labor. (f) No immigration visa shall be issued to an immigrant if it appears to the consular officer, from statements in the application, or in the papers submitted therewith, that the immigrant is inadmissible to the United States under the immigration laws, nor shall such immigration visa be issued if the application fails to comply with the provisions of this Act, nor shall such immigration visa be issued if the consular officer knows or has reason to believe that the immigrant is inadmissible to the United States under the immigration laws. (g) Nothing in this Act shall be construed to entitle an immigrant, to whom an immigration visa has been issued, to enter the United States, if, upon arrival in the United States, he is found to be inadmissible to the United States under the immigration laws. The substance of this subdivision shall be printed conspicuously upon every immigration visa. (h) A fee of $9 shall be charged for the issuance of each immigration visa, which shall be covered into the Treasury as miscellaneous receipts.

DEFINITION OF IMMIGRANT. SEC. 3. When used in this Act the term "immigrant" means an alien departing from any place outside the United States destined for the United States, except (1) a government official, his family, attendants, servants, and employees, (2) an alien visiting the United

States temporarily as a tourist or temporarily for business or pleasure, (3) an alien in continuous transit through the United States, (4) an alien lawfully admitted to the United States who later goes in transit from one part of the United States to another through foreign contiguous territory, (5) a bona fide alien seaman serving as such on a vessel arriving at a port of the United States and seeking to enter temporarily the United States solely in the pursuit of his calling as a seaman, and (6) an alien entitled to enter the United States solely to carry on trade under and in pursuance of the provisions of a present existing treaty of commerce and navigation.

NON-QUOTA IMMIGRANTS. SEC. 4. When used in this Act the term "non-quota immigrant" means- (a) An immigrant who is the unmarried child under 18 years of age, or the wife, of a citizen of the United States who resides therein at the time of the filing of a petition under section 9; (b) An immigrant previously lawfully admitted to the United States, who is returning from a temporary visit abroad; (c) An immigrant who was born in the Dominion of Canada, Newfoundland, the Republic of Mexico, the Republic of Cuba, the Republic of Haiti, the Dominican Republic, the Canal Zone, or an independent country of Central or South America, and his wife, and his unmarried children under 18 years of age, if accompanying or following to join him; (d) An immigrant who continuously for at least two years immediately preceding the time of his application for admission to the United States has been, and who seeks to enter the United States solely for the purpose of, carrying on the vocation of minister of any religious denomination, or professor of a college, academy, seminary, or university; and his wife, and his unmarried children under 18 years of age, if accompanying or following to join him; or (e) An immigrant who is a bona fide student at least 15 years of age and who seeks to enter the United States solely for the purpose of study at an accredited school, college, academy, seminary, or university, particularly designated by him and approved by, the Secretary of Labor, which shall have agreed to report to the Secretary of Labor the termination of attendance of each immigrant student, and if any such institution of learning fails to make such reports promptly the approval shall be withdrawn.

EXCLUSION FROM UNITED STATES. SEC. 13. (a) No immigrant shall be admitted to the United States unless he (1) has an unexpired immigration visa or was born subsequent to the issuance of the immigration visa of the accompanying parent, (2) is of the nationality specified in the visa in the immigration visa, (3) is a non-quota immigrant if specified in the visa in the immigration visa as such, and (4) is otherwise admissible under the immigration laws. (b) In such classes of cases and under such conditions as may be by regulations prescribed immigrants who have been legally admitted to the United States and who depart therefrom temporarily may be admitted to the United States without being required to obtain an immigration visa. (c) No alien ineligible to citizenship shall be admitted to the United States unless such alien (1) is admissible as a non-quota immigrant under the provisions of subdivision (b), (d), or (e) of section 4, or (2) is the wife, or the unmarried child under 18 years of age, of an immigrant admissible under such subdivision (d), and is accompanying or following to join him, or (3) is not an immigrant as defined in section 3.

(d) The Secretary of Labor may admit to the United States any otherwise admissible immigrant not admissible under clause (2) or (3) of subdivision (a) of this section, if satisfied that such inadmissibility was not known to, and could not have been ascertained by the exercise of reasonable diligence by, such immigrant prior to the departure of the vessel from the last port outside the United States and outside foreign contiguous territory or, in the case of an immigrant coming from foreign contiguous territory, prior to the application of the immigrant for admission. (e) No quota immigrant shall be admitted under subdivision (d) if the entire number of immigration visas which may be issued to quota immigrants of the same nationality for the fiscal year has already been issued. If such entire number of immigration visas has not been issued, then the Secretary of State, upon the admission of a quota immigrant under subdivision (d), shall reduce by one the number of immigration visas which may be issued to quota immigrants of the same nationality during the fiscal year in which such immigrant is admitted; but if the Secretary of State finds that it will not be practicable to make such reduction before the end of such fiscal year, then such immigrant shall not be admitted. (f) Nothing in this section shall authorize the remission or refunding of a fine, liability to which has accrued under section 16.

DEPORTATION SEC. 14. Any alien who at any time after entering the United States is found to have been at the time of entry not entitled under this Act to enter the United States, or to have remained therein for a longer time than permitted under this Act or regulations made thereunder, shall be taken into custody and deported in the same manner as provided for in sections 19 and 20 of the Immigration Act of 1917: Provided, That the Secretary of Labor may, under such conditions and restrictions as to support and care as he may deem necessary, permit permanently to remain in the United States, any alien child who, when under sixteen years of age was heretofore temporarily admitted to the United States and who is now within the United States and either of whose parents is a citizen of the United States.

"An act to limit the migration of aliens into the United States ... " (approved May 26, 1924). *The Statutes at Large of the United States of America, from December 1923 to March 1925.* Vol. XLII, Part 1, pp. 153–169 (Washington, D.C.: Government Printing Office, 1925).

Sheppard-Towner Maternity and Infancy Protection Act (1921)

This was the first such social legislation providing matching federal funds as a way to reduce infant mortality rates. The idea of protecting the health and well-being of women and children was not new. The 1908 U.S. Supreme Court case *Muller v. Oregon* upheld a law that limited the number of hours women could work in order to protect their health, especially for those women of childbearing years. The Sheppard Act provided for $1 million in annual appropriations. Many criticized the law for federal intrusion into states' authority. Funding for this program lapsed in 1929.

An Act for the promotion of the welfare and hygiene of maternity and infancy, and for other purposes.

Be it enacted by the Senate and House of Representatives of the United States of America in Congress assembled, That there is hereby authorized to be appropriated annually, out of any money in the Treasury not otherwise appropriated, the sums specified in section 2 of this Act, to be paid to the several States for the purpose of cooperating with them in promoting the welfare and hygiene of maternity and infancy as hereinafter provided.

Sec. 2. For the purpose of carrying out the provisions of this Act, there is authorized to be appropriated, out of any money in the Treasury not otherwise appropriated, for the current fiscal year $480,000, to be equally apportioned among the several States, and for each subsequent year, for the period of five years, $240,000, to be equally apportioned among the several States in the manner hereinafter provided: *Provided*, That there is hereby authorized to be appropriated for the use of the States, subject to the provisions of this Act, for the fiscal year ending June 30, 1922, an additional sum of $1,000,000, and annually thereafter, for the period of five years, an additional sum not to exceed $1,000,000: *Provided further*, That the additional appropriations herein authorized shall be apportioned $5,000 to each State and the balance among the States in the proportion which their population bears to the total population of the States of the United States, according to the last preceding United States census: *And provided further*, That no payment out of the additional appropriation herein authorized shall be made in any year to any State until an equal sum has been appropriated for that year by the legislature of such State for the maintenance of the services and facilities provided for in this Act.

So much of the amount apportioned to any State for any fiscal year as remains unpaid to such State at the close thereof shall be available for expenditures in that State until the close of the succeeding fiscal year.

Sec. 3. There is hereby created a Board of Maternity and Infant Hygiene, which shall consist of the Chief of the Children's Bureau, the Surgeon General of the United States Public Health Service, and the United States Board of Education, and which is hereafter designated in this Act as the Board. The Board shall elect its own chairman and perform the duties for in this Act . . .

Sec. 4. In order to secure the benefits of the appropriations authorized in section 2 of this Act, any State shall, through the legislative authority thereof, accept the provisions of this Act and designate or authorize the creation of a State agency with which the Children's Bureau shall have all necessary powers to cooperate herein provided in the administration of the provisions of this Act: *Provided*, That in any State having a child-welfare or child-hygiene division in its State agency of health, the said State agency of health shall administer the provisions of this Act through such divisions. If the legislature of any State has not made provision for accepting the provisions of this Act, the governor of each State may in so far as he is authorized to do so by the laws of such State accept the provisions of this Act and designate or create a State agency to cooperate with the Children's Bureau until six months after the adjournment of the first regular session of the legislature in such State following the passage of this Act . . .

Sec. 8. Any State desiring to receive the benefits of this Act shall, by its agency described in section 4, submit to the Children's Bureau detailed plans for carrying out the provisions of this Act within such State which plan shall be subject to the approval of the board: *Provided,* That the plans of the States under this Act shall provide that no official, or agent, or representative in carrying out the provisions of this Act shall enter any home or take charge of any child over the objection of the parents, or either of them, or the person standing in loco parentis or having custody of such child. If these plans shall be in conformity with the provisions of the Act and reasonably appropriate and adequate to carry out its purposes they shall be approved by the board and due notice of such approval shall be sent to the State agency by the chief of the Children's Bureau.

Sec. 9. No official, agent, or representative of the Children's Bureau shall by virtue of this Act have any right to enter any home over the objection of the owner thereof, or to take charge of any child over the objection of the parents, or either of them, or of the person standing in loco parentis or having custody of such child. Nothing in the Act shall be construed as limiting the power of a parent or guardian or person standing in loco parentis to determine what treatment of correction shall be provided for a child or the agency or agencies to be employed for such purpose . . .

Sec. 13. The Children's Bureau shall perform the duties assigned to it by this Act under the supervision of the Secretary of Labor, and he shall include in his annual report to Congress a full account of the administration of this Act and expenditures of the moneys herein authorized.

Sec. 14. This Act shall be construed as intending to secure to the various States control of the administration of this Act within their respective States, subject only to the provisions and purposes of this Act.

U.S. Congress. Sheppard-Towner Maternity and Infancy Protection Act. P.L. 67-97. Approved November 23, 1921.

American Education Week Announcements (1920–1926)

In what started as a week to promote and celebrate the American educational system, American Education Week (AEW) began to be seen as an ultraconservative movement to squelch any real, or perceived, left-wing thinking. In 1923, not too long after the end of the Red Scare, radicals were still very much denounced as dangerous to American values. In 1924, however, the wording of AEW came to criticize not just radicals but also pacifists, or any other minority ideas. To AEW supporters, there was nothing to fear; they were merely protecting American society. To its critics, it was seen as a form of oppression. Many religious leaders pointed out that Jesus was a pacifist, and advocated peace and love toward one's fellow people. The controversy was not repeated. The 1925 AEW returned to the earlier sentiments of promoting the educational system in America and not using the week as a platform to denounce divergent viewpoints. What follows is a sampling of the various announcements to this annual event.

ANNOUNCEMENT IN SCHOOL LIFE, A JOURNAL OF THE BUREAU OF EDUCATION, 1920
As part of the nation-wide campaign for the improvement of the schools and other agencies of education, the Commissioner of Education is designating the week of December 5-11 as "school week," . . . to take such action as may be necessary to cause the people to use this week as will most effectively disseminate among the people accurate information in regard to the conditions and needs of the schools, enhance appreciation of the value of education, and create such interest as will result in better opportunities for education.

BUREAU OF EDUCATION, SUGGESTIONS FOR THE OBSERVANCE OF SCHOOL WEEK IN THE ELEMENTARY AND SECONDARY SCHOOLS (1920)

1. Teachers in all the grades should give the children such instruction as they can comprehend in regard to the American public school system, its purpose, methods, and means of support.
2. They should give detailed information in regard to the school of their own city and country.
3. They should give special attention to the relation of education to the every day life and activities of the people, pointing out the relation of education to the production of material wealth, to the preservation of health, to the manners and customs of society, to moral conduct, to civic relations, to government, and to the strength and safety of the State and Nation.
4. The importance of regular school attendance and the right use of time in school should be discussed.
5. During this week all compositions should be on topics pertaining to the schools, as should all oral discussions and debates.

ANNOUNCEMENT FOR 1922 AMERICAN EDUCATION WEEK
Sunday shall be observed as God and Country Day; Monday, Citizenship Day; Tuesday, Patriotism Day; Wednesday, School and Teacher Day; Thursday, Illiteracy Day; Friday, Equality of Opportunity Day; and Saturday, Physical Education Day.

SLOGANS FOR 1923 AMERICAN EDUCATION WEEK
"Revolutionists and Radicals a menace to [constitutional] guarantees."
"No immigration until illiteracy among native and foreign born is removed."

ANNOUNCEMENT FOR 1924 AMERICAN EDUCATION WEEK
Monday, Constitution Day

1. Life, liberty, justice, security, and opportunity.
2. How our Constitution guarantees these rights.
3. Revolutionists, communists, and extreme pacifists are a menace to these guarantees.

Tuesday, Patriotism Day

1. The red flag means death, destruction, poverty, starvation, disease, anarchy, and dictatorship.
2. Help the immigrants and aliens to become American citizens.

ANNOUNCEMENT FOR 1925 AMERICAN EDUCATION WEEK

1. Monday, Constitution Day
2. Tuesday, Patriotism Day; "The Flag of the United States of America is the symbol of the ideals and institutions of our republic."
3. Wednesday, School and Teacher Day; Trained teachers require adequate compensation, the teaching of patriotism is the duty of all public servants.
4. Friday, Know Your School Day; "Progressive civilization depends upon progressive education."

*BUREAU OF EDUCATION, 1926 ANNOUNCEMENT CONCERNING
AMERICAN EDUCATION WEEK INVOLVEMENT*
Promotion of American Education Week in the future will be discontinued by the Bureau of Education and turned over to the States and organizations interested in its observance. The Bureau has accomplished all that can be properly done by a Government agency and seems to have achieved much more than could have been reasonably expected. The Bureau hopes that observance of the Week will be continued with the same enthusiasm that has marked its recent history.

All documents National Archives and Records Administration. Records of the Office of Education, Record Group 12.

John Fitzpatrick's Speech to the Chicago Federation of Labor Minutes, May 18, 1924

Longtime Chicago Federation of Labor (CFL) president John Fitzpatrick had dreams of a major labor party, especially because the two major political parties seemed to be oblivious to the needs of the working class. The CFL, a creation of the American Federation of Labor (AFL), knew it was courting trouble with its parent organization, especially as AFL president Samuel Gompers believed in political nonpartisanship. Although the movement started off with high hopes, and even some minor victories, the party, which became known as the Farmer-Labor Party in 1920, was a dismal failure. The party was eventually taken over by communists, led by William Z. Foster, a former colleague and fellow organizer partner of Fitzpatrick's. In 1924, the CFL completely abandoned the party and returned solidly to the AFL fold.

Some years ago, in 1918, the political situation in the city and in the state was such that the representatives of the Chicago Federation of Labor felt called upon to present these matters very definitely to the federation and to ask the federation to draw its own conclusions as to what it would do, and in order to meet that situation when this presentation was made, the Chicago Federation of Labor authorized the submission to the local organizations, by a referendum vote, the question as to whether certain political activities would be followed and as a result of that consideration and discussion the Labor Party was formed and it was formed by the vote of a vast majority of the organizations in the Chicago Federation of Labor, about 200 out of 300 organizations voting in favor. Whether they represented the majority of members I don't recall, but we proceeded on that line and entered into the first political campaign that happened which was the mayoralty campaign and in which I happened to be the burnt offering as a candidate for mayor, but we are ready to do that again in a similar situation.

Out of that came a very costly procedure and when it came to financing it we were considerably short of what was really necessary, and there was some deficit, and other campaigns came along and in which we engaged and these were costly and it was difficult to carry on because of the expense and lack of interest.

Then a national situation developed and a convention was held in Chicago, which was another costly procedure and which left considerable deficit and left the Federation holding the bag in that kind of situation. Out of that convention was born the Farmer-Labor Party and they went through their activities in the various states and in the national campaign. And then we went on down through all the other situations until we got into the year 1924, and out of this situation the Chicago Federation of Labor had a deliberate purpose and what those who are actuated by the situation feel was a real object and that was to have a political organization subscribed to and supported and participated in by the members of the organizations paying their dues and per capita tax, and the federation would be the economic organization and the Labor Party the political organization, but as far as the purpose was concerned it was all right and would have worked except for what is liable to happen in any political situation, where other programs will be injected and where there is no responsibility and free lances are trying to carry through their own political notions and trying to tie and hitch everyone to their kite, and if they can't do that to destroy it, and we have been in that situation long enough for the federation.

We feel we have held the bag long enough and that the thing should be changed, and as chairman, one who is responsible to the Federation to bring these matters to your attention, after consultation, I have outlined the following as a statement of the situation and a recommendation as to what we ought to subscribe to now:

Possibly the greatest opportunity for the workers and farmers to more effectively establish their own political party is upon us now, and possibly there is no other situation in which so much confusion and misunderstanding has been injected by self-seeking individuals in order to serve their own ends.

The only bona fide Farmer-Labor Party is the one launched by the Chicago Federation of Labor. All others are masquerading under various titles and for various reasons, and all are seceding or dual organizations and no thoughtful union man or woman will have anything to do with them.

Labor organizations, individuals and farmers are the prey of these conflicting groups and not a single principle of the labor movement actuates them. Instead of striving for more cohesive action they will only confound and bewilder the entire situation and the hope of using this great opportunity is shattered.

The bona fide Farmer-Labor Party was created to serve the workers and the farmers and not to confound and despoil their political hopes, but with the chaotic condition of all these conflicting, seceding and dual groups there is only one honest position that can be taken by the bona fide Farmer-Labor Party and that is to cease activities until this hysteria or mania for control has passed over.

After the Cleveland Conference for Progressive Political Action the National Farmer-Labor Party made the declaration that if it ever became necessary we would accept the political program of the American Federation of Labor as against all others who are more or less irresponsible and all wedded to their own political hobby, while the American Federation of Labor is responsible and acts for the bona fide labor movement.

The present situation compels action. The time has arrived when this decision must be made, and in order to end this confusion and prevent further exploitations of labor unions and farmer organizations and whatever the fates have in store for the political future of the labor movement, we cast our lot with that of the American Federation of Labor.

It seems to me to be the only way to meet the present situation. If I tried to enumerate the different groups that claim to represent labor and the farmers it would be considerable of a list and you can't keep track of them. There is only one thing for us to do and that is to cut loose and stand by our own guns in this movement we are a part of, and which holds our hope for the future, and after this thing has gone by then labor may be able to find its own political position when the skies are clear. The rank and file have not subscribed to the program we launched and when they did not and will not there is no hope for that to happen now or in the near future, and we feel this is the only real and honest thing that can be done.

John Fitzpatrick's Speech to the Chicago Federation of Labor. Chicago Federation of Labor. Minutes, May 18, 1924.

Corrigan v. Buckley

Corrigan v. Buckley was an important early civil rights case concerning restrictive covenants. In Washington, D.C., such covenants existed between white property owners to restrict the sale of property to African Americans. To force the issue into the courts, Irene Corrigan tried to sell her house to Dr. Arthur Curtis and his wife Helen. A neighbor took the issue to the District Supreme Court, which upheld the covenant. Corrigan and Curtis invoked the Fourteenth Amendment to argue their case, but, on appeal, the U.S. Supreme Court refused to hear the case on the basis of jurisdiction, leaving the covenant in place. Restrictive covenants would stand until the 1948 case of *Shelley v. Kramer.*

Mr. Justice Sanford delivered the opinion of the Court.

This is a suit in equity brought by John J. Buckley in the Supreme Court of the District of Columbia against Irene H. Corrigan and Helen Curtis, to enjoin the conveyance of certain real estate from one to the other of the defendants.

The case made by the bill is this: The parties are citizens of the United States, residing in the District. The plaintiff and the defendant Corrigan are white persons, and the defendant Curtis is a person of the negro race. In 1921, thirty white persons, including the plaintiff and the defendant Corrigan, owning twenty-five parcels of land, improved by dwelling houses, situated on Street, between 18th and New Hampshire Avenue, in the City of Washington, executed an indenture, duly recorded, in which they recited that for their mutual benefit and the best interests of the neighborhood comprising these properties, they mutually covenanted and agreed that no part of these properties should ever be used or occupied by, or sold, leased or given to, any person of the negro race or blood; and that this covenant should run with the land and bind their respective heirs and assigns for twenty-one years from and after its date.

In 1922, the defendants entered into a contract by which the defendant Corrigan, although knowing the defendant Curtis to be a person of the negro race, agreed to [271 U.S. 323, 328] sell her a certain lot, with dwelling house, included within the terms of the indenture, and the defendant Curtis, although knowing of the existence and terms of the indenture, agreed to purchase it. The defendant Curtis demanded that this contract of sale be carried out, and, despite the protest of other parties to the indenture, the defendant Corrigan had stated that she would convey the lot to the defendant Curtis.

The bill alleged that this would cause irreparable injury to the plaintiff and the other parties to the indenture, and that the plaintiff, having no adequate remedy at law, was entitled to have the covenant of the defendant Corrigan specifically enforced in equity by an injunction preventing the defendants from carrying the contract of sale into effect; and prayed, in substance, that the defendant Corrigan be enjoined during twenty-one years from the date of the indenture, from conveying the lot to the defendant Curtis, and that the defendant Curtis be enjoined from taking title to the lot during such period, and from using or occupying it.

The defendant Corrigan moved to dismiss the bill on the grounds that the "indenture or covenant made the basis of said bill" is (1) "void in that the same is contrary to and in violation of the Constitution of the United States," and (2) "is void in that the same is contrary to public policy." And the defendant Curtis moved to dismiss the bill on the ground that it appears therein that the indenture or covenant "is void, in that it attempts to deprive the defendant, the said Helen Curtis, and others of property, without due process of law; abridges the privilege and immunities of citizens of the United States, including the defendant Helen Curtis, and other persons within this jurisdiction (and denies them) the equal protection of the law, and therefore, is forbidden by the Constitution of the United States, and especially by the Fifth, Thirteenth, and Fourteenth [271 U.S. 323, 329] Amendments thereof, and the Laws enacted is aid and under the sanction of the said Thirteenth and Fourteenth Amendments."

Both of these motions to dismiss were overruled, with leave to answer. 52 Wash. Law Rep. 402. And the defendants having elected to stand on their motions, a final decree was entered enjoining them as prayed in the bill. This was affirmed, on appeal, by the Court of Appeals of the District. 55 App. D. C. 30, 299 F. 899. The defendants then prayed an appeal to this Court on the ground that such review was authorized under the provisions of section 250 of the Judicial Code (Comp. St. 1227)—as it then stood, before the amendment made by the Jurisdictional Act of 1925—in that the case was one "involving the construction or application of the Constitution of the United States" (paragraph 3), and "in which the construction of" certain laws of the United States, namely, sections 1977, 1978, 1979 of the Revised Statutes (Comp. St. 3925, 3931, 3932) were "drawn in question" by them (paragraph 6). This appeal was allowed, in June, 1924

The mere assertion that the case is one involving the construction or application of the Constitution, and in which the construction of federal laws is drawn in question, does not, however, authorize this Court to entertain the appeal; and it is our duty to decline jurisdiction if the record does not present such a constitutional or statutory question substantial in character and properly raised below. *Sugarman v. United States*, 249 U.S. 182, 184, 39 S. Ct. 191; *Zucht v. King*, 260 U.S. 174, 176, 43 S. Ct. 24. And under well settled rules, jurisdiction is wanting if such questions are so unsubstantial as to be plainly without color of merit and frivolous. *Wilson v. North Carolina*, 169 U.S. 586, 595, 18 S. Ct. 435; *Delmar Jockey Club v. Missouri*, 210 U.S. 324, 335, 28 S. Ct. 732; *Binderup v. Pathe Exchange*, 263 U.S. 291, 305, 44 S. Ct. 96; *Moore v. New York Cotton Exchange*, 270 U.S. 593, 46 S. Ct. 367, No. 200, decided April 12, 1926.

Under the pleadings in the present case the only constitutional question involved was that arising under the [271 U.S. 323, 330] assertions in the motions to dismiss that the indenture or covenant which is the basis of the bill is "void" in that it is contrary to and forbidden by the Fifth, Thirteenth and Fourteenth Amendments. This contention is entirely lacking in substance or color of merit. The Fifth Amendment "is a limitation only upon the powers of the General Government," *Talton v. Mayes*, 163 U.S. 376, 382,

16 S. Ct. 986, 988 (41 L. Ed. 196), and is not directed against the action of individuals. The Thirteenth Amendment denouncing slavery and involuntary servitude, that is, a condition of enforced compulsory service of one to another, does not in other matters protect the individual rights of persons of the negro race. *Hodges v. United States*, 203 U.S. 1, 16, 18 S., 27 S. Ct. 6. And the prohibitions of the Fourteenth Amendment "have reference to State action exclusively, and not to any action of private individuals." *Virginia v. Rives*, 100 U.S. 313, 318; *United States v. Harris*, 106 U.S. 629, 639, 1 S. Ct. 601. "It is State action of a particular character that is prohibited. Individual invasion of individual rights is not the subject-matter of the Amendment." *Civil Rights Cases*, 109 U.S. 3, 11, 3 S. Ct. 18, 21 (27 L. Ed. 835). It is obvious that none of these amendments prohibited private individuals from entering into contracts respecting the control and disposition of their own property; and there is no color whatever for the contention that they rendered the indenture void. And plainly, the claim urged in this Court that they were to be looked to, in connection with the provisions of the Revised Statutes and the decisions of the courts, in determining the contention, earnestly pressed, that the indenture is void as being "against public policy," does not involve a constitutional question within the meaning of the Code provision.

The claim that the defendants drew in question the "construction" of sections 1977, 1978 and 1979 of the Revised Statutes, is equally unsubstantial. The only question raised as to these statutes under the pleadings was the [271 U.S. 323, 331] assertion in the motion interposed by the defendant Curtis, that the indenture is void in that it is forbidden by the laws enacted in aid and under the sanction of the Thirteenth and Fourteenth Amendments. Assuming that this contention drew in question the "construction" of these statutes, as distinguished from their "application," it is obvious, upon their face, that while they provide, inter alia, that all persons and citizens shall have equal right with white citizens to make contracts and acquire property, they, like the Constitutional Amendment under whose sanction they were enacted, do not in any manner prohibit or invalidate contracts entered into by private individuals in respect to the control and disposition of their own property. There is no color for the contention that they rendered the indenture void; nor was it claimed in this Court that they had, in and of themselves, any such effect.

We therefore conclude that neither the constitutional nor statutory questions relied on as grounds for the appeal to this Court have any substantial quality or color of merit, or afford any jurisdictional basis for the appeal.

And while it was further urged in this Court that the decrees of the courts below in themselves deprived the defendants of their liberty and property without due process of law, in violation of the Fifth and Fourteenth Amendments, this contention likewise cannot serve as a jurisdictional basis for the appeal. Assuming that such a contention, if of a substantial character, might have constituted ground for an appeal under paragraph 3 of the Code provision, it was not raised by the petition for the appeal or by any assignment of error, either in the Court of Appeals or in this Court; and it likewise is lacking in substance. The defendants were given a full hearing in both courts; they were not denied any constitutional or statutory right; and there is no semblance of ground for any contention that the decrees were so plainly arbitrary [271 U.S. 323, 332] and contrary to law as to be acts of mere spoliation. *See Delmar Jockey Club v. Missouri, supra*, 335 (28 S. Ct. 732). Mere error of a court, if any there be, in a judgment entered after a full hearing, does not constitute a denial of due process of law. *Central Land Co. v. Laidley*, 159 U.S. 103, 112, 16 S. Ct. 80; *Jones v. Buffalo Creek Coal Co.*, 245 U.S. 328, 329, 38 S. Ct. 121.

It results that, in the absence of any substantial constitutional or statutory question giving us jurisdiction of this appeal under the provisions of section 250 of the Judicial Code, we cannot determine upon the merits the contentions earnestly pressed by the defendants in this court that the indenture is not only void because contrary to public policy, but is also of such a discriminatory character that a court of equity will not lend its aid by enforcing the specific performance of the covenant. These are questions involving a consideration of rules not expressed in any constitutional or statutory provision, but claimed to be a part of the common or general law in force in the District of Columbia; and, plainly, they may not be reviewed under this appeal unless jurisdiction of the case is otherwise acquired.

Hence, without a consideration of these questions, the appeal must be, and is dismissed for want of jurisdiction.

Corrigan v. Buckley 271 U.S. 323 (1926)

Eighteenth Amendment (1919)

The Eighteenth Amendment prohibited the sale, manufacture, or transport of intoxicating liquors into the United States and its territories, thus beginning the era of Prohibition. The one question remains: If there was so much opposition to Prohibition, how did it manage to pass? Although there may be several answers to that question, the one issue remains: the Prohibition forces were merely better organized. There was certainly a strong anti-Prohibition force in the country, but it did not have the long legacy that Prohibition's supporters did. Even in the early decades of the 19th century there were numerous calls to severely limit, or altogether prohibit, alcoholic beverages by those who were part of the Temperance movement. Temperance supporters merely morphed into the Prohibition forces. It is already well known how Prohibition was a total failure, but this amendment demonstrates the unique nature of the Jazz Age—a seemingly conservative time (in terms of those in favor of Prohibition)—and those who openly flaunted it. Prohibition was over in 1933, especially with the passage of the Twenty-First Amendment.

Section 1. After one year from the ratification of this article, the manufacture, sale, or transportation of intoxicating liquors within, the importation thereof into, or the exportation thereof from the United States and all territory subject to the jurisdiction thereof for beverage purposes is hereby prohibited.

Section 2. The Congress and the several States shall have concurrent power to enforce this article by appropriate legislation.

Section 3. This article shall be inoperative unless it shall have been ratified as an amendment to the Constitution by the legislatures of the several States, as provided in the Constitution, within seven years from the date of the submission hereof to the States by the Congress.

U.S. Constitution. Eighteenth Amendment. 1919. Passed by Congress December 18, 1917. Ratified January 16, 1919. Repealed by the Twenty-First Amendment.

Nineteenth Amendment (1920)

After years of protest, marching, and outright civil disobedience, women finally earned the right to vote on the national level. Some states had already granted this privilege to women, such as Wyoming in 1890, but now this right was protected by the Constitution. In the presidential election of 1920, women tended to vote along with men, that is, conservatively. The White House was returned to the Republican Party in a repudiation of the two Democratic administrations under Woodrow Wilson, the same president who ran on a "no war" platform in 1916, only to get the United States embroiled in World War I. Although most women were thrilled to have the chance to speak their minds in the political arena, other women believed it was something better left alone. Politics was considered to be corrupt and best left to men.

The right of citizens of the United States to vote shall not be denied or abridged by the United States or any State on account of sex.

Congress shall have power to enforce this article by appropriate legislation.

U.S. Constitution. Nineteenth Amendment. 1920. Passed by Congress June 4, 1919. Ratified August 18, 1920.

National Prohibition Enforcement Act/Volstead Act (1919)

The Eighteenth Amendment began the era of Prohibition, and the amendment allowed Congress to enforce the amendment through appropriate legislation. Named for Andrew Volstead, who actually did not write it, the law provided the authority to enforce Prohibition and gave more definitions. Intoxicating liquors were defined as those having more than 0.5 percent alcohol. The desire for alcoholic beverages merely helped lead to more efficient means of organized crime as gang bosses were all too willing to provide liquor. Despite the Volstead Act and its legal authority, it was quite easy to get around the law, especially because Prohibition agents were greatly outnumbered and could not enforce the law effectively. Prohibition was officially ended in 1933 with the passage of the Twenty-First Amendment, which repealed the Eighteenth Amendment. Certain portions of the law are presented here.

AN ACT

To prohibit intoxicating beverages, and to regulate the manufacture, production, use, and sale of high-proof spirits for other than beverage purposes, and to insure an ample supply of alcohol and promote its use in scientific research and in the development of fuel, dye, and other lawful industries.

Be it enacted by the Senate and House of Representatives of the United States of America in Congress assembled, That the short title of this Act shall be the "National Prohibition Act."

Title I.

To Provide for the Enforcement of War Prohibition.

The term "War Prohibition Act" used in this Act shall mean the provisions of any Act or Acts prohibiting the sale and manufacture of intoxicating liquors until the conclusion of the present war and thereafter until the termination of demobilization, the date of which shall be determined and proclaimed by the President of the United States. The words "beer, wine, or other intoxicating malt or vinous liquors" in the War Prohibition Act shall be hereafter construed to mean any such beverages which contain one-half of 1 per centum or more of alcohol by volume: *Provided,* That the foregoing definition shall not extend to dealcoholized wine nor to any beverage or liquid produced by the process by which beer, ale, porter or wine is produced, if it contains less than one-half of 1 per centum of alcohol by volume, and is made as prescribed in section 37 of Title II of this Act, and is otherwise denominated than as beer, ale, or porter, and is contained and sold in, or from, such sealed and labeled bottles, casks, or containers as the commissioner may by regulation prescribe.

SEC. 2. The Commissioner of Internal Revenue, his assistants, agents, and inspectors, shall investigate and report violations of the War Prohibition Act to the United States attorney for the district in which committed, who shall be charged with the duty of prosecuting, subject to the direction of the Attorney General, the offenders as in the case of other offense against laws of the United States; and such Commissioner of Internal Revenue, his assistants, agents, and inspectors may swear out warrants before United States commissioners or other officers or courts authorized to issue the same for the apprehension of such offenders, and may, subject to the control of the said United States attorney, conduct the prosecution at the . . . trial for the purpose of having the offenders held for the action of a grand jury.

SEC. 3. Any room, house, building, boat, vehicle, structure, or place of any kind where intoxicating liquor is sold, manufactured, kept for sale, or bartered in violation of the War Prohibition Act, and all intoxicating liquor and all property kept and used in maintaining such a place, is hereby declared to be a public and common nuisance, and any person who maintains or assists in maintaining such public and common nuisance shall be guilty of a misdemeanor, and upon conviction thereof shall be fined not less than $100 nor more than $1,000, or be imprisoned for not less than thirty days or more than one year, or both. If a person has knowledge that his property is occupied or used in violation of the provisions of the War Prohibition Act and suffers the same to be so used, such property shall be subject to a lien for, and may be sold to pay, all fines and costs assessed against the occupant of such building or property for any violation of the

War Prohibition Act occurring after the passage hereof, which said lien shall attach from the time of the filing of notice of the commencement of the suit in the office where the records of the transfer of real estate are kept; and any such lien may be established and enforced by legal action instituted for that purpose in any court having jurisdiction. Any violation of this title upon any leased premises by the lessee or occupant thereof shall, at the option of the lessor, work a forfeiture of the lease.

SEC. 4. The United States attorney for the district where such nuisance as is defined in this Act exists, or any officer designated by him or the Attorney General of the United States, may prosecute a suit in equity in the name of the United States to abate and enjoin the same. Actions in equity to enjoin and abate such nuisances may be brought in any court having jurisdiction to hear and determine equity causes. The jurisdiction of the courts of the United States under this section shall be concurrent with that of the courts of the several States.

If it be made to appear by affidavit, or other evidence under oath, to the satisfaction of the court, or judge in vacation, that the nuisance complained of exists, a temporary writ of injunction shall forthwith issue restraining the defendant or defendants from conducting or permitting the continuance of such nuisance until the conclusion of the trial. Where a temporary injunction is prayed for, the court may issue an order restraining the defendants and all other persons from removing or in any way interfering with the liquor or fixtures, or other things used in connection with the violation constituting the nuisance. No bond shall be required as a condition for making any order or issuing any writ of injunction under this Act. If the court shall find the property involved was being unlawfully used as aforesaid at or about the time alleged in the petition, the court shall order that no liquors shall be manufactured, sold, bartered, or stored in such room, house, building, boat, vehicle, structure, or places of any kind, for a period of not exceeding one year, or during the war and the period of demobilization. Whenever an action to enjoin a nuisance shall have been brought pursuant to the provisions of this Act, if the owner, lessee, tenant, or occupant appears and pays all costs of the proceedings and files a bond, with sureties to be approved by the clerk of the court in which the action is brought, in the liquidated sum of not less than $500 nor more than $1,000, conditioned that he will immediately abate said nuisance and prevent the same from being established or kept therein a period of one year thereafter, or during the war and period of demobilization, the court, or in vacation the judge, may, if satisfied of his good faith, direct by appropriate order that the property, if already closed or held under the order of abatement, be delivered to said owner, and said order of abatement canceled, so far as the same may relate to said property; or if said bond be given and costs therein paid before judgment on an order of abatement, the action shall be thereby abated as to said room, house, building, boat, vehicle, structure, or place only. The release of the property under the provisions of this section shall not release it from any judgment, lien, penalty, or liability to which it may be subject by law.

In the case of the violation of any injunction, temporary or permanent, granted pursuant to the provisions of this Title, the court, or in vacation a judge thereof, may summarily try and punish the defendant. The proceedings for punishment for contempt shall be commenced by filing with the clerk of the court from which such injunction issued information under oath setting out the alleged facts constituting the violation, whereupon the court or judge shall forthwith cause a warrant to issue under which the defendant shall be arrested. The trial may be had upon affidavits, or either party may demand the production and oral examination of the witnesses. Any person found guilty of contempt under the provisions of this section shall be punished by a fine of not less than $500 nor more than $1,000, or by imprisonment of not less than thirty days nor more than twelve months, or by both fine and imprisonment.

SEC. 5. The Commissioner of Internal Revenue, his assistants, agents, and inspectors, and all other officers of the United States whose duty it is to enforce criminal laws, shall have all the power for the enforcement of the War Prohibition Act or any provisions thereof which is conferred by law for the enforcement of existing laws relating to the manufacture or sale of intoxicating liquors under the laws of the United States.

SEC. 6. If any section or provision of this Act shall be held to be invalid, it is hereby provided that all other provisions of this Act which are not expressly held to be invalid shall continue in full force and effect.

SEC. 7. None of the provisions of this Act shall be construed to repeal any of the provisions of the "War Prohibition Act," or to limit or annul any order or regulation prohibiting the manufacture, sale, or disposition of intoxicating liquors within certain prescribed zones or districts, nor shall the provisions of this Act be construed to prohibit the use of the power of the military or naval authorities to enforce the regulations of the President or Secretary of War or Navy issued in pursuance of law, prohibiting the manufacture, use, possession, sale, or other disposition of intoxicating liquors during the period of the war and demobilization thereafter.

National Prohibition Act. Sixty-sixth Congress of the United States of America, May 19, 1919.

Twenty-First Amendment (1933)

Prohibition is officially declared dead. What was once considered to be a noble experiment turned out to be nothing more than an impetus for flagrant law-breaking and the rise of organized crime. Ratified at the beginning of President Franklin D. Roosevelt's first term, the drive to repeal Prohibition was already in full swing.

Section 1.

The eighteenth article of amendment to the Constitution of the United States is hereby repealed.

Section 2.

The transportation or importation into any State, Territory, or Possession of the United States for delivery or use therein of intoxicating liquors, in violation of the laws thereof, is hereby prohibited.

Section 3.

This article shall be inoperative unless it shall have been ratified as an amendment to the Constitution by conventions in the several States, as provided in the Constitution, within seven years from the date of the submission hereof to the States by the Congress.

U.S. Constitution. *Twenty-first Amendment.* Passed by Congress February 20, 1933. Ratified December 5, 1933.

The Butler Bill (1925)

Also known as the *Butler Act*, this 1925 Tennessee law banned the teaching of evolution in the state public schools. As a way of testing the validity of the law, John Scopes admitted to violating the law, touching off a virtual media circus as he went to trial. Defending Scopes was the noted Chicago attorney Clarence Darrow. William Jennings Bryan, a failed presidential candidate and one-time U.S. secretary of state, prosecuted the case. Scopes was convicted, as Darrow had hoped for, in order to challenge the law in the state supreme court. The law remained on the books for four decades.

CHAPTER NO. 27
House Bill No. 185
(By Mr. Butler)
AN ACT prohibiting the teaching of the Evolution Theory in all the Universities, Normals and all other public schools of Tennessee, which are supported in whole or in part by the public school funds of the State, and to provide penalties for the violations thereof.

Section 1. *Be it enacted by the General Assembly of the State of Tennessee,* That it shall be unlawful for any teacher in any of the Universities, Normals and all other public schools of the State which are supported in whole or in part by the public school funds of the State, to teach any theory that denies the story of the Divine Creation of man as taught in the Bible, and to teach instead that man has descended from a lower order of animals.

Section 2. *Be it further enacted,* That any teacher found guilty of the violation of this Act, Shall be guilty of a misdemeanor and upon conviction, shall be fined not less than One Hundred ($100.00) Dollars nor more than Five Hundred ($ 500.00) Dollars for each offense.

Section 3. *Be it further enacted,* That this Act take effect from and after its passage, the public welfare requiring it.

Passed March 13, 1925
W. F. Barry,
Speaker of the House of Representatives
L. D. Hill,
Speaker of the Senate
Approved March 21, 1925.
Austin Peay,
Governor.

State of Tennessee, Public Acts, 64th General Assembly, 1925.

President Herbert Hoover's Inaugural Address (1929)

In this excerpt, newly elected U.S. president Herbert Hoover, riding into office on the popularity of the Republican Party, addressed some of the major issues outlined in this book, especially Prohibition, education, public health, and the presence of big business in America. Hoover places a lot of blame on state and local authorities for not effectively enforcing Prohibition, although he believes the lawbreakers are a minority. In terms of business activities, Hoover makes it clear that private enterprise must remain so and must not be owned by the federal government. In terms of education, Hoover echoes the sentiments of Horace Mann, a 19th-century advocate of public education, in that an educated electorate is an informed one. With the Great Depression looming early in his administration, Hoover projected an image to America that all would be fine.

My Countrymen:

This occasion is not alone the administration of the most sacred oath which can be assumed by an American citizen. It is a dedication and consecration under God to the highest office in service of our people. I assume this trust in the humility of knowledge that only through the guidance of Almighty Providence can I hope to discharge its ever-increasing burdens.

It is in keeping with tradition throughout our history that I should express simply and directly the opinions which I hold concerning some of the matters of present importance.

ENFORCEMENT OF THE EIGHTEENTH AMENDMENT.—Of the undoubted abuses which have grown up under the eighteenth amendment, part are due to the causes I have just mentioned; but part are due to the failure of some States to accept their share of responsibility for concurrent enforcement and to the failure of many State and local officials to accept the obligation under their oath of office zealously to enforce the laws. With the failures from these many causes has come a dangerous expansion in the criminal elements who have found enlarged opportunities in dealing in illegal liquor.

****

To those of criminal mind there can be no appeal but vigorous enforcement of the law. Fortunately they are but a small percentage of our people. Their activities must be stopped.

THE RELATION OF GOVERNMENT TO BUSINESS.—The election has again confirmed the determination of the American people that regulation of private enterprise and not Government ownership or operation is the course rightly to be pursued in our relation to business. In recent years we have established a differentiation in the whole method of business regulation between the industries which produce and distribute commodities on the one hand and public utilities on the other. In the former, our laws insist upon effective competition; in the latter, because we substantially confer a monopoly by limiting competition, we must regulate their services and rates. The rigid enforcement of the laws applicable to both groups is the very base of equal opportunity and freedom from domination for all our people, and it is just as essential for the stability and prosperity of business itself as for the protection of the public at large. Such regulation should be extended by the Federal Government within the limitations of the Constitution and only when the individual States are without power to protect their citizens through their own authority. On the other hand, we should be fearless when the authority rests only in the Federal Government.

COOPERATION BY THE GOVERNMENT.—The larger purpose of our economic thought should be to establish more firmly stability and security of business and employment and thereby remove poverty still further from our borders. Our people have in recent years developed a new-found capacity for cooperation among themselves to effect high purposes in public welfare. It is an advance toward the highest conception of self-government. Self-government does not and should not imply the use of political agencies alone. Progress is born of cooperation in the community—not from governmental restraints. The Government should assist and encourage these movements of collective self-help by itself cooperating with them. Business has by cooperation made great progress in the advancement of service, in stability, in regularity of employment and in the correction of its own abuses. Such progress, however, can continue only so long as business manifests its respect for law.

*****

EDUCATION.—Although education is primarily a responsibility of the States and local communities, and rightly so, yet the Nation as a whole is vitally concerned in its development everywhere to the highest standards and to complete universality. Self-government can succeed only through an instructed electorate. Our objective is not simply to overcome illiteracy. The Nation has marched far beyond that. The more complex the problems of the Nation become, the greater is the need for more and more advanced instruction. Moreover, as our numbers increase and as our life expands with science and invention, we must discover more and more leaders for every walk of life. We cannot hope to succeed in directing this increasingly complex civilization unless we can draw all the talent of leadership from the whole people. One civilization after another has been wrecked upon the attempt to secure sufficient leadership from a single group or class. If we would prevent the growth of class distinctions and would constantly refresh our leadership with the ideals of our people, we must draw constantly from the general mass. The full opportunity for every boy and girl to rise through the selective processes of education can alone secure to us this leadership.

*****

PUBLIC HEALTH.—In public health the discoveries of science have opened a new era. Many sections of our country and many groups of our citizens suffer from diseases the eradication of which are mere matters of administration and moderate expenditure. Public health service should be as fully organized and as universally incorporated into our governmental system as is public education. The returns are a thousand fold in economic benefits, and infinitely more in reduction of suffering and promotion of human happiness.

*****

CONCLUSION.—This is not the time and place for extended discussion. The questions before our country are problems of progress to higher standards; they are not the problems of degeneration. They demand thought and they serve to quicken the conscience and enlist our sense of responsibility for their settlement. And that responsibility rests upon you, my countrymen, as much as upon those of us who have been selected for office.

Ours is a land rich in resources; stimulating in its glorious beauty; filled with millions of happy homes; blessed with comfort and opportunity. In no nation are the institutions of progress more advanced. In no nation are the fruits of accomplishment more secure. In no nation is the government more worthy of respect. No country is more loved by its people. I have an abiding faith in their capacity, integrity and high purpose. I have no fears for the future of our country. It is bright with hope.

In the presence of my countrymen, mindful of the solemnity of this occasion, knowing what the task means and the responsibility which it involves, I beg your tolerance, your aid, and your cooperation. I ask the help of Almighty God in this service to my country to which you have called me.

Herbert Hoover, Inaugural Address, March 4, 1929.

Reference

Mitchell Newton-Matza

African Blood Brotherhood (ABB)   A secret Afro-Marxist organization founded in Harlem during World War I.

Agricultural Credits Act (1924)   The act was passed in an effort to prevent agricultural goods from being dumped on the market, which could lead to farm foreclosures. Loans were provided to cooperatives and dealers in order to hold products from the marketplace. By 1932, approximately $304 million in loans had been given.

Agricultural Marketing Act (1929)   In response to the numerous economic problems farmers faced, this act provided price supports. However, many farmers did not like the federal government to intrude in their operations.

Algonquin Round Table   A group of writers, performers, and other celebrities whose daily luncheons at the Algonquin Hotel, in New York City made considerable press. Although many of the group's members used the gatherings for collaboration, their meetings were mostly concerned with exchanges of wit and critiques of society.

American Civil Liberties Union (ACLU)   The group was founded in 1920 to ensure that all Americans would be guaranteed their constitutional liberties and privileges. Leading founders include Crystal Eastman and Roger Baldwin. An early concern of the ACLU was protecting those who faced deportation as a result of the Palmer Raids.

American Education Week   An annual week-long event that promoted the improvement of education in the United States and provided Americanization programs for immigrants. The movement became controversial in 1924 as it grew excessively right wing and intolerant of divergent viewpoints.

Amos 'n' Andy   A radio show featuring black characters as the leads that debuted in 1928. Although some would decry the show as being racist, especially in more contemporary times, the show was very popular.

Arbuckle, Roscoe "Fatty" (1887–1933)   A silent film comedian and highly paid performer. In 1921, he was the center of a scandal involving the death of actress Virginia Rappe. Arbuckle was also accused of rape in this tragedy. The evidence against Arbuckle was incredibly flimsy, but rumors and innuendoes in the press doomed him. After two mistrials, Arbuckle was found not guilty, but the damage to his professional life and reputation was irreversible.

Armstrong, Louis "Satchmo" (1901–1971)   A jazz cornetist, singer, and composer whose innovations had a profound influence on the style, composition, and performance techniques of subsequent generations of musicians.

Baker, Josephine (1906–1975)   An African American singer and dancer. One of the American expatriates living abroad during the Jazz Age, Baker especially made her mark on the stages of Paris, though success in the United States eluded her for years. She was known for her beauty and risqué shows.

Beiderbecke, Bix (1903–1931)   A jazz cornetist and a significant innovator of improvisatory methods. He imitated African American musicians in his formative years, subsequently blending these and other influences into his individual style.

"Billy" Mitchell trial (1925)   A military court-martial involving Colonel William "Billy" Mitchell, an advocate of the use and importance of air power in military conflicts. His open criticism of the high brass gained him a five-year suspension from service.

Birth of a Nation (1915)   A silent film that sparked the rebirth of the Ku Klux Klan. The film is both praised for its technique and vilified for its negative portrayals of African Americans and positive images of the post–Civil War Klan. William Simmons viewed the film and saw it as a way to make money through memberships and sales of Klan paraphernalia and to revive the Klan.

Black Sox Scandal of 1919   During baseball's World Series of 1919, members of the Chicago White Sox were accused of intentionally losing to the Cincinnati Reds in exchange for payoffs from organized crime bosses. Eight members were implicated, and although some members confessed to their roles, the part others played was not so certain. Besides leaving professional baseball with serious damage to its image, the scandal also brought about the first commissioner of baseball, Judge Kenesaw Mountain Landis.

Book-of-the-Month Club   Created in 1926 as a mail-order venture that focused on a different book each month for its subscribers. It became hugely popular as it promoted the idea of a group of people who read one book and could discuss its contents together.

Bootlegger   Those who deal with the manufacture or sale of illegal liquor.

Boston police strike   In 1919, the Boston police force walked off the job. Officers had not had a raise since before World War I, and they wished to unionize. A volunteer force was assembled, and Calvin Coolidge, the governor of Massachusetts and future U.S. president, fired a goodly number of the striking officers.

Bow, Clara (1905–1965)   A silent film star who became known as the "It Girl" for her sex appeal during a time when sexuality had to be toned down in films. She was one of the most popular and successful film stars of the Jazz Age.

Brotherhood of Sleeping Car Porters   Organized in 1925 as a labor union organizing black Pullman porters. Blacks had been previously shut out of most other labor organizations, so people like A. Philip Randolph—the union's first president—saw the need to create a union on their own.

Bryan, William Jennings (1860–1925)   An American statesman who was most remembered during the Jazz Age as the special prosecutor in the Scopes "Monkey" Trial of 1925. Bryan represented the state of Tennessee in upholding the law that banned the teaching of evolution. Although Bryan won the case, he was put on the stand to support the biblical view of creation. Under the rigorous examination of defense attorney and friend Clarence Darrow, Bryan was forced to admit that the Bible's depiction of creation was open to question.

Capone, Al "Scarface" (1899–1947)   A noted organized crime boss whose operations centered in Chicago. Capone made a lot of money in the illegal liquor trade and was noted for the viciousness with which he eliminated competing gangs. In a strange twist of fate, Capone was never jailed for his violent acts but rather for income tax invasion. He died of syphilis because his fear of needles would not allow any treatment to save his life.

Carter, Howard (1873–1939)   A British archaeologist who discovered the tomb of the Egyptian pharaoh Tutankhamen.

census of 1920   The census showed that for the first time in U.S. history more people lived in urban than rural settings.

Chaney, Lon (1883–1930)   Lnown as the "Man of A Thousand Faces," this silent film star is remembered for creating notable film characters such as the phantom of the opera and the hunchback of Notre Dame. A master of screen makeup, his horror film characters were both grotesque and pitiable. His groundbreaking makeup effects, however, were often painful, and he could wear certain pieces for only short periods of time.

Charleston   A popular dance form named for the city of Charleston, South Carolina. The dance could be performed with a partner, or even solo, and often used improvisation in its moves.

Chicago Federation of Labor (CFL)   An umbrella union organization created by the American Federation of Labor in 1896. During the Jazz Age the CFL failed in its attempt to create a labor party to counterbalance what was seen as the inability of the two major parties to address the needs of workers.

Chicago Race Riot   A violent event that gripped Chicago for a week during the extremely hot summer of 1919. Racial tensions were already running high when a young black boy, swimming in Lake Michigan, accidentally crossed over into the "white" section. The boy was hit in the head and drowned, which was the catalyst of days of violence. When it was all over, 38 people had died, 23 black and 15 white, and more than 500 were injured.

Christensen, Parley Parker (1869–1954)   The failed presidential candidate for the Farmer-Labor Party in 1920. Christensen failed to receive even 1 percent of the popular vote. Eugene Debs, the socialist candidate, ran for president from a prison cell and received more votes than Christensen.

Communist Party/Communist Labor Party   Two separate political parties formed in 1919. There was a split in the Socialist Party over support for the Bolsheviks who were consolidating their control over the new Soviet Union. The left wing of the Socialist Party was expelled, and a further split ensued, creating these two entities, both of which sought recognition from the Soviets, who refused to cater to either faction, ordering the two to combine.

Coolidge, Calvin (1872–1933)   Coolidge assumed the office of president upon the death of Warren G. Harding. Under Coolidge's administration the political landscape of the country tended to lean toward the Republican/conservative side. Coolidge made a major mark for himself as Massachusetts governor when the Boston police force went on strike.

Darrow, Clarence (1857–1938)   Darrow had a reputation as an activist attorney. In 1924, he defended the child murderers Nathan Leopold and Richard Loeb, sparing them from the electric chair. In 1925, he defended John T. Scopes in the infamous Scopes "Monkey" Trial, whereby Scopes was convicted of violating a Tennessee law banning the teaching of evolution in the school system.

Davis, James John (1873–1947)   The U.S. Secretary of Labor during the Jazz Age. Although he was an immigrant from Wales, Davis advocated stringent immigration laws, especially calling for quotas.

Debs, Eugene V. (1855–1936)   A Socialist labor leader. In 1920, Debs ran for president from an Atlanta penitentiary, having been convicted for violating the Espionage and Sedition Acts, which prohibited antiwar statements during World War I.

Dempsey, Jack (1895–1983)   Dempsey held the heavyweight boxing title from 1919 to 1926, earning him a fortune. His bouts set attendance records. His famous losses to Gene Tunney in 1926 and 1927, with the controversies surrounding how the match was refereed, are still legendary in sports history.

DePriest, Oscar (1871–1951)   The first African American from the North to be elected to Congress. He was elected in 1927, representing the state of Illinois.

Dos Passos, John (1896–1970) An American writer who was part of the Lost Generation. Besides authoring 42 novels, he also wrote plays, poetry, and even produced works of art. His use of nonlinear fiction was groundbreaking and influential.

Durant, William Crapo "Billy" (1861–1947) Durant controlled, and became president of, General Motors. He was forced out of office on more than one occasion by the banks.

Dyer Anti-Lynching Bill Federal legislation first introduced by Congressman Leonidas Dyer of Missouri in 1918. The House of Representatives did not pass the measure until 1922. A Senate filibuster, however, killed the bill.

Ederle, Gertrude (1905–2003) An American swimmer who in 1926 was the first woman to swim across the English Channel. The swim took 14 hours and 30 minutes, a record that stood until 1950.

Eighteenth Amendment Established the era of Prohibition by outlawing the sale, manufacture, or importation of alcoholic beverages beginning in 1920. A controversial measure from the start, people flouted the law through bootlegging or making their own booze, even if such drinks were poisonous. With the rise of bootlegging came the rise of organized crime syndicates who made large amounts of money providing illegal liquor. Prohibition, which officially ended in 1933, was a dismal failure.

Einstein, Albert (1879–1955) Won the Nobel Prize in Physics in 1921. His theory of relativity remains important into contemporary times.

Elgin National Watch Company The company rose to prominence for its manufacture of watches and other timepieces. Manufacturers during this time faced controversy over the dangers of radium poisoning in watch dial painters.

Ellington, Edward Kennedy "Duke" (1899–1974) A jazz pianist who rose to national prominence. In 1927, he led a 12-piece group at New York's famous Cotton Club. His career and influences extended far beyond the Jazz Age, and he remains a jazz icon.

Emergency Quota Act (1921) The act limited the number of any specific group of immigrants that could enter the country. Using the 1910 census as its gauge, the number of immigrants was restricted to 3 percent of its U.S. population during that year.

Fall, Albert (1861–1944) Secretary of Interior under President Warren G. Harding who was convicted of accepting bribes in exchange for leasing federal lands in what would be called the Teapot Dome Scandal. Fall was the first cabinet member to go to prison.

Farmer-Labor Party A political party created in 1920 to provide a political alternative to the two main established parties. The party was a dismal failure and was eventually taken over by communists during 1924.

Fitzgerald, F. Scott (1896–1940)   A famed writer who is credited with creating the term "Jazz Age." His 1925 classic work, *The Great Gatsby*, was a commentary on the excesses and over-the-top behavior that is often associated with the post–World War I period.

Fitzpatrick, John (1871–1946)   An Irish-born labor leader who headed up the Chicago Federation of Labor for many decades. Fitzpatrick attempted to create a labor party as a counterbalance to the two main political parties in 1919, which then evolved into the national Farmer-Labor Party. The party was a complete failure and was eventually taken over by communists in 1924. Fitzpatrick advocated full equality in the workplace, regardless of one's gender, ethnicity, or race.

flappers   The term given to the women who flouted society's conventions as to how they should act. They were known for wearing short skirts, bobbing their hair, dancing in jazz clubs, and freely expressing their sexuality.

Ford, Henry (1863–1947)   One of the inventors of the modern automobile who helped to perfect the modern assembly line during the 1920s. During the Jazz Age more than 15 million of his famous Model T automobiles were sold. Ford believed in making autos affordable to the general public, especially through financing programs. Ford resisted changing the style of his autos for years, but competition from other car manufacturers reversed this attitude.

Garvey, Marcus (1887–1940)   A Jamaican-born leader in the Back to Africa movement. He was convicted of mail fraud under the flimsiest of evidence. President Calvin Coolidge pardoned Garvey, though he was eventually deported.

Grace, Sweet Daddy (1881–1960)   Founded the United House of Prayer for All People. He was known as a healer and a miracle worker.

Great Miami Hurricane   A Category Five hurricane that brought an end to the Florida land boom in 1926. Hundreds were killed, as many as 50,000 were made homeless, and there was approximately $100 million in damage.

Ham, Mordecai (1877–1961)   An evangelist who converted more than 300,000 people, including Billy Graham. Ham was born in Kentucky to a family that traced its lineage back through eight generations of Baptist preachers. Ham strongly supported Prohibition.

Harding, Warren G. (1865–1923)   Elected U.S. president in 1920. Harding's administration is noted mostly for its scandals, including the imprisonment of Secretary of Interior Albert Fall. Harding's post–World War I administration was a return to "normalcy," and the United States was increasingly inward looking, not concerned with world affairs.

Harlem Renaissance   A flourishing of artistic endeavors in the African American community during the Jazz Age. These endeavors ranged from literature to music to art. Although Harlem was seen as the center of the Harlem Renaissance, the artistic output could be seen around the country.

Hemingway, Ernest (1889–1961)   A famous writer who made his mark during the Jazz Age. As part of the Lost Generation of Jazz Age writers, Hemingway's writings often drew on his personal experiences, especially during World War I. Although Hemingway was known as a short story writer during the Jazz Age, his two novels during that time, *The Sun Also Rises* (1926) and *A Farewell to Arms* (1929), helped describe the mood of American expatriates.

Hoover, Herbert (1874–1964)   Elected U.S. president in 1928. Riding a wave of popularity for the Republican Party, Hoover was president at the onset of the Great Depression. His seeming inability to alleviate the economic crisis cost him the office in 1932.

Hughes, Langston (1902–1967)   A writer, poet, and columnist who rose to literary prominence as part of the Harlem Renaissance.

Hurston, Zora Neale (1891–1960)   A trained anthropologist who became noted as a writer during the Harlem Renaissance. In 1926, along with other noted Harlem Renaissance names such as Langston Hughes, she helped to publish the journal *Fire!*

Insull, Samuel, Sr. (1859–1938)   He helped to create the modern electric utility infrastructure of the United States. In the Chicago area, he established or expanded Commonwealth Edison, People's Gas, and the Northern Indiana Public Service Company.

isolationism   The attitude the United States adopted toward international affairs in the period between the two world wars. Although international relations were certainly maintained, the United States attempted to keep to itself and avoid any issues or conflicts that might lead to yet another war.

Izzie and Moe   Two U.S. Prohibition agents, Izzie Einstein (ca. 1880–1938) and Moe Smith (ca. 1887–1961), who used a variety of techniques, including disguises, to infiltrate speakeasies and catch various bootleggers. They are said to have made more than 4,900 arrests and had a 95 percent conviction rate.

jazz   A free-form style of music that gained national prominence during the 1920s. Improvisation is a key part of jazz music. Jazz numbers start with a basic melody and pattern, which members of a jazz band build on to play a solo of their own. Jazz was not accepted at first by many members of mainstream society for racist reasons as most jazz musicians were African American. Jazz remains a popular form of music today.

Jazz Singer, The   The first talking picture in the era of silent films. Although portions of the 1927 film were still silent, star Al Jolson's comment "You ain't heard nothing yet" brought about the age of talkies.

Kellogg-Briand Pact   An international treaty signed by 15 countries in 1928. Essentially outlawing war, the treaty renounced war as "an instrument of national policy." Although the treaty technically had the force of law, it did nothing to maintain world peace.

Ku Klux Klan An organization that promotes strong racist and anti-Semitic views, as well as being anti-Catholic and anti-immigrant. The first incarnation of the Klan arose after the Civil War, faded away, and then enjoyed a resurgence in 1915. During the Jazz Age the Klan rose to national prominence and had chapters in every state in the union as well as members in political positions.

Lindbergh, Charles (1902–1974) An American aviator who became famous for making the first solo transcontinental flight, going from New York to Paris in May 1924.

Lindy Hop A popular dance form named after famed American aviator Charles Lindbergh. Frankie "Musclehead" Manning, a choreographer and dancer, is said to be one of the creators of the wildly popular dance.

Lewis, Sinclair (1885–1951) A prolific author who wrote plays, short stories, and commentaries throughout his career. His most famous book, *Babbitt* (1922), is thought to be the one novel of the Jazz Age that is the best statement about conspicuous consumption during the era. His controversial 1927 work, *Elmer Gantry*, was an indictment of those who use organized religion as a way to make a fortune for themselves.

Locke, Alain (1885–1954) The "Father of the Harlem Renaissance." Locke was the first African American Rhodes Scholar. He believed black Americans should look to their African roots and move away from tradition and convention. He is best known for editing *The New Negro*.

Lost Generation A group of American writers and poets during the Jazz Age who chose to live abroad rather than in the United States.

Luciano, Charles "Lucky" (1897–1962) A Sicilian-born mob boss who is often credited with helping create modern organized crime.

Manning, Frankie "Musclehead" (1914–) A dancer and choreographer who is noted for performing the first air (or high) step in a 1935 swing dance contest. Manning is also considered one of the creators of the famed Lindy Hop dance.

McPherson, Aimee Semple (1890–1944) An evangelist known also as "Sister Aimee." Her groundbreaking use of mass media, especially the radio, to spread her message predated future televangelists. Claims of an abduction in 1926 were highly questioned, and she faced further accusations of lying and improper sexual behavior.

Micheaux, Oscar (1884–1951) A pioneering African American filmmaker specializing in what were called "race movies." He began his career as an author, even selling his books door to door. Micheaux's films addressed many important racial issues of the time, such as lynching, and avoided the stereotypes of blacks often presented during the early years of cinema.

Mickey Mouse A famed cartoon character that debuted in 1928 in "Plane Crazy" and "Steamboat Willie."

McKay, Claude (1889–1948)   An African American writer and poet who made his mark during the Harlem Renaissance. He is especially known for his 1928 novel *Home to Harlem*.

Mein Kampf   [*My Struggle*] Written by future Nazi dictator Adolf Hitler in 1925, the book outlined his plans and his severe anti-Semitism and was a frightening precursor to the 1930s and World War II.

Miss America Pageant   A beauty contest first held in 1921 in Atlantic City, New Jersey, with a total of eight contestants. The winner was Margaret Gorman of Washington, D.C.

Model T   The car that most epitomized the Ford Motor Company during the Jazz Age. For years there were no changes to the car, and Henry Ford's famous phrase "You can choose any color you like as long as it's black" summed up his views toward change. Competition from other car manufacturers forced Ford to make changes to his automobiles. Production ceased in 1927 in favor of the new Model A.

Morton, "Jelly Roll" (born Ferdinand Joseph Lamothe; 1890–1941)   Self-proclaimed inventor of jazz and an exceptional pianist and highly capable solo performer.

Museum of Modern Art (MOMA)   The New York museum opened its doors in 1929, just after the stock market crash that began the Great Depression. Despite the economic downturn, the museum managed to survive.

National Origins Act   Also known as the Johnson-Reed Act, this 1924 act severely restricted immigration to 2 percent of any particular group's U.S. presence according to the 1890 census.

National Women's Party   A political movement that fought for an Equal Rights Amendment.

nativism   A term that was quite common in America before the Jazz Age, it refers to a nation that wishes to preserve its purity by restricting immigration. During the Jazz Age, renewed calls for immigration restriction intensified.

Negro World, The   A newspaper that promoted Marcus Garvey's Back to Africa agenda. The paper would not accept advertisements for such items as skin lighteners. *Negro World* was not limited to Harlem alone, for readers across the United States could access this paper.

Ness, Eliot (1903–1957)   A U.S. Prohibition agent whose group, nicknamed the "Untouchables," achieved legendary status. Ness especially targeted Al Capone and his operations.

New Majority, The (1919–1924)   The newspaper created by the Chicago Federation of Labor (CFL) as the official organ of their newly created labor party. Besides promoting the new party, the paper also reported labor news around the country and reviewed movies and live shows. When the party was taken over by communists in 1924, the CFL abandoned the party and changed the name of the paper to *Federation News*.

New Negro This anthology of African American writings made its first appearance in 1925. According to Alain Locke, "Negro life is seizing upon its first chances for group expression and self-determination."

Nineteenth Amendment This amendment granted women the right to vote in 1920. Although some states already provided women with the right to vote, this right was now federally protected. The presidential election of 1920 was the first such federal election in which women could participate.

normalcy A term used by President Warren G. Harding to refer to the United States getting back to its normal way of life upon the conclusion of World War I (as well as the end of Wilsonian democracy under previous president Woodrow Wilson). Although many thought Harding misused the word *normality*, research has shown that the word *normalcy* had actually existed previously in the English language.

Original Dixieland Jazz Band The first commercially recorded jazz group.

Palmer Raids A series of mass arrests against political and labor agitators in 1919. Noncitizens were subjected to deportation. The legality of the raids remains highly questioned.

Pound, Ezra (1885–1972) An artist before, during, and even after the Jazz Age who had an enormous impact on the break from traditionalism in art in all its many forms. Before the Jazz Age, Pound already had a reputation as a poet, but during that time he continued to experiment with many different forms of expression.

Prohibition The period in American history (1920–1933) during which it was constitutionally illegal to make, sell, or possess alcoholic beverages. The consumption of alcohol hardly ceased as people who desired liquor obtained it through the black market or in illegal drinking establishments called speakeasies. Prohibition contributed to the rise of organized crime as gangsters competed for control of the illegal liquor trade. Prohibition was controversial from its institution in 1920 with the ratification of the Eighteenth Amendment to the Constitution. Prohibition was repealed by the Twenty-first Amendment in 1933.

Protocols of the Elders of Zion, The An anti-Semitic document containing false information about how the Jewish race was going to take over the world. During a strong resurgence of anti-immigrant and anti-Semitic feelings, especially led by the Ku Klux Klan, many accepted the protocols as fact.

Rader, Daniel Paul (1879–1935) A Jazz Age evangelist who saw the importance of radio and other forms of mass media to spread Gospel messages.

Randolph, A. Philip (1889–1979) An African American labor leader and civil rights crusader. In 1925 he helped to create, and assumed the presidency of, the Brotherhood of Sleeping Car Porters, a labor organization for the black Pullman porters.

Roaring Twenties   The phrase that came to stereotype the dominant decade of the Jazz Age. It mostly refers to the changes in music, dance, social interaction, and overall lifestyle of the time, which were in stark contrast to the Victorian era that preceded it.

Reed, John (1887–1920)   An American socialist who witnessed the Russian Bolshevik Revolution of 1917, writing about it in his famous book *Ten Days that Shook the World*. Reed was instrumental in creating the Communist Labor Party, which later fused with the Communist Party.

Remus, George (1873?–1952)   A noted bootlegger in the Cincinnati area. Remus is said to be the inspiration for Jay Gatsby in F. Scott Fitzgerald's *The Great Gatsby*.

rent parties   Social events in which guests were charged admission and then provided with music and alcohol. These were especially popular in Harlem where African Americans were faced with high rents, and rent parties were a way to make money. Jazz music, especially played on a piano, was a favorite form of music.

Roaring Twenties   A name given to the decade of the 1920s in the United States, which refers to the numerous cultural changes, especially in terms of music, dancing, social relations, and even participation in the stock market. The Victorian values of the pre–World War I era were rejected in favor of a more open society.

Ruth, George Herman "Babe" (1895–1948)   Regarded by many to be the greatest baseball player in history, Ruth became the first player to hit 60 home runs in a single season (1927), a record that stood for decades.

Sacco and Vanzetti Trial   Two Italian immigrants, Nicola Sacco and Bartolomeo Vanzetti, were arrested for a 1920 robbery/murder. Although the evidence was highly questionable, the two were convicted in 1921. Despite worldwide protests, Sacco and Vanzetti were executed in the electric chair in 1927. The famed socialist writer/politician Upton Sinclair immortalized their story in his historical fiction work *Boston* (1928).

Scopes, John T. (1900–1970)   A schoolteacher convicted for violating the Tennessee law banning the teaching of evolution. His arrest and subsequent trial were set up as a means to challenge the law, and Scopes became a symbol for those who sought scientific free thinking and progress against religious fundamentalists who opposed such actions.

Scopes "Monkey" Trial   The infamous 1925 court case that challenged a Tennessee law banning the teaching of evolution in the public schools. In a scenario set up by the American Civil Liberties Union, John Scopes stood trial for teaching evolution, represented by the Chicago attorney Clarence Darrow. Representing the state was the noted politician and failed presidential candidate William Jennings Bryan. Darrow's scientific evidence was denied in the trial, but in a twist he put Bryan on the stand to discuss the biblical view, a move that made the latter look hypocritical. Scopes was convicted, as Darrow had hoped for, in order to challenge the law in the state supreme court. The law remained on the books for four decades.

Sheppard-Towner Maternity and Infancy Protection Act   In 1921 this became the first such social legislation providing matching federal funds as a way to reduce infant mortality rates.

Simmons, William (1880–1945)   Simmons was responsible for reviving the Ku Klux Klan in 1915. During the Jazz Age, the Klan reached national prominence and even political power.

Smith, Alfred E. (1873–1944)   The Democratic candidate for president in the 1928 election, and the first Catholic to be nominated to the post. Strong anti-Catholic sentiment, coupled with the popularity of the Republican Party, contributed to his defeat.

Soviet Ark   The USS *Buford*, a boat that carried 294 people who were being deported to Russia in the wake of the infamous Palmer Raids. One of the passengers was the famed anarchist Emma Goldman.

speakeasies   Illegal drinking establishments during the era of Prohibition. Many were operated by organized crime units, and in many cases law enforcement officers were paid to stay away.

Stein, Gertrude (1874–1946)   She is generally attributed with coining the phrase "Lost Generation" to describe a group of American writers and poets during the Jazz Age who chose to live abroad rather than in the United States.

stock market crash   Also dubbed the "Great Crash," this was the collapse of the stock market that helped to usher in the Great Depression. The first collapse occurred on Thursday, October 24, 1929, and carried on for the next month. Although it is argued whether the crash itself was an immediate cause for the Depression, for there was a slight economic upturn after it, there is no denying the event contributed to the end of one period and the beginning of another.

strike wave of 1919   A massive labor strike across the United States. Approximately 25 percent of the workforce walked off their jobs. In Seattle, workers temporarily seized control of the city, but pressure from labor leaders and the government ended the movement.

St. Valentine's Day Massacre   A vicious gangland murder taking place in a Chicago garage in 1929. Mob boss Al Capone ordered the murder of seven members of rival gang boss George Clarence "Bugs" Moran. The massacre still has legendary status in contemporary times.

Sunday, Billy (1862–1935)   A Jazz Age evangelist who used his athletic skills and squeaky clean Christian image in sports and preaching. He used sports metaphors in his sermons, incorporated athletic physicality in his revival preaching, and was a keen advocate of the Prohibition movement.

Taft, William Howard (1857–1930)   A former U.S. president who became Supreme Court chief justice in 1921. Under his guidance, the Supreme Court gained better control over its docket. Although some refer to the conservatism of the Court under his administration, Taft had a previous reputation as being a "trust buster." Through his actions, the Court would eventually have its own building (it had previously met in other government offices). Taft died before the building was completed in 1935.

Tatem, William "Big Bill" (1893–1953)   In 1920, he became the first American to win at Wimbledon, a feat he would repeat in 1921 and 1930.

Teapot Dome Scandal   A corruption scandal that broke in 1923 during the Harding administration. Secretary of Interior Albert Fall was convicted for accepting bribes concerning the leasing of federal lands. Fall would be the first Cabinet member to go to prison.

Tunney, Gene (1897–1978)   Held the heavyweight boxing title between 1926 and 1928. His two victories over the enormously popular Jack Dempsey had some controversies over how the matches were refereed.

Universal Negro Improvement Association   An organization created by Marcus Garvey, leader of the Back to Africa movement. A major focus of the group was promoting positive feelings among African Americans toward their own heritage.

Valentino, Rudolph (1895–1926)   Silent film star noted for his sex appeal and also called the "Latin Lover." Although his films were not always favorites with critics, audiences, especially women, flocked to see his films.

Volstead Act   Named for Andrew Volstead, this 1919 act helped provide the federal government with the legislative authority to enforce Prohibition. Intoxicating liquors were defined as having more than 0.5 percent alcohol. The rise of organized crime syndicates dealing in the sales of illegal liquor, along with increased opposition, led to the repeal of Prohibition in 1933.

Walgreen, Charles R., Sr. (1873–1939)   He helped to create the pharmacy store chain Walgreen's. Pharmacies were no longer places to obtain just medicine; they also served as an early form of convenience store and typically sported a soda fountain whereby people could obtain various treats such as milkshakes.

Walker, Madam C. J. (1867–1919)   An African American businesswoman whose hair care products for black women helped to make her the first woman to become a millionaire not through inheritance but through her own hard work.

welfare capitalism   Programs enacted by corporations to provide benefits to their employees, such as pensions and vacation time. Although some companies did so out of true concern for their workers, in most cases these programs were enacted to reduce labor union influence, which pushed for similar measures.

Whiteman, Paul (1890–1967)   Whiteman dubbed himself the "King of Jazz." Classically trained on viola, he became famous as a jazz band leader and helped launch the music careers of many members.

Bibliography

Alft, E. C., and William H. Briska. *Elgin Time: A History of the Elgin National Watch Company*. Elgin: Elgin Historical Society, 2003.

This is a good overview of an important and influential watch-making company. It also covers the health risks many employees faced painting watch dials with radium.

Allen, Frederick Lewis. *Only Yesterday: An Informal History of the 1920s*. New York: John Wiley and Sons, 1997.

In this reprint of a timeless classic work (originally published in 1931, by Harper & Row) on the cultural side of the Jazz Age, Allen leads up to the stock market crash and presents a social side of America that many did not want to admit.

Anderson, Jervis. *This Was Harlem: 1900–1950*. New York: Farrar, Straus and Giroux, 1987.

This history of how Harlem became a mecca for black culture mentions the major names as well as the lesser known characters who contributed to the development of Harlem culture.

Arnensen, Eric. *Black Protest and the Great Migration*. Boston: Bedford/St. Martin's, 2003.

This is a short history, with documents, about the movement of thousands of African Americans from the southern states to the northern urban centers. The author also addresses how southern blacks were not always welcomed by northern blacks, as northerners often considered southerners to be inferior.

Bailey, Beth L. *From the Front Porch to Back Seat: Courtship in Twentieth Century America*. Baltimore: Johns Hopkins University Press, 1989.

This study concerns dating rituals in the 20th century. In terms of the Jazz Age, the author addresses how these rituals went from Victorian standards to dance halls and automobiles.

Bainbridge, John. *Little Wonder. Or, the Reader's Digest and How It Grew*. New York: Reynal & Hitchcock, 1945.

This interesting history of the publication that became part of the American cultural scene also covers its influences.

Baker, Carlos. *Hemingway: The Writer as Artist*. Princeton, NJ: Princeton University Press, 1972.

This is a good biography of one of the most famous members of the Lost Generation.

Barron, Hal S. *Mixed Harvest: The Second Great Transformation of the Rural North, 1870–1930*. Chapel Hill: University of North Carolina Press, 1997.

This book examines not just the development of rural areas but also how these areas responded to the growing changes in the urban centers. Despite the ever-growing importance and influence of the cities, rural settings maintained their own culture and identity.

Berger, Michael L. *The Devil Wagon in God's Country: The Automobile and Social Change in Rural America, 1893–1929*. Hamden, CT: Archon, 1979.

Berger looks at the cultural and social impacts of the automobile upon American society.

Bogart, Max. *The Jazz Age*. New York: Charles Scribner's Sons, 1969.

This is a collection of representative works of the time by those who lived through it. The writers selected for this edition are all from the literary tradition, such as Floyd Dell, Ernest Hemingway, and Langston Hughes.

Boyle, Kevin. *Arc of Justice: A Saga of Race, Civil Rights and Murder in the Jazz Age*. New York: Henry Holt and Company, 2004.

The author relates the experiences of Dr. Ossian Sweet who moves his family into an all-white Detroit neighborhood during the Great Migration. When attempts to drive him out result in violence and the death of a white man, Sweet is tried for murder. He is defended by Clarence Darrow in a trial that became a sensation.

Brecher, Jeremy. *Strike!* San Francisco: Straight Arrow, 1972.

This is a good overview of the various labor upheavals throughout American history. Brecher provides vital insights into the mass strike wave of 1919, including the workers' takeover of Seattle.

Brody, David. *Labor in Crisis: The Steel Strike of 1919*. Philadelphia: Lippincott, 1965.

This classic work examines not just the great steel strike of 1919 but also the overall atmosphere of the year when one quarter of America's workforce went on strike.

Buhle, Paul. *Marxism in the United States*. London: Verso, 1987.

This book looks at Marxism and left-wing thought in the context of American culture, although it does not address the economic portions of leftist theory. This book is meant more for those who already have a grounding in radical history.

Calder, Lendol Glen. *Financing the American Dream: A Cultural History of Consumer Credit*. Princeton, NJ: Princeton University Press, 1999.

In tracing the history of consumer credit back to the 19th century, this work examines how new forms of credit were created and popularized during the Jazz Age.

Canaan, Gareth. "Part of the Loaf: Economic Conditions of Chicago's African American Working Class During the 1920s." *Journal of Social History* 35, no. 1 (Fall 2001): 147–74.

This working-class history of blacks during the Jazz Age discusses the participation of African Americans in the economic system in the wake of the Great Migration.

Canterbury, Ray E., and Thomas Birch. *F. Scott Fitzgerald: Under the Influence*. St. Paul, MN: Paragon House, 2006.

This is a good biography about the life and lifestyle of one of the Jazz Age's most famous writers. This book also describes the personal demons Fitzgerald faced, including his firm belief that he was a failure professionally.

Carpenter, Humphrey. *A Serious Character: The Life of Ezra Pound*. Boston: Houghton Mifflin, 1988.

This is a good biography about the life of an important Jazz Age writer.

Carter, Paul. *The Twenties in America*. New York: Harlan, 1975.

This is an examination of the Jazz Age from the cultural to the political arenas. The Jazz Age is seen as a transitional period.

Chafe, William H. *The Paradox of Change: American Women in the Twentieth Century*. Cambridge, UK: Oxford University Press, 1992.

This study shows how women improved their status in America without achieving full equality. This is not just a study of struggle, but of victory.

Clark, Claudia. *Radium Girls: Women and Industrial Health Reform, 1910–1935*. Chapel Hill: University of North Carolina Press, 1997.

This is a vital work about the role of women in the manufacturing workplace and the many dangers they faced to their health and well-being. Also covered are the many ways people tried to alleviate health dangers, both privately and through government actions.

Cowan, Ruth Schwartz. *More Work for Mother: The Ironies of Household Technologies from the Open Hearth to the Microwave*. New York: Basic Books, 1982.

Despite the growing number of so-called labor-saving devices, Cowan shows that housewives' workloads were actually increased, in part because of having to operate these new machines. Women were still expected to fulfill their motherly role of keeping the house in order.

Cowley, Malcolm, and Robert Cowley. *Fitzgerald and the Jazz Age*. New York: Charles Scribner's Sons, 1966.

This is a series of essays about the Jazz Age by those who lived through the period. It is mostly a cultural and literary view of the Jazz Age. What all the essays have in common is that the authors view the Jazz Age as a period of transition.

Cox, James A. *A Century of Light*. New York: Benjamin Company, 1979.

This is an overview of the development of filament, the light bulb, and its subsequent importance.

Danbom, David. *The Resisted Revolution: Urban America and the Industrialization of Agriculture, 1900–1930*. Ames: Iowa State University Press, 1979.

This work takes a look at the many changes in the country's agricultural system and its interaction with urban settings.

Davis, Angela Y. *Blues Legacies and Black Feminism*. New York: Vintage Books, 1998.

Written by the famous radical and future professor, this is an interesting examination of the blues and its importance and influence on the lives of African American women. The author discusses some of the issues present in the lyrics of Blues, such as open sexuality and even domestic abuse.

Dicaire, David. *Jazz Musicians of the Early Years, to 1945*. Jefferson, NC: McFarland and Company, 2003.

This look at the vital formative years of jazz music moves from its beginnings to the end of World War II. Especially examined are the names of those, both famous and otherwise, who contributed to this musical form.

Dinnerstein, Leonard, and David M. Reimers. *Ethnic Americans: A History of Immigration and Assimilation*. New York: Harper and Row, 1975.

This book provides a good general overview of the history of immigration in the United States. The authors also focus on the many ways in which the country sought to incorporate the newcomers.

Drowne, Kathleen, and Patrick Huber. *The 1920s*. Westport, CT: Greenwood Press, 2004.

The authors portray the Jazz Age as the birth of modern America. This is mostly a cultural view of the Jazz Age with topics ranging from the cultural to the technical.

Esedebe, P. Olisanwuche. *Pan Africanism: The Idea and Movement, 1776–1991*. Washington, D.C.: Howard University Press, 1994.

This fresh look at Pan-Africanism acknowledges that there is no one single way to define the movement. The author contends that the study of this topic is still very new and in development.

Ewen, David. *The Life and Death of Tin Pan Alley: The Golden Age of American Popular Music*. New York: Funk and Wagnalls, 1964.

Ewen presents a lively description of Tin Pan Alley music. As with other books about musical genres, he examines both the famous and not so famous, people who participated in this art form.

Fass, Paula S. *The Damned and the Beautiful: American Youth in the 1920s*. New York: Oxford University Press, 1977.

This interesting social history and examination of the lives of America's youth during the Jazz Age holds that youth became a "social problem" during this period.

Forte, Allen. *The American Popular Ballad of the Golden Era, 1924–1950.* Princeton, NJ: Princeton University Press, 1995.

Forte analyzes the construction and influence of love songs written for the theater. Rather than dismissing ballads as popular tripe, the author holds that a much more serious analysis and appreciation of the form is deserved.

Fowler, Gene. *Skyline: A Reporter's Reminiscence of the 1920s.* New York: Viking Press, 1962.

Fowler, a journalist turned screenwriter, lived through the very era he wrote about. Although the book is mostly an autobiography, the author knew many of the important figures of the time. The book is an interesting self-character study.

Fox, Philip. *Adler Planetarium and Astronomy Museum Operated and Maintained by Chicago Park District: An Account of the Optical Planetarium and a Brief Guide to the Museum.* Chicago: Lakeside Press, 1935.

This is a brief overview of the opening and exhibits of the first such planetarium in the United States.

Gabbard, Krin. *Jammin' at the Margins: Jazz and the American Cinema.* Chicago: University of Chicago Press, 1996.

This book is an examination of the relationship between two burgeoning arts—jazz music and cinema.

Giddins, Gary. *Visions of Jazz: The First Century.* New York: Oxford University Press, 1998.

This examination of jazz music moves from its earliest roots and forms through its development and eventual acceptance by mainstream society.

Glickman, Lawrence B. *A Living Wage: American Workers and the Making of Consumer Society.* Ithaca, NY: Cornell University Press, 1997.

Besides examining how workers went from being skilled labor to mere wage earners, the author also addresses how the working classes contributed to the development of a consumer society.

Goldman, Jonathan. *The Empire State Building Book.* New York: St. Martin's Press, 1980.

This book chronicles the construction, importance, and influence of New York's famous Empire State Building, as well as its place in American culture.

Hamilton, David E. *From New Day to New Deal: American Farm Policy from Hoover to Roosevelt, 1928–1933.* Chapel Hill: University of North Carolina Press, 1991.

This is not just an overview of farm policies, but it also presents many sides of each issue.

Hansen, John M. "Choosing Sides: The Creation of an Agricultural Policy Network in Congress, 1919–1932." *Studies in American Political Development* 2 (1987): 183–229.

This is a good essay that describes the development of American farm policy in the post–World War I years.

Heidenry, John. *Theirs Was the Kingdom: Lila and DeWitt Wallace and the Story of the Reader's Digest.* New York: W.W. Norton, 1993.

In this detailed account of the rise of one of America's most famous publications, the author recounts those who founded the magazine and how it came to be part of American culture.

Henri, Florette. *Black Migration: Movement North, 1900–1920.* Garden City, NY: Anchor Press/Doubleday, 1975.

Henri describes not only the mass movement of African Americans to the North but also the social conditions, employment opportunities, and race relations they would encounter.

Herrmann, Dorothy. *With Malice Toward All: The Quips, Lives and Loves of Some Celebrated Twentieth Century American Wits.* New York: G. P. Putnam's Sons, 1982.

This amusing book is filled with anecdotes and sayings from some of America's most famous celebrities. The antics of the Algonquin Round Table are related in particular.

Higham, John. *Send These to Me: Jews and Other Immigrants in Urban America.* New York: Antheum, 1975.

This is an important work by one of the most preeminent historians of immigration history. Although the Jewish population is certainly a central focus, so are other groups that had an impact in major urban centers.

Hill, Daniel Delis. *Advertising to the American Woman, 1900–1999.* Columbus: Ohio State University Press, 2002.

Hill provides a good examination about the role and influence of women in the development of modern advertising.

Hine, Darlene Clark. "Black Migration in the Urban Midwest: The Gender Dimension, 1915–1945." In *The Great Migration in Historical Perspective,* edited by Joe William Trotter, 127–46. Bloomington: Indiana University Press, 1991.

This essay looks at the Great Migration not just from a racial perspective, but it also incorporates the role of gender.

Howells, Trevor, ed. *A Guide to the World's Greatest Buildings: Masterpieces of Architecture and Engineering.* San Francisco: Fog City Press, 1996.

This is a sweeping overview of some of the most famous structures in world history.

Jacobson, Lisa. "Manly Boys and Enterprising Dreamers: Business Ideology and the Construction of the Boy Consumer, 1910–1930." *Enterprise & Society* 2 (2001): 225–258.

This essay provides an interesting examination about the role and influence of advertising on everyday life.

Jellison, Katherine. *Entitled to Power: Farm Women and Technology, 1913–1963.* Chapel Hill: University of North Carolina Press, 1993.

A much overlooked topic in American agricultural history is the role women played in its development. Jellison offers an important look at the role and influence of women in agriculture.

Jenkins, Alan. *The Twenties*. New York: Universe Books, 1974.

This extensively illustrated work is more of a pop history of the Jazz Age or a social history of the United States. The lively narrative covers some technological and scientific issues, but they are presented in a manner that ties in well with the cultural changes during the period.

Johnson, James Weldon. *The Book of American Negro Poetry*. New York: Harcourt Brace, 1959.

This anthology of African American poetry includes such authors as Paul Lawrence Dunbar and James Edwin Campbell.

Kallen, Stuart E., ed. *The Roaring Twenties*. San Diego: Greenhaven Press, 2002.

This collection of essays was written by those who lived through the Jazz Age. The volume concentrates on mostly social and economic issues.

Kenner, Hugh. *The Pound Era*. Berkeley: University of California Press, 1973.

Kenner examines not just the life of Ezra Pound but also the time in which he lived.

Kirschner, Don S. *City and Country: Rural Responses to the Urbanization in the 1920s*. Westport, CT: Greenwood Publishing, 1970.

An examination of rural life and how those who lived in such settings saw their roles within their regional cultures. The work compares the rural view with that of the growing urban centers.

Kraut, Alan M. *The Huddled Masses*. Arlington Heights, IL: Harlan Davidson, 1982.

This is a good general overview of immigration history that consolidated the most current research and bibliography at the time it was written.

Kuykendall, Ronald A. "African Blood Brotherhood, Independent Marxist During the Harlem Renaissance." *The Western Journal of Black Studies* 26, no. 1 (2002): 16–21.

This essay looks at the role of Marxism/communism on the black community, a topic that is not addressed as frequently as others in African American histories.

Kyvig, David E. *Daily Life in the United States, 1920–1940*. Chicago: Ivan R. Dee, 2002.

In this cultural view of America through the decades, Kyvig explains how everyday life was changed through a variety of innovations. The author examines a variety of urban locales across the country instead of just focusing on major cities.

Landes, David S. *Dynasties: Fortunes and Misfortunes of the World's Great Family Businesses*. New York: Penguin Books, 2006.

This book examines 11 different powerful families from around the world. This is not just a book about how business moguls operated in the economic world, but it is also about how their family interactions were equally important.

Leach, William. *Land of Desire: Merchants, Power, and the Rise of a New American Culture*. New York: Vintage Books, 1994.

This work examines the rise of the consumer culture and the many forces behind it, including business moguls, government officials, or even the clergy. This book also examines how consumers are enticed to participate, whether through advertising or other forms of clever visualizations.

Lears, T. J. Jackson. *Fables of Abundance: A Cultural History of Advertising in America*. New York: Basic Books, 1994.

In this interesting take on how advertising became part of American culture, the author rejects the idea of advertising as portraying itself as important and useful to the American public, an action he considers harmful because it relied too much on false assumptions as to what constituted a good life.

Lewis, David Levering. *When Harlem Was in Vogue*. New York: Penguin Books, 1997.

Focusing on the period 1905 to 1935, the author traces the history of African Americans in Harlem. He covers the many aspects of their lives ranging from artistic endeavors to economic and political movements.

Lewis, Earl. "Expectations, Economic Opportunities, and Life in the Industrial Age: Black Migration to Norfolk, Virginia, 1910–1940." In *The Great Migration in Historical Perspective*, edited by Joe William Trotter, 22–45. Bloomington: Indiana University Press, 1991.

This examination of African Americans during the Black Migration is interesting because of its focus on a locale other than the major northern industrial centers.

Lingeman, Richard. *Sinclair Lewis: Rebel from Main Street*. New York: Random House, 2002.

This is an involving biography of one of the most famous writers of the Jazz Age. Although the author portrays Lewis's enormous talent, he also shows much of the sadness that engulfed his life.

Marks, Carole. *Farewell—We're Good and Gone: The Great Black Migration*. Bloomington: Indiana University Press, 1989.

In this neo-Marxist view of the Great Migration, the author sees the movement as being mostly the result of actions on the part of northern industrialists to obtain a cheap source of labor.

Martin, Tony. *Race First: The Ideological and Organizational Struggles of Marcus Garvey and the Universal Negro Improvement Association*. Westport, CT: Greenwood Press, 1976.

This work looks at Marcus Garvey and his influence, which went beyond U.S. borders. The author looks at the psychological aspects of the movement that Garvey helped to create.

McClymer, John. "The Federal Government and the Americanization Movement, 1915–1924." *Prologue* 10 (Spring 1978): 10–28.

This journal article examines the role of the federal government in assimilating immigrants into American society.

McDonald, Forrest, *A Constitutional History of the United States*. Malabar, FL: Robert Krieger, 1986.

In this brief overview of the role of the U.S. Constitution in American life, the author notes the legal struggles of such groups as African Americans and immigrants.

McMillen, Neil R. "The Migration and Black Protest in Jim Crow Mississippi." In *Black Exodus: The Great Migration from the American South*, edited by Harrison Alferdteen, 83–100. Jackson: University of Mississippi Press, 1991.

This essay looks at the lives of African Americans during a crucial time in their history. In this and other works, McMillen chronicles African Americans' many struggles with the legal and economic system and their attempts to carve out a niche for themselves.

Meade, Marion. *Dorothy Parker: What Fresh Hell Is This?* New York: Penguin Books, 1987.

In this biography, the author examines the many facets of famed American writer Dorothy Parker, both her comedic and misanthropic sides as well as her personal struggles with alcohol abuse.

Mordden, Ethan. *That Jazz: An Idiosyncratic Social History of the American Twenties*. New York: G. P. Putnam's Sons, 1978.

Mordden's book makes no pretenses about how he views America during the 1920s. As much a personal view of the Jazz Age as anything, jazz music is certainly a central focus of the book. Since jazz is a free from sort of music, so is this period.

Mowry, George, ed. *The Twenties: Fords, Flappers and Fanatics*. Englewood Cliffs, NJ: Prentice-Hall, 1963.

In this older work, the editor comments that historians have described the Jazz Age as retrograde, concentrating on the economic landscape. This is a collection of essays written by people across the spectrum, from businesspeople to lawyers to politicians. The contributors were participants in or eyewitnesses to the very events they describe.

Naison, Mark. *Communists in Harlem during the Depression*. Urbana: University of Illinois Press, 1983.

Naison looks at the communists' attempts to recruit from the African American community. The author notes that despite promises of liberation the communists had difficulty persuading blacks to join.

Nasaw, David. *Going Out: The Rise and Fall of Public Amusements*. New York: Basic Books, 1993.

This is a description of how certain forms of public amusement, including amusement parks, vaudeville, and baseball, arose beginning in the late 19th century. The author shows how European immigrants enjoyed these pleasures but native-born blacks were not allowed to participate.

Nelson, William T. *Fresh Water Submarines: The Manitowoc Story*. Manitowoc, WI: Hoeffner Printing, 1986.

This is an important story about how the Manitowoc Shipbuilding Company came to be awarded a contract to produce submarines for the U.S. government.

Olneck, Michael R., and Marvin Lazerson. "The School Achievement of Immigrant Children: 1900–1930." *History of Education Quarterly* (Winter 1974): 430–465.

A major focus of this journal article is the debate about whether school systems were trying to help assimilate newly arrived immigrants for their own benefit or were trying to indoctrinate them to be good, nonconfrontational citizens.

Olney, Martha L. *Buy Now, Pay Later: Advertising, Credit, and Consumer Durables in the 1920s*. Chapel Hill: University of North Carolina Press, 1991.

Olney's discussion about the development of consumer culture during the Jazz Age also covers the development and new uses of credit.

Ottley, Roi, and William Weatherby, eds. *The Negro in New York: An Informal Social History, 1626–1940*. New York: Praeger Publishers, 1969.

This book provides a sweeping view of African American history. It is a fascinating study of not just how blacks viewed themselves and the world they lived in but also how they helped to create Harlem.

Perrett, Geoffrey. *America in the Twenties*. New York: Simon and Schuster, 1982.

This volume views the Jazz Age as still having the trappings of post–World War I Victorian-era values. To the author, there was still a battle between the old ways and the new.

Pietruskza, David. *1920: The Year of Six Presidents*. New York: Carroll and Graf Publishers, 2007.

In a very focused work, the author concentrates on a single year—the presidential election year of 1920—and how the numerous events during that year had long-reaching effects. From the political to the social, 1920 is shown to be one of the most pivotal years in U.S. history

Platt, Harold L. *The Electric City: Energy and the Growth of the Chicago Area, 1880–1930*. Chicago: University of Chicago Press, 1991.

Using Chicago as a background, the author examines how electricity and public utilities had a profound impact on the rise of the modern city.

Popular and Social Dance. Microsoft Encarta Online Encyclopedia. 2006. http://encarta.msn.com.

This encyclopedia article describes the development of popular dance styles, their innovators, and public acceptance.

Renshaw, Patrick. *The Wobblies: The Story of Syndicalism in the United States*. New York: Doubleday and Company, 1967.

This is a dated but important work about not just the Industrial Workers of the World but also how syndicalism itself was addressed in the United States.

Robinson, Dean. *Black Nationalism in American Politics and Thought*. New York: Cambridge University Press, 2001.

In this focus on the idea of black nationalism, which the author translates to mean separatism, he reflects upon the different ideologies that played a role in African American activities. He also addresses how white America did not always view blacks as being as "American" as whites, especially as blacks embraced their African roots.

Schneider, Mark Robert. *"We Return Fighting": The Civil Rights Movement in the Jazz Age*. Boston: Northeastern University Press, 2002.

This is a bottom-up view of African American history, concentrating more on the rank-and-file members of the NAACP rather than the major names in the fight for civil rights. These struggles took place in the courtrooms, workplace, and in various venues across the country.

Schorer, Mark. *Sinclair Lewis: An American life*. New York: McGraw-Hill, 1961.

An older biography of Lewis published not too long after his death. While recognizing the talent of Lewis, the book also shows that he might not have been too pleased with his professional life. Prior critiques of this biography are that the author here might not have cared much for his subject.

Schrum, Kelly. *Some Wore Bobby Sox: The Emergence of Teenage Girls' Culture, 1920–1945*. New York: Palgrave Macmillan, 2004.

This is a look at the changes in the lives of teenage girls—not just in the cultural sphere, but also the impacts of advertising and popular culture on their lives, especially in the new consumer culture.

Shawki, Ahmed, *Black Liberation and Socialism*. Chicago: Haymarket Books, 2006.

An examination of the many ways African Americans fought against racism in the United States. The author examines movements from Marcus Garvey to contemporary times. The author points out that there is still much to achieve.

Sinclair, Upton. *The Flivver King*. 1937; reprint Chicago: Charles H. Kerr, 1987.

This is one of Sinclair's historical fiction works whereby he combines actual historical facts within the context of a fictional story. This is an indictment of Henry Ford and the Ford Motor Corporation. The central character is Abner Shutt, a Ford employee, who blindly follows what his beloved employers supposedly tell him. A good portion of the book deals with the KKK resurgence, as well as the rampant anti-Semitism during the Jazz Age.

Sivulka, Juliann. *Soap, Sex, and Cigarettes. A Cultural History of American Advertising*. Belmont, CA: Wadsworth Publishing, 1998.

A good overview of how the development of modern advertising became an integral part of American cultural life.

Sivulka, Juliann. *Stronger than Dirt: A Cultural History of Advertising Personal Hygiene in America, 1875–1940.* Amherst, NY: Humanity Books, 2001.

This is a cultural view of the influence of advertising in American culture, in particular how advertising campaigns convinced women that using their products would improve their personal lives.

Sklar, Robert. *Movie-Made America: A Cultural History of Movies.* New York: Vintage, 1994.

This history of American cinema includes a look at the old studio system and its demise. A main focus of the book is on film as an art form and its cultural influences.

Smulyan, Susan. *Selling Radio: The Commercialization of American Broadcasting, 1920–1934.* Washington, D.C.: Smithsonian Institution Press, 1994.

This history of radio in the post–World War I years describes how the increasing costs of broadcasting, coupled with the growing high demand for programming, led to the commercialization of a still new form of media.

Sobel, Robert. *The Great Bull Market: Wall Street in the 1920s.* New York: W.W. Norton, 1968.

This is not the average book about the stock market. Rather, it is an examination of the presence of the market in the lives of U.S. citizens and how the two interacted with each other.

Spurlock, John C., and Cynthia A. Magistro. *New and Improved: The Transformation of American Women's Emotional Culture.* New York: New York University Press, 1998.

This work is a look at the lives of educated women during the early 20th century and the roles they were expected to play.

Stein, Judith. *The World of Marcus Garvey: Race and Class in Modern Society.* Baton Rouge: Louisiana State University Press, 1986.

In a look at the extremely colorful figure of Marcus Garvey, the author contends that his Back to Africa movement was just as much about blacks being part of the middle class as it was about race. The book also looks at the place of blacks not just in the United States but also in other world locales.

Stephens, Judith. "Racial Violence and Representation: Performance Strategies in Lynching Dramas of the 1920s." *African American Review* 33, no. 4 (Winter 1999): 655–671.

This article is an overview of the struggles against the racist and illegal lynchings that were an unfortunate part of American history and the Jazz Age.

Stevenson, Elizabeth. *Babbitts and Bohemians: The American 1920s.* New York: Macmillan Company, 1967.

Writing as a child of the 1960s, the author looks at the plethora of activities of the era, many of which seem to contradict each other. Stevenson notes how any era has numerous complexities that can have long-reaching effects.

Stock, Noel. *Life of Ezra Pound*. London: Routledge and Kegan Paul, 1970.

This is a good biography about the life and influence of an important Jazz Age writer.

Stovel, Katherine. "Local Sequential Patterns: The Structure of Lynching in the Deep South, 1882–1930." *Social Forces* 79, no. 3 (March 2001): 843–880.

This is a study of the legacy of lynching in the Deep South and the attempts to put an end to the terrible practice.

Strasser, Susan. *Satisfaction Guaranteed: The Making of the American Mass Market*. New York: Pantheon Books, 1989.

This look at consumer culture ranges from the 19th century all the way to the development of the modern malls. The author traces the development of name brands on products that were previously considered generic.

Thompson, Neal. *Driving with the Devil: Southern Moonshine, Detroit Wheels, and the Birth of NASCAR*. New York: Crown, 2006.

This is a look at the rise of stock car racing, especially how its earliest drivers honed their high-speed craft running illegal liquor for bootleggers.

Tirro, Frank. *Jazz: A History*. New York: Norton and Company, 1993.

This is a good general history of the development of jazz music from its origins to modern times.

Trotter, Joe William, Jr. "Race, Class, and Industrial Change: Black Migration to Southern West Virginia." In *The Great Migration in Historical Perspective*, edited by Joe William Trotter, 46–67. Bloomington: Indiana University Press, 1991.

In an essay about the Great Migration the author examines an area not usually considered about the movement.

Waller, Maurice, and Anthony Calabrese. *Fats Waller*. New York: Macmillan Publishing Company, 1977.

Written by the son of Fats Waller, this biography is filled with lively anecdotes and shows how the groundbreaking musician went about his craft. Although the book naturally shows admiration for Waller, it also presents a balanced view of his life.

Wintz, Cary D. *Black Culture and the Harlem Renaissance*. Houston: Rice University Press, 1988.

Although this work certainly discusses the more prominent names connected with the Harlem Renaissance, it also relates the era to previous time periods. The author also demonstrates how the Harlem Renaissance incorporated more than just artistic endeavors.

Wondrick, David. *Stomp and Swerve: American Music Gets Hot, 1843–1924*. Chicago: A Cappella, 2003.

This is an examination of what is termed "hot music" and its development. Starting with the minstrel shows through the blending of Afro-Caribbean rhythms to ragtime and to the blues, the author also looks at how the public accepted such musical forms.

Wood, James Playsted. *Of Lasting Interest: The Story of the Reader's Digest.* Westport, CT: Greenwood Press, 1958.

This is a dated but interesting look at the rise of *Reader's Digest* and its influence in American culture.

Wukovits, John F. *The 1920s.* San Diego: Greenhaven Press, 2000.

Each essay in this collection of academic essays examines a different aspect of the Jazz Age. This is mostly a political and social study of the period.

Young, Al. *African American Literature: A Brief Introduction and Anthology.* New York: HarperCollins, 1996

As the title indicates, this is a brief overview and sampling of important works of African American literature.

Zolberg, Aristide. *A Nation by Design: Immigration Policy in the Fashioning of America.* Cambridge, MA: Harvard University Press, 2006.

This excellent contemporary work examines U.S. immigration policy from the colonial era to the present. The author, a Jewish World War II refugee, provides fresh insights into how the nation accepted new peoples into its culture.

Index

Abbott, Robert, 7
Abbott, William Rufus, 182
Addams, Jane, 117
Adler Planetarium and Astronomy Museum, 183, 184
Adler, Max, 183
Adler, Sophie, 183, 184
Adolescents, rural, 25
Adonis, Joe, 44
Advertising, 79–80, 88–90
African Americans, 152
    African Blood Brotherhood, 7–9
    and Communist Party, 8–9
    and consumer culture, 83–84
    and evangelism, 64–66
    Garvey and UNIA, 5–7
    Great Migration, 1–3
    Harlem renaissance, 10–13
    jazz music, importance of, 13
    NAACP, 10
    northern promises and realities, 3–5
    pan–African congresses, 9–10
    perceptions of, 1
    political actions and aspirations, 5
African Blood Brotherhood (ABB), 7–9
African Diaspora, 6, 9 *See also* African Americans
Age of Reform, 38, 113
Agricultural Credits Act (1924), 21
Agricultural Marketing Act (1929), 21, 34
Agricultural mobilization, 19
Al Smith, 34
Algonquin Round Table, 164
Ali, Noble Drew, 64
America First Party, 71
American Automobile Association, 33
American Civil Liberties Union (ACLU), 139

American Cotton Association, 23
American Education Week(AEW), 134–137
    1924 controversy, 136–137
    beginnings, 134
American Farm Bureau Federation (AFBF), 20
American Federation of Labor (AFL), 31, 132, 141, 142, 168
American Legion, 119, 136
American Magazine, 59
American Negro Labor Congress (ANLC), 8
American Waltham Watch Company, 174
Americanism, 109–112
Americanization programs, 117–118
Amusements, public, 77
Angeline, 67
Antheil, George, 159
Anti-Saloon League, 39
Appearance and consumer culture, 79–80
Argentina, 114
Armstrong, Garner Ted, 72
Armstrong, Herbert W., 70–71
Armstrong, Loma, 70–71
Armstrong, Louis, 12, 98, 101, 102–104
Arrowsmith, 164
Art Deco, 170, 171
Association of Methodist Women Preachers, 60
Atwood, Charles, 182
Austin High Gang, 98
Austin, Lovie, 98
Australia, 57
Austria, 114
Automobile, 82–83
    farmer-owned, 27
    impact on American culture, 83
    and impact on farmers, 24
Avery, Sewell, 182

Babbitt, 164

Ballard School and International Institute, 119

Banjo, 154

Bank of North Dakota, 30, 31

Barrow, Clyde, 49

Bauersfeld, Walther, 184

Beatty, Warren, 49

The Beautiful and the Damned, 161

Beiderbecke, Bix, 101, 104–105

Belgium, 9

Bennet, Edward H., 181

Berardelli, Alessandro, 143

Berkebile, Mary Louise, 70

"Bernice Bobs Her Hair," 161

Better Homes and Gardens, 81

Better Homes in America movement, 28

The Big Money, 158

Big Steel Tent, 60

Birth of a Nation, 122, 152

Black Cross Navigation and Trading Company, shipping ventures, 7

Black evangelism. *See* African Americans

Black Star Line, 6, 7

Blair & Company, 179

Bless You, Sister, 59

Bliss, Cornelius Newton, 180

Bliss, Lizzie Plummer, 180

Blues tradition, 12, 67

Boll weevil, 3

Bonanno family, 43

Borah, William, 31

Boston, 146

Bowman, L. E., 137

Bradford, Perry, 93

Bradfute, Oscar, 32

Brazil, 114

The Bridal Call, 57

Brinkley, John R., 70

Broadway Mob, 44

Brookhart, Smith, 32

Bryan, William Jennings, 71, 139, 140

Buchman, Frank, 59

Budd, Britton I., 179

Bugs and Meyer Mob gang, 45

Bugsy, 50

Bureau of Alcohol, Tobacco, and Firearms, 48

Bureau of Education, 119, 120, 134

Bureau of Naturalization, 119, 134

Bureau of Prohibition, 48

Burlingame Treaty, 114

Burnham, Daniel, 181

Burns, Ken, 106

Burrell, Ben E., 8

Burrell, Theodore, 8

Business persons, 167

    Charles Walgreen and rise of chain pharmacies, 176–177

    clock-and-watch manufacturing industry, 172–176

    philanthropy, 180–184

    Samuel Insull and utilities and transportation empire, expansion and collapse of, 177–180

    skyscrapers, 168–172

Butler bill, 138

Cadillac, 83

California Fruit Growers' Association, 20

California Tabernacle, 61

Campbell, Grace, 8

Campbell, Thomas, 22–23

Canada, 41, 45, 63, 117

Capone, Al "Scarface," 37, 40–44, 48, 49

"Carolina Shout," 96

Casual racism, 93–94

Cathay, 158

Catholic Church, 40

Catholicism and evangelism, 68–69

CBS, 60, 68

Celler, Emanuel, 117

Central Valley Project, 23

A Century of Progress World's Fair, 177

Chain farms, 22

Chapman, J. Wilbur, 55

Charleston, 106

Cherry, Prophet, 64

Chestnut, Charles, 13

Chevrolet, 83

Chicago & Oak Park Elevated Railroad Company, 179

Chicago Defender, 3

Chicago Elevated Railways Collateral Trust, 179, 180

Chicago Federation of Labor (CFL), 26, 133, 141, 142

Chicago Gospel Tabernacle, 61

Chicago jazz, 97–98

Chicago North Shore & Milwaukee interurban railroad, 179

Chicago Outfit, 42

Chicago Rapid Transit Company, 180

Chicago Rapid Transit Line, 179

Chicago Tribune, 168

Chicago White Stockings, 55

China, 57

Chinese exclusionary laws (1882), 114
Chomsky, Noam, 168
Christensen, Parley Parker, 141
Christian and Missionary Alliance (C&MA), 60
Christian Front, 68
Chrysler Building, 170
Chrysler, Walter, 170
Church of God (COG)–7th Day doctrine, 71
Civil War, 114
The Clansman, 122
Clark, Claudia, 176
Claxton, P. P., 119
Clayborn, E. W., 67
Cleveland, Grover, 115
Clock-and-watch manufacturing industry,
    172–176
Collective improvisation, 94–95
Colombo family, 43
Columbia Records, 67
Combo, 95
Comintern. *See* Communist Third International
Commercial Club, 181, 182
Committee of One Hundred, 5
Committee of One Million, 71
Commonwealth Edison, 177, 179
Communist Labor Party, 143
Communist Manifesto, 147
Communist Party of America, 143
Communist Third International, 143
Community morality, concerns about, 33
Condon, Eddie, 98
Constab Ballads, 12
Consumer culture, 75
    advertising, 88–90
    African-American consumers, 83–84
    appearance, 79–80
    automobiles, 82–83
    consumer credit availability, 90–91
    in the country, 84–86
    home, 80–82
    immigrants, 86
    leisure, 78
    market research development, 90
    as mass culture, 76–78
    mass market development, 86–87
    new, opportunity to participate in, 88–89
    rise of, 75–76
Consumer's League, 175
Consumerism and mass consumption, 27–30
Coolidge, Calvin, 17, 31, 116, 117, 132, 153, 180
Cora Dow, 176
Cornet, 105

Cosmetics industry, 79–80
Costello, Frank, 44
Cotton Club, 100
Coué, Emile, 59
Coughlin, Charles Edward, 68, 71
Coulson, Ivar "Pop," 177
Countercultural rebellion, 25
Counter-culture, 130–131
Country Life Commission, 18
Cox, James, 126
Crawford, Janie, 155
Crazy Blues, 12, 93
Creole Jazz Band, 96, 102
Crisis, 10
Crooner, 99
Crosby, Bing, 101
Crowninshield, Francis, 181
Culture, meaning of, 130
Czechoslovakia, 151

Darrow, Clarence, 139, 140
Darwin's evolution theory and Bible, 139–140
Davis, James John, 118, 136
Dawes, Rufus, 182
Dearborn Independent, 125
Debs, Eugene V., 121, 126, 142
Debussy, Claude, 105
Denver Symphony Orchestra, 101
Devil's music, 106
Deyenka Sr., Peter, 62
Dial painters and radium poisoning, 174–176
Dickinson, Lester J., 32
Dillinger, John, 38, 49
Disenfranchisement, 3
Divine, Father, 59, 64, 65–66
Dixon Jr., Thomas, 122
Dodds, Johnny, 98
Dodge, Horace, 71
Dodsworth, 165
Domingo, W. A., 8
Dorsey, Jimmy, 101, 105
Dorsey, Thomas A., 67
Dorsey, Tommy, 101, 105
Dos Passos, John, 150, 157–158
Dranes, Arizona, 67
Drinker, Cecil, 176
Drinker, Philip, 176
Drug, Inc., 177
DuBois, W. E. B., 7, 9, 10, 154, 155
Dunaway, Faye, 49
Dunbar, Paul Lawrence, 13
Dunlop, Merrill, 62

E. Ingraham Company, 175

Eastman, Max, 130

Edison General Electric Company, 178

Edison, Thomas Alva, 177, 178

Eiffel Tower, 170

Einstein, Isidore "Izzy," 48

Elgin Clock Company, 172

Elgin National Watch Company, 172

Elgin Watchmakers College, 172

Ellington, Duke, 12, 94, 99, 100–101

Elmer Gantry, 56, 165

Emergency Quota Act, 116

Emotional appeal and advertising, 89

Empire State Building, 170, 171

England, 41, 63, 114, 127, 176

Espionage Act (1917), 130

Europe, 63

Evangelism, of Jazz Age:

> African-American community and, 64–66

Aimee Semple McPherson, 57–59

Billy Sunday, 55–56

Catholicism and, 68–69

Charles Price, 63–64

Cora Fauss, 72

Daniel Paul Rader, 60–62

Doc Springer, 69–70

Dwight Moody, 53–54

Ethel Musick, 63

Father Divine, 65–66

Gerald Lyman Kenneth Smith, 71–72

Herbert W. Armstrong, 70–71

John R. Brinkley, 70

Mordecai Ham, 56–57

Morris Plotts, 62–63

music and, 67–68

and national mortality, 56–57

origins, 53

outsiders in, 69–72

Robert Reynolds Jones, 64

Smith Wigglesworth, 62

Sweet Daddy Grace, 64–65

Uldine Utley, 59–60

Williams Simmons, 59

women and, 66–67

Evans, Hiram, 125

Ever-increasing Faith, 62

Evolution theory and controversy, 137–140

Extension Service, 28

Fall, Albert, 135

A Farewell to Arms, 162, 163

Farm Bureau Federation, 32

Farmer-Labor Party, 26, 31, 141, 142

Farmers, 17

> associations, 20–21

consumerism and mass consumption, 27–30

country life movement, 18–19

cultural interactions, 26–27

facing changes, 17–18

politics of protest, 30–34

recreation and culture, 24

and resistance to mechanization, 23

rural economy, 19–20

rural participation in new cultural pursuits, 24–26

and struggle to survive, 20–21

work initiatives, 22–23

"Farmers' night," 24

Father Time's Family, 174

Fausett, Redmon Jessie, 9

Fauss, Cora, 72

Fauss, Milton, 72

Feature-length moving pictures, 78

Federal Farm Board, 34–35

Federal Farm Loan System (1916), 35

Federal Highway Act (1921), 32–33

Federal Trade Commission, 180

Federation News, 142

Field Columbian Museum, 183

Field Museum of Natural History, 181

Fine Clothes to the Jew, 12

Fire!, 155

Fitzgerald, F. Scott, 45, 149, 160–162

Fitzpatrick, John, 133, 141

Five Families, 43

The Flivver King, 124

Florida land boom, 170–171

Fogg Art Museum, Harvard, 181

Food Production Act, 19

Ford, Henry, 82, 124

Forrest, Nathan Bedford, 122

The 42nd Parallel, 158

Foster, William Z., 133, 142

Foursquare movement, 58

Fox, Lorne, 63

Fox, Philip, 183

Fraina, Louis, 143

France, 9, 41, 113, 127, 156, 159

Frazier, Lynn, 30, 31

Freeman, Bud, 98

Freud, Sigmund, 152

Fuller, Charles, 62

Fuller Theological Seminary, 62

Furlong, William E., 183

Gambino family, 43
Gangsters and bootleggers. *See* Illicit alcohol
Garvey, Marcus: and mail fraud, 7
    and UNIA, 5–7
Gary, Elbert H., 132
General Electric, 177
General Mills, 82
General Motors Acceptance Corporation, 91
General Strike Committee, 132
Genovese family, 43, 44
Germany, 114, 127, 184
Gershwin, George, 101
Gitlow, Benjamin, 143
The Godfather Part II, 121
Golden Grain, 63
Goldman, Emma, 116, 130
Goldman, Sachs, 181
Gompers, Samuel, 141, 168
Goodman, Benny, 98, 105
Goodwin, Philip, 181
Goodyear, A. Conger, 180–181
Gothic Rouen Cathedral, 169
Gouraud, George A., 178
Grace, Sweet Daddy, 64–65
Graham, Anderson, Probst, and White, 181
Graham, Billy, 56, 72
Grapes of Wrath, 165
Grateful Dead, 46
Great Depression, 39, 43, 63, 71, 158, 181
The Great Gatsby, 45, 161
Great Migration, 1–3, 152
Griffith, D. W., 122
Grunsfeld, Ernest, 184

Hall & Lyon Company of Providence, 176
Ham, Mordecai, 56–57
Hamilton, Alexander, 38
Hamilton, Alice, 175, 176
Hardin, Lillian, 102
Harding, Warren, G., 17, 31, 129, 135, 141
Harlem Renaissance, 10–13
    Alaine Locke and *The New Negro*, 155
    and beyond, 13–14
    black pride, rising, 153
    Claude McKay, 153–154
    Great Migration, 152
    Harlem School, 99
    roots of Renaissance, 153
    Zora Neale Hurston, 155
Harlem: Negro Metropolis, 154
Hayes, Max, 141, 142
Hayes, Rutherford B., 122

Hearst Corporation newspapers, 175
Hegeman & Company, 176
Hemingway, Ernest, 156, 162–163
Henderson, Fletcher, 12, 102
Henderson, Fletcher, 99
Hi and Lois, 46
Hillquit, Morris, 121
Hinn, Benny, 72
Hodes, Art, 98
Home to Harlem, 154
Hood, Raymond M., 168, 169
Hoover, J. Edgar, 49, 50
Hoover, Herbert, 34, 126, 171
Hot jazz. *See* Chicago jazz
House Beautiful, 81
Howard, Mattie, 59
Howard, William, 115
Howells, John Mead, 168
Hughes, Howard, 45
Hughes, Langston, 11, 12, 155
Huiswood, Ottow, 8
Hungary, 114
Hurston, Zora Neale, 155

Idaho Farmers' Political Association, 31
Illicit alcohol, 37
    Al Capone, 40–48
    bootlegging industry and organized crime
        rise, 40–41
    Charles "Lucky" Luciano, 44
    criminal activities outside Prohibition, 49–50
    Joe "The Boss" Masseria, 44
    legacy of Jazz Age crime, 50–51
    liquor trade, battling, 48–49
    outside organized crime, 46–48
    progressive movement, 38–39
    Prohibition movement and Eighteenth
        Amendment, 39–40
    temperance movement, 38
Imagism, 158
Immigrants and nativists, 109
    Americanism, 109–112
    Americanization programs, 117–118
    congressional legislation, 116–117
    early nativism, 113–114
    government concerns and involvement,
        118–120
    immigration, changing face of, 114–115
    immigration concerns in early 20th century,
        115–116
    isolationism, 112
    Ku Klux Klan, 121–125

Immigrants, *continued*
    native-born citizens, deep-rooted prejudices
        against, 125–126
    Old World identities, maintaining, 120–121
    xenophobia, 115
Impressionism, 105
Independent Voter's Association (IVA), 30, 31
Industrial Revolution, 114
Industrial Workers of the World (IWW), 142
Inherit the Wind, 140
Insull, Samuel: and utilities and transportation
    empire, expansion and collapse of, 177–180
International Church of the Foursquare Gospel,
    58–59
Intolerance, 122
Irwin, Vermonter Clive, 46
Isolationism, 112
Italy, 114, 159, 160
Ivy League, 59

J. Walter Thompson Company, 90
Jackson, Charlie, 67
Japan, 117
Japanese and Korean Exclusion League, 114
Jardine, Edith L., 119, 120
Jaynes, Charles B., 176
Jazz music, importance of, 13. *See also* Musicians
    and entertainers
Jeweler's Building, 172–173
Jim Crow system, 3
John G. Shedd Aquarium, 181
Johnson, Albert, 117
Johnson, Charles, 11
Johnson, James P., 93, 96, 99, 106
Johnson, James Weldon, 11
Johnson, Mamie, 93
Johnson, Torrey, 62
Johnson, Willie, 67
Johnson-Reed Act (1924), 86, 117
Jones Jr., Bob, 72
Jones, Clarence, 61, 62
Jones, Robert Reynolds (Bob Jones Sr.), 64
Jones, Sam, 59
Jones, William, 8
The Jungle, 150
"Jungle style" jazz, 100

Kahn, Julius, 129
Kansas City Star, 162
"Kanvas Kathedral," 63
Katzmann, Frederick, 145
Kaufman, George S., 163
Kelly, George R. "Machine Gun," 49

Kennedy, Aimee Elizabeth, 57
Kennedy Sr., Joseph, 48
Kenyon, William S., 32
Keppard, Freddie, 98
Kern County Land Company, 23
Know-Nothing Party, 113
Krupa, Gene, 98
Ku Klux Klan, 59, 68, 110, 121–125
    backlash, 125
    early history, 122
    images in radical literature, 124–125
    influence, 123–124
    rebirth of, 122–123

Labor Party, of Cook County, 141
Labor strife: Boston, 132
    Seattle, 131–132
    steel industry, 132–134
LaFollette, Robert, 32, 141, 142
Lamb, William, 170
Land O'Lakes Creamery, 20
Langer, William, 30
Lanigan, Jim, 98
Lansky, Meyer, 45
The Last Tycoon, 162
Latham, Lance, 61
League of Nations, 9
Leisure, and consumer culture, 78
Lemke, William, 68
The Leopard's Spots, 122
Lewis, Sinclair, 56, 163–164
Lewis-Pacific Dairymen's Association, 20
Liggett, Louis K., 177
Lindbergh, Charles, 106
Lindy Hop, 106
Lindy Hoppers, 106
Locke, Alain, 12
    and *The New Negro*, 155
Lombardo, Guy, 101
Long, Huey, 68, 71
A Long Way from Home, 154
"Loping," 94
Lost Generation, 155–153
    Ernest Hemingway, 162–163
    Ezra Pound, 158–160
    F. Scott Fitzgerald, 160–162
    John Dos Passos, 157–158
Love, Clarence, 12
Lucchese family 43
Luciano, Charles "Lucky," 44
Lynching, 3
Lyric Opera House, 180

Madeiros, Celestino, 145

Main Street, 164

Manhattan Company Building, 170

Manhattan Transfer, 158

Manning, Frankie, 106

Manone, Wingy, 98

Maranzano, Salvatore, 45

Marshall Field & Company, 89, 180, 181

Martin, Sallie, 67

Martland, Harrison, 175

Marx, Harpo, 163

Mass-produced clothing, 79

Masseria, Joe ''The Boss,'' 44

Mauer, Harold, 171

McCormick, Col. Robert R., 168

McGurn, Jack ''Machine Gun,'' 42

McKaig, Ray, 31, 32

McKay, Claude, 11, 12, 153–154

McNary-Haugen legislation, 21, 23

McParland, Dick, 98

McPartland, Jimmy, 98

McPherson, Aimee Semple, 57–59, 62, 63

McPherson, Harold, 57

Mencken, H. L., 71, 163

Messenger, 8

Mexico, 3, 117

Mezzrow, Mezz, 98

Miami Herald, 170

Michaux, Elder Lightfoot Solomon, 64

Middle East, 63

Middle West Utilities Co. *See* Midland Utilities Co.

Midland Utilities Co., 179

Miley, James ''Bubber,'' 100

Miller, Herbert A., 137

Minnesota Theatre, 78

Model T Fords, 27

Montana Farming Corporation, 22

Moody, Dwight , 53–54

Moonshine, 46–47

Moralists and jazz music, 93

Moran, George Clarence ''Bugs,'' 42

Morton, Ferdinand Joseph Lamothe ''Jelly Roll,'' 95

Morton, Jelly Roll, 12

''Mother to Son,'' 12

Muckrakers, influence on Jazz Age, 150–151

Murray, Bill, 112

Museum of Modern Art (MOMA), 180, 181

Museum of Science and Industry (MSI), 181

Music and evangelism, 67–68

Musicians and entertainers, 93

    Chicago jazz, 97–98

    defining jazz of the period, 94–96

    jazz beyond delta, 96–97

    jazz in modern age, 106–107

    and New York, 98

    New York big bands, 99–101

    popular dance and jazz, 105–106

    stride piano style, 98–99

    Tin Pan Alley, 101–105

Musick, Ethel, 63, 72

NASCAR racing, 46–48

National Association for the Advancement of Colored People (NAACP), 9, 10

National Barn Dance, 30

National Crime Syndicate, 44

National Education Association, 137

National Farm and Home Hour, 28

National Origins Act (1921). *See* Johnson-Reed Act

National Union of Social Justice, 68

Nebraska Tractor Test, 22

''The Negro Speaks of Rivers,'' 12

Negro World, 6, 7, 153

Nelson, George ''Baby Face,'' 38, 49

Ness, Eliot, 37, 48

New Colonial Theater, 106

New Haven Clock Company, 175

New Majority, 141

New Negro, 7

The New Negro, 12, 155

New Orleans jazz, 97

New York big bands, 99–101

New York Daily News, 169

1919, 158

No Siree, 163

Nonpartisan League (NPL), 30

Noone, Jimmie, 98

Norris, Frank, 150

North, Dave, 98

Northern Indiana Public Service Company, 177

Nubin, Katie, 66

O'Banion, Dean Charles, 42

Office of the Commissioner of Immigration, 114

Okeh Record Company, 12

Old World identities, maintaining, 120–121

Oliver, Joseph ''King,'' 95, 98, 102, 104

Olson, Floyd B., 68

On the Condition of the Working Class, 68

One Man's Initiation, 157

Original Dixieland Jazz Band, 93, 94

Ory, Kid, 102
Owen, Chandler, 7, 8
Palace of Fine Arts, 181, 183
Palmer, A. Mitchell, 116, 130
Palmer raids, 116, 130
Pan–African congresses, 9–10
Parker, Bonnie, 49
Parker, Dorothy, 163
Parmenter, Frederick, 143
Peace Mission movement, 65
Peay, Austin, 138
Peek, George N., 21, 32
People's Gas, 177
Philanthropy, 180–184
The Plain Truth, 71
Plan of Chicago, 181
Plotts, Morris, 62–63
Poland, 112, 114
Polly, 62
Polyrhythms, 96
Portugal, 9
Post-Civil War years, 122
Postwar world, 151–152, 161
Pound, Ezra, 158–160
Powell Sr., Adam Clayton, 153
Prejudice, 115
Price, Charles, 63–64
Princeton Triangle Club, 160
Procter & Gamble, 87
Producers' News, 26
Progressive Era, 113, 129
Progressive movement, 38–39
Progressive Party, 31–32
Prohibition, 33
    criminal activities outside, 49–50
    and Eighteenth Amendment, 39–40
Prohibition Unit of the Bureau of Internal
    Revenue, 48
Protestant revivalism, 26
Protestantism, 64
The Protocols of the Elders of Zion, 125
Public Ownership League, 31
Pullman Strike (1894), 126
Purple Gang, 45

Racism, 110, 152
    casual, 93–94
Rader, Daniel Paul, 60–62
    Chicago Gospel Tabernacle, 61
    influencing future evangelists, 62
    radical identity, 130–131
    use of media, 60–61

Radio, 85
    and farm families, 29–30
    and jazz, 96–97
Radium Chemical Company, 176
Radium Dial Company, 176
*Radium Girls: Women and Industrial Health Reform,
    1910–1935*, 176
Radium poisoning, 174–176
Ragtime, 94
Randolph, Philip, A., 7, 8
Raskob, John Jakob, 170
Raulston, John T., 139, 140
Reader's Digest, 165
"Reason-Why" copy, 89
Recreation and culture: farmers and, 24
Red Hot Peppers, 95
Reed, David, 117
Reed, John, 143
Reeves, George, 170
Reformers, radicals, and socialists, 129
    AEW, 134–137
    beginnings, 134
    1924 controversy, 136–137
    communist party creation, 143
    evolution and controversy, 137–140
    radical identity, 130–131
    Sacco and Vanzetti case SPA, 142–143
    third political party, move toward,
        141–142
Remus, George, 45
Reno, Milo, 68
Restrictive covenants, 10
Rhapsody in Blue, 101
Rialto Theater, 78
Richards, Charles R., 182
Riker-Hegman-Jaynes stores, 177
Roaring Twenties, 49, 177
Rockefeller, Abby Aldrich, 180
Rockefeller Jr., John D., 180
Rodeheaver, Homer, 55
The Romantic Egotist, 161
Roosevelt, Franklin, 35, 39, 68, 71, 172
Rosenwald, Julius, 181, 182, 183, 184
Rotgut. *See* Moonshine
Rudge, Olga, 159
Rum Line, 41
Rumrunners, 40–41
"Rural suburbs," 27
Russell, Pee Wee, 98
Russia, 114, 115, 116, 129, 130
Russian revolutions, 116, 129

Ruthenberg, Charles, 143

Saarinen, Eliel, 169

Sacco and Vanzetti case, execution and legacy, 145–146

    execution and legacy, 145–146

    origins, 143–145

    trial, 145

Sacco, Nicola, 143

Sachs, Paul J., 181

St. Valentine's Day Massacre (1929), 42

Salvation Army, 62

San Francisco Symphony Orchestra, 101

Saturday Evening Post, 161

Sayre, Zelda, 160

Scandinavia, 114, 127

Schwellenbach, L. B., 119

Scopes, John, 138, 139

Scopes "Monkey" Trial (1925), 138

Scotland, 176

Scott, Sam, 59

Sears, Roebuck & Company, 80, 180, 184

Seay, Lloyd, 46

Sedition Act (1918), 130

Segregation, residential, 10

Selected Poems, 154

Self-Mastery Through Conscious Autosuggestion, 59

Semple, Robert, 57

Senate Committee of Education, 135

Seth Thomas Clock Company, 175

Severance, H. Craig, 170

Sharecropping, 2

Shedd Aquarium Society, 181

Shedd, John Graves, 181

Shedd, Mary R., 181

Shipstead, Henrik, 30, 31

Sicilians and organized crime, 44, 45

Siegel, Benjamin Bugsy, 45, 50

The Significance of the Frontier in American History, 110

Silver, Gray, 32

Simmons, William, 59, 122–123

Sinclair, Upton, 124, 125, 146, 149, 150

Skyscrapers, 168–172

Sloan, Alfred P., 82, 83

Small, Sam, 59

Smith, Alfred E., 126

Smith, Bessie, 12

Smith, Gerald Lyman Kenneth, 68, 71–72

Smith, Moe, 48

Smith, Willie "The Lion," 99

Smooth jazz, 106

Snowden, Elmer, 100

Social Democratic Party, 142

Social Justice Weekly, 68

Socialist Labor Party of America, 142

Socialist Party of America (SPA), 142–143

Socialist Party, 141, 147

Songs of Jamaica, 12, 154

South Park Commission (SPC), 183

Soviet Ark, 116, 130

Soviet Union, 158 *See also* Russia

Spain, 162

Spanier, Muggsy, 98

Speakeasies, 37

Splettstocher, Frances, 175

Springer, Curtis Howe "Doc," 69–70

Standard Chemical Company, 176

State highway commission (1921), 34

Stein, Gertrude, 156

Stewart-Warner Corporation, 172

Stone, Durell, Edward, 181

Straton, John Roach, 59

Stride piano style, 98–99

Stripes, 112

Sullivan, Cornelius J., 180

Sullivan, Joe, 98

The Sun Also Rises, 162–163

Sunday, Billy, 55–56, 59

Sunday, Helen Amelia Thompson, 56

Survey Graphic, 155

Swing feeling, 94, 96

Symphonic jazz, 99

Syncopation, 94, 96

Taft, Lorado, 183

Taylor, Charles, 26

Taylor, Frederick Winslow, 168

Teagarden, Jack, 101

Temperance movement, 38

Ten Days That Shook the World, 143

Tender is the Night, 162

Teschemacher, Frank, 98

Tesla-Westinghouse victory, 179

Tharpe, Rosetta, 66

Thayer, Webster, 144

Their Eyes Were Watching God, 155

Third political party, move toward, 141–142

This Side of Paradise, 161

Thompson, Sam, 32

Three Soldiers, 157

Tigert, John, 135, 136, 137

Time-Life Building, 181

Tin Pan Alley, 98, 101–105

Toiletry industry, 83, 87

Tomson, Sister, 63
Torrio, Johnny, 41, 42
Tough, Dave, 98
Townsend, Francis, 68
Trumbauer, Frankie, 101, 104
Turner, Frederick Jackson, 110, 111, 127

Union church, 26
United Drug Company, 177
Universal Negro Improvement Association
    (UNIA)
    and Garvey, 5–7, 153
"Untouchables," 37, 48
Urban blues, 12
U.S. Department of Agriculture (USDA), 19,
    21, 35
    and modernization of rural environment, 28
U.S. Grain Growers Inc., 20–21
U.S. Radium Corporation, 175, 176
U.S. Steel, 132
U.S.A. Trilogy, 158
Utley, Uldine, 59–60

Van Alen, William, 170
Van Slicken Speedometer Company, 172
Vanzetti, Bartolomeo, 143
Vein of Iron, 165
Venuti, Joe, 101
Victorian era, end of, 149–150
Victorian morality, 76
Violence, 3, 50, 53, 113, 125, 174
Volstead Act, 39
    problems facing, 48

Walgreen, Charles: and rise of chain
    pharmacies, 176–177
Walker, Jimmy, 172
Walker, Madame C. J., 6
Wallace Jr., Henry, 35
Wallace Sr., Henry, 32
Wallace, DeWitt, 163
Wallace, Lila Bell, 163
Waller, Fats, 99
Wannamaker, J. S., 23
Washington State Legionnaire, 119
The Watch Word, 174
Waterbury Clock Company (Timex), 175
The Weary Blues, 12
Weiss, Earl "Hymie," 42
Welfare capitalism, 168

Welk, Lawrence, 101
Wettling, George, 98
Whiskey Rebellion, 38
White, Walter, 9
Whitefield, George, 54
Whiteman, Paul, 99, 101, 105
WHT programs, 60
Wigglesworth, Smith, 62
Wilson, Roma, 67
Wilson, Woodrow, 115, 129
Wobblies. *See* Industrial Workers of the
    World (IWW)
Wolverines, 104
Women and evangelism, 66–67
Women's Christian Temperance Union, 39
Wood, Robert E., 184
Woolworth Building, 168–169
World War I, 39, 59, 129, 142, 149
    advertising during, 88
    and agricultural mobilization, 19, 21
    American entry into, 19, 130, 162
    clothing, 79
    and immigration, 86
    labor during, 131, 168
    movies during, 78
    World War II, 69, 71, 174
World Wide Christian Courier clubs, 61
World's Columbian Exposition, 183
Wrigley Building, 181
Wristwatches, 173–175
    and health of dial painters, 174
Writers, 149. *See also* by name
    Algonquin Round Table, 163
    Black pride, rising, 153
    Great Migration, 152
    Harlem Renaissance, 152
    Lost Generation, 155–163
    postwar world, 151–152
    roots of Renaissance, 153
    Victorian era, end of, 149–150

Xenophobia, 110, 115

Young Men's Christian Association
    (YMCA), 55
Young Women's Christian Association
    (YWCA), 119

Zeiss Projector, 184